GREAT
BRITISH
SPEECHES

To my mother

GREAT BRITISH SPEECHES

SIMON HEFFER

Quercus

Contents

INTRODUCTION

With the overwhelming variety of media available to us today, we are perhaps liable to take for granted the power of spoken communication. These days politicians and other public figures tend to concentrate on getting their messages across via television, radio, the internet, and of course powerful PR machines; but for centuries the prime means of communication was the set-piece speech. This book selects fifty highlights from over 600 years of British speechmaking, from the disgruntled voices of the Peasants' Revolt to the triumphalism of New Labour. Taken individually they are landmarks, because they stake out positions at particular historical moments; and they often contribute to the reputations (mostly for good, sometimes for ill) of those who spoke them. Collectively they amount to a concise history of the art of the speech.

Most of them, too, prove the point that when a man or woman speaks from the heart, and uses sincerity of feeling as a prime weapon of communication, the result is often striking and compelling. The second most recent speech in the book, that given by Earl Spencer at the funeral of his sister Diana, Princess of Wales, in 1997, makes that quite clear: it stimulated a spontaneous public reaction of a kind hardly ever seen in modern times. Yet striking too, in their different ways, are some other of the more recent, and more political, speeches made at times when their speakers had escaped from a prevailing orthodoxy and were fighting for survival – whether it was Labour leader Neil Kinnock determined to see off the Militant Tendency, or Geoffrey Howe at last saying what he really thought of Margaret Thatcher, or Margaret Thatcher herself, at Bruges, finally saying what she really thought of Europe. These speeches will be familiar to many of us because they are from the recent past; but they are likely, too, to prove significant in our history for some time to come.

To go to the beginning of the sequence, one reads into the words of earlier speakers nothing but a genuine passion or conviction, and one sees the raw power of words to make an immediate difference to history. Whether in the proto-Marxist words of John Ball during the Peasants' Revolt, or in the inspiring determination of Queen Elizabeth I at Tilbury to give backbone to the scratch army that might have to fight the Spanish invaders, or in the sheer anger of Oliver Cromwell as he throws out the Rump Parliament – in all these one detects the pure energy and will of leadership.

Later, that leadership takes on a different tone. It ceases, for a time, to be about matters of life and death, but becomes instead about shaping the constitutional tenor of Britain (and the United Kingdom). It is about breaking out of a post-feudal world, in which criticism of the sovereign or his ministers might be punishable by death, and moving into a society in which freedom of speech, and free expression of spiritual and religious opinions, is being established. In speeches by Charles James Fox and Richard Brinsley Sheridan in the 18th century, we see a crucial step being taken on the way to the two-party system of Whigs and Tories (and later the Liberals and Conservatives of the 19th century), with demands for freedom of the press, religious toleration, and the right of public meeting. William Wilberforce's epic campaign to abolish slavery is perhaps the most striking example here of the use of a rhetorical campaign to achieve freedom for the oppressed; but it should be compared with Thomas Erskine's defence of Tom Paine and his right to publish *The Rights of Man*, which was taking place contemporaneously. Black Africans were indeed subjected to an extreme form of oppression, but Paine, too, was lucky to escape with his life.

By the mid-19th century politics becomes more organised, and with the expansion of the electorate after the Reform Acts, from 1832, speeches start to become more formulaic; but there is still scope for passion and conviction. Lord Palmerston's defence of his actions in the case of Don Pacifico (with its vigorous assertion of the rights of British citizens in classical terms, *'Civis Romanus sum'*) is one such example, but so too, and in a context familiar to us once again following the events in Iraq, is John Bright's speech on the Crimean War. Sitting on the Opposition benches enables great statesmen, freed of the constraints of office and collective responsibility, to make their pitches in an unfettered form, as Benjamin Disraeli's Manchester speech and Gladstone's electioneering during the Midlothian campaign exemplify.

The arrival first of a popular press during the 19th century, and of the wireless in the 20th century, presented conflicting challenges to the politician. On the one hand he could attract an infinitely larger audience than ever before for his words; on the other, any gaffe (or perceived gaffe) on his part could have career-damaging implications that could no longer be concealed. F.E. Smith, the first Earl of Birkenhead, made a speech 17 years after his auspicious beginnings as an MP (and, incidentally, a stunning maiden speech), which contained a phrase that passed into the language; but his view that war was sometimes necessary, that 'the world continues to offer glittering prizes to those who have stout hearts and sharp swords', caused an immediate outcry, coming as it did just five years after the traumatic slaughter of the Great War, and the speech did him no favours. That speech appears here, as does one that caused problems nearly a quarter of a century earlier for the Liberal leader Henry Campbell-Bannerman, who found himself vilified for describing British policy against the Boers as 'methods of barbarism'. As with Birkenhead, he qualified his controversial points, but found that the headline-writers are no respecters of context.

With the coming of the Second World War oratory becomes once more a means to inspire a nation in its struggle for deliverance from a potentially overwhelming threat. No fewer than four speeches by Winston Churchill sum up that mood, and they are reprinted in part here, as is a fifth by him, made in 1946, in which he warned of the 'iron curtain' coming down across Central Europe, signifying the change of enemies for the West from Nazi Germany to the Soviet Union. By the time Churchill made these speeches he had the experience of nearly 40 years in public life; he had also demonstrated a brilliance with the written word in several published volumes of history and had for some time earned a living as a gifted journalist. His speechmaking was borne out of deep conviction, reflected through a titanic personality, and articulated by a man drawing on a deep knowledge of English literature. As his biographers have pointed out, too, when Churchill came across or invented a powerful phrase he would store it away for the right moment. For all his genius, this proves that the greatest oratory is borne not only of natural gifts but also of years of hard work, dedication and experience. Churchill shows too that the greatest orators never underestimate their public, or fail to understand its willingness to be led and inspired.

Moving into the modern era, the selection contains the most famous – or notorious – speeches of the post-1945 years. The cautious nature of Harold Macmillan's 'Never had it so good' and 'Wind of change' speeches is in contrast to those from the same period by two of his backbenchers: Enoch Powell denouncing the atrocities in Kenya's Hola Camp in 1959, in which the colonial policy of his own Party is forensically and passionately assaulted, and Nigel Birch's mordant, breathakingly witty but ultimately lethal attack on Macmillan four years later in the Profumo debate. This was almost the last time in British political history when the House of Commons had men of sufficient oratorical skill and independent fearlessness to drop depth-charges in this way: Michael Foot's ridiculing of his own government's policy on reform of the House of Lords is another fine example. Another speech by Powell, his so-called 'Rivers of Blood' speech, is one of the last instances of a politician commanding universal headlines for a speech made at a routine political meeting, and it was, admittedly, something of a 'detonation' (Powell's own word). Today, though, it is what is said in the broadcasting studio that counts.

There are still examples of the set-piece speech in Britain, of course: every autumn the leaders of the main political parties give big speeches at their Party Conferences. These have become almost the only occasions in the calendar, apart from the chancellor's budget, when a whole speech will be broadcast, and it represents a marvellous opportunity for politicians to set out their own and their Party's stalls before the electorate. But even in this environment much has changed over a relatively short period. A comparison between the last speech in this book – Tony Blair's 'Forces of Conservatism' Conference speech of 1999 – and the two by a former Labour Party leader, Hugh Gaitskell, from the 1960s are revealing. Gaitskell's two speeches – one on nuclear disarmament, the other opposing Britain's membership of the Common Market – display an almost classical rhetoric. Gladstone, Palmerston or even Sheridan would have been able to listen to them with comprehension and to recognise a medium that they themselves used, and used in the same way. Gaitskell speaks in paragraphs and develops his argument with the use of various classical rhetorical devices. By the time we get to a modern politician such as Blair, whose own classical education

The 14th century in England was a time of great misery and instability. From 1337 there were sporadic wars with France – the so-called Hundred Years War, deemed to have finished in 1453. In 1348–9 there was the first occurrence of the Black Death, which reduced the population of England from 5–6 million to around 3 million.

This catastrophic outbreak of plague can be interpreted as the original cause of the Peasants' Revolt more than 30 years later. The authorities at the time tried to prevent the price of labour rising in accordance with the prevailing shortage of manpower caused by the calamity: a Statute of Labourers of 1351 sought to enforce lower pay rates, and a large proportion of adults were prosecuted and fined in succeeding years for breaches of this restrictive law. In the 1370s an intensifying of the war with France put huge demands on the public purse. This led, in 1377, to the imposition of a poll tax, at 4d a head for everyone over 14 except mendicant friars. A second tax was brought in during 1379, this one graduated in the light of unrest caused by the earlier one, so that the wealthy paid more. However, this raised inadequate funds, and in late 1380 a third tax was introduced at one shilling per head on all adults over 15, with no exceptions. There was massive evasion, with a third of 1377's taxpayers 'disappearing' by 1380.

In the spring of 1381 commissioners were sent out to many English counties to enforce payment, and there were outbreaks of rioting in Essex and Kent by the beginning of June. Wat Tyler emerged as the leader of the Kentish rebels, and his campaign was encouraged by a rogue priest, John Ball (d.1381). Ball had been a preacher for 20 years and had three times been locked up in the Archbishop of Canterbury's prison, for indisciplined behaviour. He was excommunicated some time before 1376 and made a second career as a rabble-rouser, subscribing to the anti-ecclesiastical Lollard views of William Wycliffe. He was effectively a proto-communist, arguing that all men were equal under God. He was once more in the Archbishop's prison in Maidstone at the end of May 1381, but the mob sprang him. As the rebels marched on London, Ball preached the following sermon at Blackheath on the morning of 12 June. This is one of several alternative translations from Middle English made by near-contemporary chroniclers.

THE PEASANTS' REVOLT 1381

MAY
The revolt begins in Essex.

EARLY JUNE
Wat Tyler and John Ball lead Kentish rebels to Blackheath, while Essex rebels gather at Mile End.

13 JUNE
John of Gaunt's palace is destroyed.

14 JUNE
Rebels storm the Tower of London; they behead Archbishop Sudbury, who, as chancellor, is blamed for the taxes.

15 JUNE
Tyler is killed at Smithfield, but Richard II placates rebels and promises to consider their grievances.

15–23/4 JUNE
East Anglia and other areas witness further disturbances, and the king revokes his concessions.

JULY
End of the revolt; the leading rebels, including Ball are executed.

'When Adam dalf ♥, and Eve span,
Who was then a gentilman?

In the beginning all men were created equal: servitude of man to man was introduced by the unjust dealings of the wicked, and contrary to God's will. For if God had intended some to be serfs and others lords, He would have made a distinction between them at the beginning. Englishmen had now an opportunity given them, if they chose to take it, of casting off the yoke they had borne so long, and winning the freedom that they had always desired: Wherefore they should take good courage, and behave like the wise husbandman♦ of scripture, who gathered the wheat into his barn, but uprooted and burned the tares that had half-choked the good grain. The tares♣ of England were her oppressive rulers, and harvest-time had come, in which it was their duty to pluck up and make away with them all – evil lords, unjust judges, lawyers, every man who was dangerous to the common good. Then they would have peace for the present and security for the future; for when the great ones had been cut off, all men would enjoy equal freedom, all would have the same nobility, rank, and power.'

♥ dalf = dug, delved.
♦ husbandman = a type of tenant-farmer, formally below the rank of yeoman.
♣ tares = types of weed.

Ball's sermon was interpreted as incitement to murderous rebellion, and the rebels marched on London burning and pillaging. Ball is believed to have been present at Smithfield on 15 June when Tyler presented his demands to the 14-year-old King Richard II. They included equality of all men in law, and the end of serfdom and outlawry. A scuffle broke out, Tyler was killed, the rebel band dispersed on the promise of a pardon, and Ball fled into the Midlands. He was soon captured at Coventry, brought before Richard at St Albans, and sentenced to death by hanging, drawing and quartering. The sentence was quickly carried out at St Albans on 15 July, with the king watching; the quarters of Ball's dismembered corpse were sent to four different towns to be publicly displayed, *pour encourager les autres*.

'We few, we happy few'

Agincourt, France, 24 October 1415

Shakespeare's Henry V
emboldens his troops before the
Battle of Agincourt

One of the best versions we have of a speech credited to the later Middle Ages is from the realms of drama. This dramatisation by William Shakespeare (1564–1616) of the remarks made by King Henry V before the Battle of Agincourt has become one of the most famous speeches in the English language, and it has been one frequently alluded to, or directly quoted, by the more literate orators down the centuries.

Henry left England on 7 August 1415 for France with an expeditionary force of perhaps 30,000 men. By early October the English army had been severely reduced by disease during an eight-week campaign across northern France; Henry chose to send the sick home by sea and to march the remainder to Calais. On the night of 24 October the French army, spoiling for a fight, had encamped at Agincourt. The next day the English advanced towards the enemy, but not until Henry had made a speech to his soldiers: one account of the speech has Henry saying 'for me this day shall England never ransom pay'.

Taken from Act IV, Scene III, of the *The Life of King Henry V*, the speech as imagined by Shakespeare in the late 16th century is delivered after observations from the king's most senior courtiers about the overwhelming odds the English face. The 'three score thousand' at the disposal of the French king means the English are outnumbered five to one and, as Lord Salisbury says in a tone consistent with the spirit of defeatism, 'besides, they are all fresh'. King Henry, of course, is having none of that.

Westmoreland: O that we now had here
But one ten thousand of those men in England
That do no work to-day!

King: What's he that wishes so?
My cousin Westmoreland? No, my fair cousin;
If we are mark'd to die, we are enow
To do our country loss; and if to live,
The fewer men, the greater share of honour.
God's will! I pray thee, wish not one man more.
By Jove, I am not covetous for gold,
Nor care I who doth feed upon my cost;
It yearns [grieves] me not if men my garments wear;
Such outward things dwell not in my desires.
But if it be a sin to covet honour,
I am the most offending soul alive.
No, faith, my coz, wish not a man from England.
God's peace! I would not lose so great an honour
As one man more methinks would share from me
For the best hope I have. O, do not wish one more!
Rather proclaim it, Westmoreland, through my host,
That he which hath no stomach to this fight,

Let him depart; his passport shall be made,
And crowns for convoy put into his purse;
We would not die in that man's company
That fears his fellowship to die with us.
This day is call'd the feast of Crispian.
He that outlives this day, and comes safe home,
Will stand a tip-toe when this day is nam'd,
And rouse him at the name of Crispian.
He that shall live this day, and see old age,
Will yearly on the vigil feast his neighbours,
And say 'To-morrow is Saint Crispian.'
Then will he strip his sleeve and show his scars,
And say 'These wounds I had on Crispian's day.'
Old men forget; yet all shall be forgot,
But he'll remember, with advantages,
What feats he did that day. Then shall our names,
Familiar in his mouth as household words –
Harry the King, Bedford and Exeter,
Warwick and Talbot, Salisbury and Gloucester –
Be in their flowing cups freshly rememb'red.
This story shall the good man teach his son;
And Crispin♥ Crispian shall ne'er go by,
From this day to the ending of the world,
But we in it shall be remembered –
We few, we happy few, we band of brothers;
For he today that sheds his blood with me
Shall be my brother; be he ne'er so vile,
This day shall gentle his condition;
And gentlemen in England now-a-bed
Shall think themselves accurs'd they were not here,
And hold their manhoods cheap whiles any speaks
That fought with us upon Saint Crispin's day.

♥ Crispian and Crispin were brothers and Christian martyrs during the
reign of Emperor Diocletian, 3rd century AD, and later celebrated on
St Crispin's Day, 25 October.

After three hours' fighting, the French had lost 10,000
men, including many from their aristocracy, mainly
slaughtered by repeated volleys of arrows; the English
losses have been put at between 1,400 and 1,600.
The sheer numbers of the French casualties, and
the confusion caused by so many wounded horses,
prevented a regrouping that might have taken more
of a fight to the English. Henry returned to London
in triumph on 23 November.

LIFE OF KING HENRY V

1399
Henry Bolingbroke is
crowned Henry IV, and his
son Henry is made
Prince of Wales (among
other titles).

1403
As Prince Henry
(Shakespeare's 'Prince
Hal'), he takes part in the
Battle of Shrewsbury
(21 July), defeating rebels;
vanquishes Owain
Glendower, Welsh leader,
at the Battle of Usk.

1413
Is crowned Henry V
(21 March).

1414
Defeats a Lollard uprising
(Jan.).

1415
Is victorious, against the
odds, at Agincourt
(25 Aug.).

1417–19
His military victories in
Normandy over this
period give the English
control over the territory.

1420
Is named heir to the
French throne by the
terms of the Treaty of
Troyes; marries Catherine,
the daughter of Charles VI
of France.

1422
Dies in France.

'*I have the heart and stomach of a king*'

Tilbury, Essex, 9 August 1588

Elizabeth I
inspires her troops to face the
Spanish Armada

Throughout the first 30 years of her reign Elizabeth (1533–1603, r.1558–1603), daughter of Henry VIII and his second wife Anne Boleyn, had faced countless threats from the continental Catholic interest in general, and from Spain in particular. English support for the Protestant rebels in the Spanish Netherlands proved particularly irksome to Philip II, the Spanish king, who was also Elizabeth's brother-in-law (having been married to Mary I and briefly king of England himself in the 1550s).

By 1588 Philip had decided to launch a conquest of England, and for that purpose he sent the Spanish Armada, consisting of over 130 ships under the command of the Duke of Medina Sidonia, to within sight of the English coast. There was no standing army in England to resist a landing, and so a militia had to be assembled hurriedly and turned into a force to fight the apparently imminent invasion. When the queen went to Tilbury, some 15 miles east of the city of London on the Thames estuary, she found 4,000 men there, and she rode up and down their lines on horseback and was recorded as giving these words of encouragement to her forces.

THE SPANISH ARMADA
1588

31 MAY
The Armada sets sail from Spain.

JUNE–JULY
Lord Howard of Effingham, Francis Drake, John Hawkins and Martin Frobisher organise the English fleet.

19 JULY
The Armada is sighted off coast of Cornwall.

20 JULY
The first fighting at sea takes place.

27 JULY
The Armada lays anchor off Calais.

28 JULY
The 'Battle of Gravelines' sees Spanish losses in the English Channel.

29 JULY
The remaining Spanish ships head into the North Sea, eventually to round Scotland.

SEPTEMBER–OCTOBER
Violent gales wreck many of the remaining Armada ships off the Irish coast, as they attempt to head back to Spain, and invasion of England is averted.

My loving people,

We have been persuaded by some that are careful of our safety, to take heed how we commit our selves to armed multitudes, for fear of treachery; but I assure you I do not desire to live to distrust my faithful and loving people. Let tyrants fear, I have always so behaved myself that, under God, I have placed my chiefest strength and safeguard in the loyal hearts and good-will of my subjects; and therefore I am come amongst you, as you see, at this time, not for my recreation and disport, but being resolved, in the midst and heat of the battle, to live and die amongst you all; to lay down for my God, and for my kingdom, and my people, my honour and my blood, even in the dust.

I know I have the body but of a weak and feeble woman; but I have the heart and stomach of a king, and of a king of England too, and think foul scorn that Parma♥ or Spain, or any prince of Europe, should dare to invade the borders of my realm; to which rather than any dishonour shall grow by me, I myself will take up arms, I myself will be your general, judge, and rewarder of every one of your virtues in the field. I know already, for your forwardness you have deserved rewards and crowns; and We do assure you in the word of a prince, they shall be duly paid you. In the mean time, my lieutenant general♦ shall be in my stead, than whom never prince commanded a more noble or worthy subject; not doubting but by your obedience to my general, by your concord in the camp, and your valour in the field, we shall shortly have a famous victory over those enemies of my God, of my kingdom, and of my people.

♥ The Duke of Parma was supposed to add 16,000 men and more ships to the might of the Armada at Dunkirk, but this proved impossible.
♦ Elizabeth refers to Robert Dudley, Earl of Leicester (1532–88), one of her favourites, though a man regarded as an upstart by the older nobility.

In fact, by the time 'Gloriana' (as Elizabeth would become known) made her address, the threat of invasion had already passed, and the Spanish fleet was busy trying to cope with adverse weather conditions and to evade attack from the Royal Navy that Philip had, only weeks earlier, been confident he could blow from the seas. Lord Leicester died just three weeks after this review, in Oxfordshire.

'Remember, I am your king'

Westminster Hall, London, 20 January 1649

Charles I
at his trial for treason

Charles I (1600–49) succeeded his father, James I of England and VI of Scotland, in 1625 as the second Stuart monarch. From the start he took the view that his conduct of an executive monarchy was none of Parliament's business, and this became all the more vexatious to the House of Commons when he sought to mitigate the position of Catholics in England. He told Parliament that if it would not do what he wished he would dissolve it, and he was quite happy to carry out that threat, though this put him in severe financial difficulties. In 1629 his theological difficulties with Parliament led to a dissolution, which in turn led to his ruling without it for 11 years. This exacerbated the tensions that led to two civil wars in the 1640s and, ultimately, the king's arrest.

A council of senior New Model Army officers adopted a remonstrance to Parliament in the autumn of 1648 demanding that:

> … the capital and grand author of our troubles, the person of the king, by whose commissions, commands, or procurement, and in whose behalf and for whose interest only, of will and power, all our wars and troubles have been, with all the miseries attending them, may be speedily brought to justice for treason, blood, and mischief he is therein guilty of.

This call – not just to depose the king, but to execute him – immediately divided opinion. To facilitate matters, Parliament was 'purged' by one Colonel Thomas Pride of members thought likely to be favourable to the sovereign. On 1 January 1649, the newly compliant House of Commons confirmed the view that Charles had committed treason, and subsequently it established a High Court of Justice to hear the case against him. Outraged, Charles refused either to plead or to recognise the authority of the court.

'I would know by what power I am called hither … I would know by what authority, I mean lawful; there are many unlawful authorities in the world; thieves and robbers by the highways … Remember, I am your king, your lawful king, and what sins you bring upon your heads, and the judgment of God upon this land. Think well upon it, I say, think well upon it, before you go further from one sin to a greater … I have a trust committed to me by God, by old and lawful descent, I will not betray it, to answer a new unlawful authority; therefore resolve me that, and you shall hear more of me.

I do stand more for the liberty of my people, than any here that come to be my pretended judges … I do not come here as submitting to the court. I will stand as much for the privilege of the House of Commons, rightly understood, as any man here whatsoever: I see no House of Lords here, that may constitute a Parliament … Let me see a legal authority warranted by the Word of God, the Scriptures, or warranted by the constitutions of the kingdom, and I will answer.

It is not a slight thing you are about. I am sworn to keep the peace, by that duty I owe to God and my country; and I will do it to the last breath of my body. And therefore you shall do well to satisfy, first, God, and then the country, by what authority you do it. If you do it by an usurped authority, you cannot answer it; there is a God in Heaven, that will call you, and all that give you power, to account.

If it were only my own particular case, I would have satisfied myself with the protestation I made the last time I was here, against the legality of the court, and that a king cannot be tried by any superior jurisdiction on earth: but it is not my case alone, it is the freedom and the liberty of the people of England; and do you pretend what you will, I stand more for their liberties. For if power without law, may make laws, may alter the fundamental laws of the Kingdom, I do not know what subject he is in England that can be sure of his life, or any thing that he calls his own.

'I do plead for the liberties of the people of England more than you do'

I do not know the forms of law; I do know law and reason, though I am no lawyer professed: but I know as much law as any gentleman in England, and therefore, under favour, I do plead for the liberties of the people of England more than you do; and therefore if I should impose a belief upon any man without reasons given for it, it were unreasonable ... The Commons of England was never a court of judicature; I would know how they came to be so.

It was the liberty, freedom, and laws of the subject that ever I took – defended myself with arms. I never took up arms against the people, but for the laws ... For the charge, I value it not a rush. It is the liberty of the people of England that I stand for. For me to acknowledge a new court that I never heard of before, I that am your king, that should be an example to all the people of England, for to uphold justice, to maintain the old laws, indeed I do not know how to do it.

CHARLES I IN THE CIVIL WARS

1642
Enters House of Commons in a failed bid to arrest 5 MPs (Jan.); raises the royal standard at Nottingham (Aug.); establishes a new royal court at Oxford (Oct.).

1645
Suffers a serious defeat at Battle of Naseby (14 June).

1646
Following further Royalist defeats, surrenders to Scottish Covenanter army (allied to Parliamentarians) in Nottinghamshire (May); after negotiations with Parliament, attempts unsuccessfully to escape (Dec.).

1646
Is imprisoned by Parliament at Holdenby House in Northamptonshire (Feb.).

1647
Is transferred to Hampton Court (Aug.), from which he escapes to the Isle of Wight (Nov.); begins alliance with Scottish Presbyterians (Dec.).

1648
War breaks out again, and Scots supporting Charles are defeated at the Battle of Preston (17–19 Aug.).

1649
After a purged Parliament refuses further negotiations with Charles, the king is put on trial for treason and executed (Jan.).

This many-a-day all things have been taken away from me, but that that I call more dear to me than my life, which is my conscience, and my honour: and if I had a respect to my life more than the peace of the kingdom, and the liberty of the subject, certainly I should have made a particular defence for my self; for by that at leastwise I might have delayed an ugly sentence, which I believe will pass upon me ... Now, sir, I conceive that an hasty sentence once passed, may sooner be repented of than recalled: and truly, the self-same desire that I have for the peace of the kingdom, and the liberty of the subject, more than my own particular ends, makes me now at least desire, before sentence be given, that I may be heard ... before the Lords and Commons ... If I cannot get this liberty, I do protest, that these fair shows of liberty and peace are pure shows and that you will not hear your king.

John Bradshaw (1602–59), the presiding judge, responded unsympathetically:

> There is a contract and a bargain made between the king and his people, and your oath is taken: and certainly, sir, the bond is reciprocal; for as you are the liege lord, so they liege subjects ... This we know, the one tie, the one bond, is the bond of protection that is due from the sovereign; the other is the bond of subjection that is due from the subject. Sir, if this bond be once broken, farewell sovereignty! ... These things may not be denied, sir ... Whether you have been, as by your office you ought to be, a protector of England, or the destroyer of England, let all England judge, or all the world, that hath look'd upon it ... You disavow us as a court; and therefore for you to address yourself to us, not acknowledging us as a court to judge of what you say, it is not to be permitted. And the truth is, all along, from the first time you were pleased to disavow and disown us, the court needed not to have heard you one word.

Charles was found guilty of treason and sentenced to death on 27 January; he was beheaded in Whitehall on 30 January.

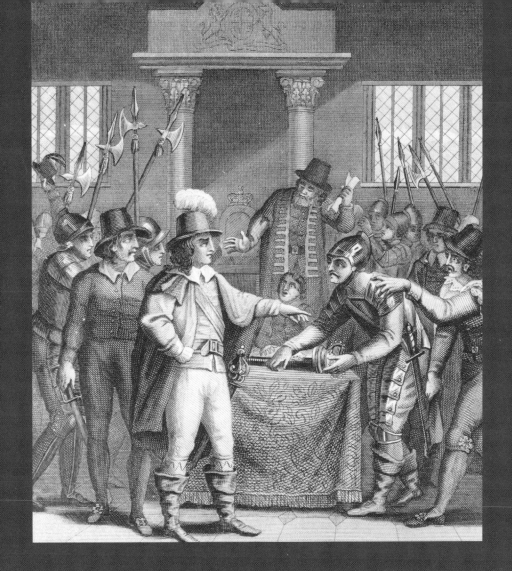

'Ye are a pack of
mercenary wretches'

Westminster Hall, London, 20 April 1653

Oliver Cromwell
lambasts members of the Rump Parliament

Oliver Cromwell (1599–1658) came from a family of impoverished Huntingdonshire gentry. He entered Parliament for Huntingdon in 1628 and, until his late thirties, lived a life untouched by the growing puritanism of the times. However, shortly before his 40th birthday he had a religious experience, which led to his obsession with a sense of his own sinfulness, and explains the religiose rhetoric of this speech. As civil war neared, he had a leading political role in ensuring that there was a Parliamentary army, and he commanded a troop of horse at the Battle of Edgehill in 1642. He showed a natural capacity for military leadership, and devoted himself to the need to improve the professionalism and training of the army. The victory of the Parliamentary army at Marston Moor in 1644 was largely because of him and his crack troops, and the boost to his reputation which that conflict provided confirmed him as one of the leading figures in Parliament.

While exasperated by the move towards puritanism and its prescriptiveness, he was motivated strongly by his Christian beliefs, and by the end of the second civil war in 1648 he was the principal figure in the new order. He was also one of the most assiduous prosecutors of Charles I. He became a temporary president of the council of state after the king's execution, though he soon found himself attacked for being insufficiently democratic by those in the army who wanted a more radical upheaval of the social and constitutional order. With rebellions to put down in Ireland, Scotland and the English provinces, Cromwell was away leading his army for much of the next three years, becoming captain-general and commander-in-chief of the Commonwealth forces early in 1650.

Now confirmed as the most powerful man in the kingdom, all that remained was for that role to be given some political authority. He watched with dismay as what remained of Parliament, after its 1648 purge of Royalist sympathisers, struggled to find the right direction for the nation. His instincts were conciliatory – he wanted religious toleration as well as an accommodation with the defeated Royalists – but Parliament was factionalised and ineffective. Talks between officers of the army and MPs in the autumn of 1652 failed to agree on a way forward for the Commons.

When in April 1653 MPs gave a promise to the army that a controversial bill giving rights to certain electors would be stopped, but then proceeded to arrange for a third reading of it, Cromwell acted. He went to the Commons and, after listening for a few minutes to the debate, began to walk up and down the chamber to demonstrate his impatience. He then decided to speak. A contemporary account says that 'at the first and for a good while he spake in commendation of the Parliament for their pains and care of the public good; afterwards he changed his style, told them of their injustice, self-interest and other faults.' What followed, according to most accounts, was a masterpiece of invective. Cromwell then called in some musketeers and told them to take away the mace, the symbol of Parliament's authority. Although some expected him to send for Prince Charles and make him king, and others thought Cromwell would take the crown himself, he did neither: he took for his immediate authority the fact that he was commander-in-chief of the army, and in December 1653, having been offered the title of king by a council of officers, instead assumed the title of 'Lord Protector'.

Ye are a pack of mercenary wretches

CROMWELL'S COMMONWEALTH

1649
The monarchy and House of Lords are abolished, and England is proclaimed a 'commonwealth'.

1649–50
Cromwell subdues Irish Catholic opposition and defeats the Scots at the Battle of Dunbar (3 Sept. 1650).

1651
Cromwell defeats Prince Charles's Royalist army at Worcester (3 Sept.); Thomas Hobbes publishes *Leviathan*.

1652–4
War at sea with the Dutch Republic.

1654–5
The first Parliament since the Rump Parliament meets (Sept.–Jan.).

1655
England is divided into 11 areas for administration by major-generals.

1656–7
Admiral Blake fights the Spanish at sea.

1657
Cromwell becomes Lord Protector of England, Scotland and Ireland.

1658
Cromwell dies (3 Sept.), and is succeeded by his son Richard.

1659
Richard Cromwell resigns office.

1660
After intervention by General Monk and his army from Scotland, the monarchy is restored and Charles II enters London (29 May) from continental exile; the living signatories to the death warrant of Charles I are executed (Oct.).

1661
Oliver Cromwell's body is exhumed and strung up at Tyburn.

It is high time for me to put an end to your sitting in this place, which you have dishonoured by your contempt of all virtue, and defiled by your practice of every vice; ye are a factious crew, and enemies to all good government; ye are a pack of mercenary wretches, and would like Esau sell your country for a mess of pottage, and like Judas betray your God for a few pieces of money; is there a single virtue now remaining amongst you? Is there one vice you do not possess? Ye have no more religion than my horse; gold is your God; which of you have not barter'd your conscience for bribes? Is there a man amongst you that has the least care for the good of the Commonwealth? Ye sordid prostitutes have you not defil'd this sacred place, and turn'd the Lord's temple into a den of thieves, by your immortal principles and wicked practices?

'Ye are grown intolerably odious'

Ye are grown intolerably odious to the whole nation; you were deputed here by the people to get grievances redress'd, are yourselves become the greatest grievance. Your country therefore calls upon me to cleanse this Augean stable♥, by putting a final period to your iniquitous proceedings in this House; and which by God's help, and the strength he has given me, I am now come to do; I command ye therefore, upon the peril of your lives, to depart immediately out of this place; go, get you out! Make haste! Ye venal slaves be gone! So! Take away that shining bauble [the mace] there, and lock up the doors. In the name of God, go!

♥ In Greek mythology, the sixth labour of Hercules was to clean out the long-neglected and filthy stables of Augeas, King of Elis.

'A flatterer
you do not
wish for'

Bristol, 3 November 1774

Edmund Burke
on the responsibilities
of a Member of
Parliament

Edmund Burke (1729–97) has come to be regarded, particularly by conservatives, as one of the foremost constitutional authorities in British political history. His father was an attorney in Dublin, and Burke initially intended to follow him into the law. Joining the Middle Temple, he found the profession unappealing, and soon embarked on a career as a writer, historian and pamphleteer. In 1759 he had become private secretary to William Gerard Hamilton, who was subsequently promoted to Chief Secretary for Ireland, taking Burke with him. In this post Burke deepened his interest in politics and made wider connections, and in 1765 he became private secretary to the Whig prime minister, Lord Rockingham. Within months Burke had secured the patronage to be elected to the Commons as MP for Wendover in Buckinghamshire. He quickly made a name for himself as a speaker on the growing crisis in the American colonies, and was much noticed in 1770 for his pamphlet *Thoughts on the Present Discontents*, which provided much of the rationale for successive generations of the Whig Party in tackling the overbearing nature of executive power.

In 1774 Burke was invited to stand for Bristol, then the second most important city in Britain, where he was described to the electors as 'indisputably the first literary character in the kingdom'. He won; the result of the poll (as was frequent in those pre-Reform days) was challenged by the losing candidate, but Burke was installed in the end. To mark his return to the House of Commons he made the following speech, in which he first defended his victory against his challenger, but then defined the duties of an MP, making it clear that he would be his constituents' representative, not their delegate. It is an understanding of the role of an MP that has remained unchanged in British political life to this day, despite occasional attempts by electors to try to make it otherwise. It certainly caused tensions between Burke and the electors of Bristol, and by the next election in 1780 he realised he would stand no chance of their re-electing him, so did not stand there again.

Burke played a leading role in both politics and literature for the rest of his life, acting as prosecutor in the impeachment of Warren Hastings, and publishing perhaps his most famous work, *Reflections on the Revolution in France*, in 1790.

I was brought hither under the disadvantage of being unknown, even by sight, to any of you. No previous canvass was made for me. I was put in nomination after the poll was opened. I did not appear until it was far advanced. If, under all these accumulated disadvantages, your good opinion has carried me to this happy point of success; you will pardon me, if I can only say to you collectively, as I said to you individually, simply and plainly, I thank you – I am obliged to you – I am not insensible of your kindness ...

I am sorry I cannot conclude, without saying a word on a topic touched upon by my worthy colleagueᵛ. I wish that topic had been passed by; at a time when I have so little leisure to discuss it. But since he has thought proper to throw it out, I owe you a clear explanation of my poor sentiments on that subject.

He tells you, that 'the topic of Instructions has occasioned much altercation and uneasiness in this City'; and he expresses himself (if I understand him rightly) in favour of the coercive authority of such instructions.

Certainly, Gentlemen, it ought to be the happiness and glory of a representative, to live in the strictest union, the closest correspondence, and the most unreserved communication with his constituents. Their wishes ought to have great weight with him; their opinion high respect; their business unremitted attention. It is his duty to sacrifice his repose, his pleasures, his satisfactions, to theirs; and, above all, ever, and in all cases, to prefer their interest to his own. But, his unbiassed opinion, his mature judgment, his enlightened conscience, he ought not to sacrifice to you; to any man, or to any set of men living. These he does not derive from your pleasure; no, nor from the law and the constitution. They are a trust from Providence, for the abuse of which he is deeply answerable. Your representative owes you, not his industry only, but his judgement; and he betrays, instead of serving you, if he sacrifices it to your opinion.

'Parliament is not a congress of ambassadors'

My worthy colleague says, his will ought to be subservient to yours. If that be all, the thing is innocent. If government were a matter of will upon any side, yours, without question, ought to be superior. But government and legislation are matters of reason and judgement, and not of inclination; and, what sort of reason is that, in which the determination precedes the discussion; in which one set of men deliberate, and another decide; and where those who form the conclusion are perhaps three hundred miles distant from those who hear the arguments?

To deliver an opinion, is the right of all men; that of constituents is a weighty and respectable opinion, which a representative ought always to rejoice to hear; and which he ought always most seriously to consider. But authoritative instructions; mandates issued, which the member is bound blindly and implicitly to obey, to vote, and to argue for, though contrary to the clearest conviction of his judgment and conscience; these are things utterly unknown to the laws of this land, and which arise from a fundamental mistake of the whole order and tenor of our constitution.

Parliament is not a congress of ambassadors from different and hostile interests; which interests each must maintain, as an agent and advocate, against other agents and advocates; but Parliament is a deliberative assembly of one nation, with one interest, that of the whole;

THE CAREER OF EDMUND BURKE

1756
Publishes *Philosophical Inquiry into ... the Sublime and the Beautiful.*

1765
Becomes private secretary to Marquess of Rockingham, the Whig prime minister.

1770
Publishes the pamphlet *Thoughts on the Present Discontents.*

1770s
Opposes Lord North's Tory administration, particularly on American policy and official corruption.

where, not local purposes, not local prejudices ought to guide, but the general good, resulting from the general reason of the whole. You choose a member indeed; but when you have chosen him, he is not Member of Bristol, but he is a Member of Parliament. If the local constituent should have an interest, or should form an hasty opinion, evidently opposite to the real good of the rest of the community, the Member for that place ought to be as far, as any other, from any endeavour to give it effect. I beg pardon for saying so much on this subject. I have been unwillingly drawn into it; but I shall ever use a respectful frankness of communication with you. Your faithful friend, your devoted servant, I shall be to the end of my life: A flatterer you do not wish for. On this point of instructions, however, I think it scarcely possible, we ever can have any sort of difference. Perhaps I may give you too much, rather than too little trouble.

'We are Members for a free country'

From the first hour I was encouraged to court your favour to this happy day of obtaining it, I have never promised you any thing, but humble and persevering endeavours to do my duty. The weight of that duty, I confess, makes me tremble; and whoever well considers what it is, of all things in the world will fly from what has the least likeness to a positive and precipitate engagement. To be a good Member of Parliament, is, let me tell you, no easy task; especially at this time, when there is so strong a disposition to run into the perilous extremes of servile compliance, or wild popularity. To unite circumspection with vigour, is absolutely necessary; but it is extremely difficult. We are now Members for a rich commercial city; this city, however, is but a part of a rich commercial nation, the interests of which are various, multiform, and intricate. We are Members for that great nation, which however is itself but part of a great empire, extended by our virtue and our fortune to the farthest limits of the east and of the west. All these widespread interests must be considered; must be compared; must be reconciled if possible. We are Members for a free country; and surely we all know, that the machine of a free constitution is no simple thing; but as intricate and as delicate, as it is valuable. We are Members in a great and ancient monarchy; and we must preserve religiously, the true legal rights of the sovereign, which form the keystone that binds together the noble and well-constructed arch of our empire and our constitution. A constitution made up of balanced powers must ever be a critical thing. As such I mean to touch that part of it which comes within my reach.

♥ Henry Cruger, who had also been returned as a Whig for this two-member constituency, and who, unlike Burke, was quite happy to do what he was told by his voters.

1774–5	1782–3	
Publishes the influential speeches *American Taxation* and *Conciliaton with America*.	Serves as Army paymaster for the new Whig government.	maladministration in India (but Hastings is acquitted years later).
1774–80	**1788**	
MP for Bristol during these years.	Speaks powerfully for the prosecution in the impeachment and subsequent trial of Warren Hastings for corruption and	**1790** His *Reflections on the Revolution in France*, opposing the revolution, lose him sympathy among progressive Whigs.
1780–94		
Serves as MP for Malton.		

'The representation of the many by a few'

House of Commons, London, 21 March 1776

John Wilkes

on the need for Parliamentary reform

The son of a malt distiller, John Wilkes (1725–97) took to politics in 1757 when elected for Aylesbury, where his heiress wife owned an estate. Something of a rake – he was a member of the Hellfire Club – he was one of the many who objected in 1762 to George III's appointment of his friend the Earl of Bute as prime minister: Bute was thought to be corrupt and incompetent. Wilkes founded, as a vehicle for his protests, the *North Briton* newspaper. An article in No. 45 attacking Bute and the king (in which Wilkes described the king's speech that opened that session of Parliament as a lie) caused Wilkes to be prosecuted, in 1763, for seditious libel. However, the case was thrown out on the grounds of Wilkes's privilege as an MP, and he was fêted as a champion of liberty.

Wilkes was then badly wounded in a duel and, Parliament deciding that the privileges of its members did not after all extend to freedom from arrest, he went into exile in Paris. Returning in 1768, once his money had run out, he was elected for Middlesex but was immediately (and at his own instigation, seeking political martyrdom) arrested for his earlier libel. He was taken to the King's Bench prison at St George's Fields in London, and the building was soon surrounded by a baying crowd of 15,000 people shouting 'Wilkes and Liberty!' Fearing a riot the militia opened fire, killing seven. Wilkes was subsequently convicted of libel and sentenced to 22 months in prison.

On his release, and still banned from sitting in the Commons, he joined a campaign for the freedom of the press, including protesting against Parliament's decision not to allow reports of its debates to be published. The public mood on this question quickly became so ugly that the authorities soon abandoned their attempts to suppress the accounts of Parliament's proceedings. The ban on Wilkes holding public office was lifted, and in 1774 he became both lord mayor of London and the MP for Middlesex. Once back in the Commons he initiated what would become a century-long campaign for parliamentary reform, and set out his arguments in this speech. He particularly draws distinctions between the lack of parliamentary constituencies in the industrialising towns and cities as opposed to the over-representation in now-decayed, underpopulated constituencies – the so-called 'rotten boroughs'.

All wise governments and well-regulated states have been particularly careful to mark and correct the various abuses which a considerable length of time almost necessarily creates. Among these, one of the most striking and important in our country is the present unfair and inadequate state of the representation of the people of England in Parliament. It is now become so partial and unequal, from the lapse of time, that I believe almost every gentleman in the House will agree with me in the necessity of its being taken into our most serious consideration, and of our endeavouring to find a remedy for this great and growing evil.

I wish, sir, my slender abilities were equal to a thorough investigation of this momentous business; very diligent and well-meant endeavours have not been wanting to trace it from the first origin. The most natural and perfect idea of a free government is, in my mind, that of the people themselves assembling to determine by what laws they choose to be governed, and to establish the regulations they think necessary for the protection of their property and liberty against all violence and fraud. Every member of such a community would submit with alacrity to the observance of whatever had been enacted by himself, and assist with spirit in giving efficacy and vigour to laws and ordinances which derived all their authority from his own approbation and concurrence. In small inconsiderable states, this mode of legislation has been happily followed, both in ancient and modern times. The extent and populousness of a great empire seems scarcely to admit it without confusion or tumult, and therefore, our ancestors, more wise in this than the ancient Romans, adopted the representation of the many by a few, as answering more fully the true ends of government. Rome was enslaved from inattention to this very circumstance, and by one other fatal act, which ought to be a strong warning to the people, even against their own representatives here – the leaving power too long in the hands of the same person, by which the armies of the republic became the armies of Sulla, Pompey, and Caesar. When all the burghers of Italy obtained the freedom of Rome, and voted in public assemblies, their multitudes rendered the distinction of the citizen of Rome, and the alien, impossible. Their assemblies and deliberations became disorderly and tumultuous. Unprincipled and ambitious men found out the secret of turning them to the ruin of the Roman liberty and the commonwealth. Among us this evil is avoided by representation, and yet the justice of this principle is preserved. Every Englishman is supposed to be present in Parliament, either in person or by deputy chosen by himself; and therefore the resolution of Parliament is taken to be the resolution of every individual, and to give to the public the consent and approbation of every free agent of the community.

'The ancient representation of this kingdom'

… The southern part of this island, to which I now confine my ideas, consists of about five millions of people, according to the most received calculation. I will state by what number the majority of this House is elected, and I suppose the largest number present of any recorded in our journals, which was in the famous year 1741. In that year the three largest divisions appear in our journals. The first is that on the 21st of January; when the numbers were 253 to 250; the second on the 25th day of the same month, 236 to 235; the third on the 9th of March, 242 to 242. In these divisions the members of Scotland are included but I will state my calculations only for England, because it gives the argument more force. The division, therefore, I adopt is that of January 21st; the number of members present on that day were 503. Let me, however, suppose the number of 254 to be the majority of members who will ever be able to attend in their places. I state it high, from the accidents of sickness, service in foreign parts, travelling, and necessary avocations. From the majority of electors in the boroughs which returned members to this House, it has been demonstrated that this number of 254 members are actually elected by no more than 5,723 persons, generally the inhabitants of Cornish and other boroughs, and perhaps not the most respectable part of the community. Is our sovereign, then, to learn the sense of his whole people from these few persons? Are these the men to give laws to this vast empire, and to tax this wealthy nation? … Lord Chancellor Talbot[v] supposed that the majority of this House was elected by 50,000 persons, and he exclaimed against the injustice of that idea. More accurate calculators than his lordship, and the unerring rules of political arithmetic, have shown the injustice to be vastly

PARLIAMENTARY REFORM TO 1832

1720s
At this time, about 5 per cent of adults are eligible to vote.

1787–9
The signing of the US constitution and the outbreak of the French Revolution increase pressures for reform in Britain.

1791–2
Thomas Paine publishes the controversial *The Rights of Man*.

1792
Thomas Hardy founds the pro-reform London Corresponding Society.

1795
Acts of Parliament limit people's rights to protest and gather.

1800
The Act of Union means that Irish MPs (but not Catholics) sit henceforth at Westminster.

1802
William Cobbett begins publishing the *Weekly Political Register*.

1810
The radical MP Sir Francis Burdett is arrested for advocating reform; riots follow in support of him.

1817–19
The activities of political radicals, Luddites and the Cato Street conspirators (who plan the assassination of the Cabinet) prompt repressive measures.

1819
At the 'Peterloo Massacre', in Manchester, 11 people are killed at a reform meeting by yeomanry.

1829
Roman Catholics are finally allowed to sit in House of Commons.

1831
The Whig government's first and second Reform bills fail to pass all stages, partly because of opposition by bishops in the Lords; in Exeter and Bristol mobs threaten the bishops' residences.

1832
The Reform Act finally receives royal assent: rotten boroughs (i.e. depopulated ones) and pocket boroughs (those in the gift of powerful individuals) are abolished, the growing industrial towns receive constituencies, and the property-holding threshold for voting rights is reformed nationally.

beyond what his lordship even suspected. When we consider, sir, that the most important powers of this House, the levying taxes on, and enacting laws for five million of persons, is thus usurped and unconstitutionally exercised by the small number I have mentioned, it becomes our duty to the people to restore to them their clear rights, their original share in the legislature. The ancient representation of this kingdom, we find, was founded by our ancestors in justice, wisdom, and equality. The present state of it would be continued by us in folly, obstinacy, and injustice. The evil has been complained of by some of the wisest patriots our country has ever produced. I shall beg leave to give that close reasoner, Mr Locke's• ideas, in his own words. He says, in the treatise on civil government:

Things not always changing equally, and private interests often keeping up customs and privileges, when the reasons of them are ceased, it often comes to pass, that in governments where part of the legislature consists of representatives chosen by the people, that in tract of time this representation becomes very unequal and disproportionate to the reasons it was at first established upon. To what gross absurdities the following of a custom, when reason has left it, may lead, we may be satisfied, when we see the bare name of a town, of which there remains not so much as the ruins, where scarce so much housing as a sheep-cot, or more inhabitants than a shepherd, is to be found, sends as many representatives to the grand assembly of law-makers, as a whole county, numerous in people and powerful in riches. This strangers stand amazed at, and every one must confess, needs a remedy.

After so great an authority as that of Mr Locke, I shall not be treated on this occasion as a mere visionary, and the propriety of the motion I shall have the honour of submitting to the House will scarcely be disputed. Even the members for such places as Old Sarum⁕ and Gatton, who I may venture to say at present stant nominis umbrae,⁕ will, I am persuaded, have too much candour to complain of the right of their few constituents, if indeed they have constituents, if they are not self-created, self-elected, self-existent, of this pretended right being transferred to the county, while the rich and populous manufacturing towns of Birmingham, Manchester, Leeds, Sheffield, and others, may have at least an equitable share in the formation of those laws by which they are governed. My idea, sir, in this case, as to the wretched and depopulated towns and boroughs in general, I own is amputation …

'Monstrous absurdities in a free state'

Our history furnishes frequent instances of the sense of Parliament running directly counter to the sense of the nation. It was notoriously of late the case in the business of the Middlesex election. I believe the fact to be equally certain in the grand American dispute, at least as to the actual hostilities now carrying on against our brethren and fellow-subjects. The proposal before us will bring the case to an issue, and from a fair and equal representation of the people, America may at length distinguish the real sentiments of freemen and Englishmen. I do not mean, sir, at this time, to go into a tedious detail of all the various proposals which have been made for redressing this irregularity in the representation of the people. I will not intrude on the indulgence of the House, which I have always found so favourable to me. When the bill is brought in, and sent to a committee, it will be the proper time to examine all the minutiae of this great plan, and to determine on the propriety of what ought now to be done, as well as of what formerly actually was accomplished. The journals of Cromwell's Parliaments prove that a more equal representation was settled, and carried by him into execution. That wonderful, comprehensive mind embraced the whole of this powerful empire. Ireland was put on a par with Scotland, and each kingdom sent 30 members to Parliament, which consisted likewise of 400 from England and Wales, and was to be triennial. Our colonies were then a speck on the face of the globe; now they cover half the New World. I will at this time, sir, only throw out general ideas, that every free agent in this kingdom should, in my wish, be represented in Parliament; that the metropolis, which contains in itself a ninth part of the people, and the counties of Middlesex, York, and others, which so greatly abound with inhabitants, should receive an increase in their representation; that the mean and insignificant boroughs, so emphatically styled the rotten part of our constitution, should be lopped off, and the electors in them thrown into the counties; and the rich, populous, trading towns, Birmingham, Manchester, Sheffield, Leeds, and others, be permitted to send deputies to the great council of the nation. The disfranchising of the mean, venal, and dependent boroughs, would be laying the axe to the root of corruption and treasury influence, as well as aristocratical tyranny. We ought equally to guard against those who sell themselves, or whose lords sell them. Burgage tenures▾▾, and private property in a share of the legislature, are monstrous absurdities in a free state, as well as an insult to common sense. I wish, sir, an English Parliament to speak the free, unbiased sense of the body of the English people, and of every man among us, of each individual who may be justly supposed to be comprehended in a fair majority.

'For the good of the mass of the people'

The meanest mechanic, the poorest peasant and day-labourer, has important rights respecting his personal liberty, that of his wife and children, his property, however inconsiderable, his wages, his earnings, the very price and value of each day's hard labour, which are in many trades and manufactures regulated by the power of Parliament. Every law relative to marriage, to the protection of a wife, sister, or daughter, against violence and brutal lust, to every contract or agreement with a rapacious or unjust master, interest the manufacturer, the cottager, the servant, as well as the rich subjects of the state. Some share, therefore, in the power of making those laws which deeply interest them, and to which they are expected to pay obedience, should be referred even to this inferior, but most useful set of men in the community; and we ought always to remember this important truth, acknowledged by every free state – that all government is instituted for the good of the mass of the people to be governed; that they are the original fountain of power, and even of revenue, and in all events, the last resource.

♥ Charles, Lord Talbot of Hensol (1685–1737), who was lord chancellor in 1733–7.
♦ John Locke (1632–1704), philosopher. His *Treatise concerning the true original extent and end of Civil Government* was published in 1690.
♣ Old Sarum, which became almost entirely depopulated but still yielded two MPs, came to epitomize the 'rotten boroughs'.
♠ i.e. 'They stand in the shadow of the name'.
♥♥ Tenures of land from the crown or an aristocrat requiring annual rent or service from the tenant.

'The *total abolition of the slave trade*'

House of Commons, London, 12 May 1789

William Wilberforce
advocates the ending of slavery

William Wilberforce (1759–1833) had been a contemporary of Pitt the Younger at Cambridge University and, like him, pursued a political career from the moment he was old enough to do so: he was elected for his home borough of Hull at the 1780 general election, just days after his 21st birthday. Pitt was instrumental, in about 1787, in persuading Wilberforce to bring up the question of the abolition of slavery before Parliament. As the *Dictionary of National Biography* reported, Wilberforce's 'independent position, his high principles, and the singular charm of character which made him popular even with his antagonists, marked him out as an ideal leader of the cause'. A long illness interrupted his campaign, but on 12 May 1789 he tabled 12 resolutions condemning slavery, and he delivered a speech lasting some three-and-a-half hours. With the support of the great men of the day – including Pitt, Edmund Burke and Charles James Fox – the resolutions were carried without a vote. However, the vested interests of traders and planters ensured that there was no easy victory for Wilberforce. An attempt in 1791 to ask for leave to introduce a bill to abolish the trade was defeated by 163 votes to 88.

In succeeding years, a succession of similar defeats and near-misses followed. The campaign was overshadowed by the revolution in France and the Napoleonic wars, and it was not until January 1807 that the bill abolishing the trade was finally carried, on second reading in the House of Lords, by 100 votes to 36. The Commons passed it by 283 votes to 15 on 23 February, and the royal assent was finally given on 25 March. The Slave Trade Abolition Act banned the practice by British subjects or ships, but until other nations followed Britain's lead, it drove the trade into other hands.

Wilberforce's great speech was made in an era before Parliament had agreed to having an official report made of its proceedings, so the account below – extracted from the *Morning Star* newspaper of 13 May 1789 – varies in some particulars from other extant versions of the speech; newspapers were not above recording a version of events that tied in best with their own editorial line.

'Mr Wilberforce then called the attention of the House to what he was about to propose. He said that he rose with a confession of what operated in his mind relative to the abolition of the Slave Trade. When I consider, says he, how long this has been suggested by many, and of what importance it is to a race of men, possessing qualities equally commendable with our own – how many millions are at present involved in the decision of the question – It is impossible for me to object in being instrumental to the business. He then remarked, that he was convinced, whatever should be the decision, that in bringing forward the discussion, he performed nothing more than his duty; and he was so fully persuaded of the rectitude of his conduct, that no consideration whatever would make him swerve from his honour so far, as to dissuade him from marching boldly forward on the occasion. It was no party question, and he flattered himself that the voice of reason and truth would be heard. He was resolved to be regulated by temper and coolness, and challenged a fair discussion. – It was not a proposition grounded upon particular motives of policy, but founded in principles of philanthropy. It was no idle expedient or speculation of the moment, but derived from the most mature deliberation. He came not to accuse the merchants, but to appeal to their feelings and humanity. He confessed, that in the weak state of health in which he now appeared, and precarious as it might seem to many, he would stand against every personal idea, and bear the burthen [burden] destined for a person who stood in his situation. The subject had already undergone many discussions, and he apprehended that previous to a final decision, it would undergo many more. What must make every man of feeling shudder was, that, after examining the annals of Africa, numbers had been carried every year from their native country, in order to satiate the avarice of a certain description of men whose whole thoughts were bent upon tyranny and oppression …

'The poor wretches were in such a deplorable state'

MR WILBERFORCE then noticed that he had carefully examined the histories of the West Indies, and had attended to the times, when forgetting every idea of humanity, they were torn from the protection of their friends. To delude them particularly from their native country, they generally set sail from Africa in the night time, and thus evaded reflections, which might be roused concerning their friends and relations ashore. This was a dreadful expedient; and till now, he could not believe that so much misery could be condensed in so little room. He could wish to rouse the feelings of every man on the occasion, and convince the people that their intention and aid were the result of consideration, which did awaken him. With regard to the gentlemen of Liverpool, he could do them the justice to believe, that they would not seriously interrupt the abolition of the slave trade, especially when they understood that the characters of the people of this country were sullied by the outrages alluded to. Nothing, certainly, could excite them sooner to an acquiescence, than the sight of 600 linked two and two; consequently to hear the gentlemen of Liverpool affirm, that the situation of these poor unhappy mortals, was comfortable, rather appeared strange and ridiculous. He then adverted to what had been adduced by Mr Norris, in his evidence, who had made a comparison between an African monarch, and an European, and declared that was called a palace, was nothing more than a house of mud, where, however, every attention was made for that tenor of tranquillity which was so very desireable. – The manner of treating negroes, during a long voyage, was to the following effect:– the space between the decks is appointed entirely for

THE END OF TRANSATLANTIC SLAVERY

1772
The 'Somerset Case' rules that slaves arriving in England acquire automatic freedom and cannot be returned to the West Indies.

1787
The Society for the Abolition of the Slave Trade is founded.

1791
Wilberforce's bill for abolition of the slave trade to the West Indies fails in the Commons.

1794
Revolutionary France abolishes slavery in its colonies; Napoleon restores it two years later.

their lodging; every attention is paid to keep that as clean as possible; the negroes are kept on deck all day, if the weather be fine; they are fed with two meals of comfortable victuals; they are supplied with the luxuries of pipe and tobacco, and a dram occasionally, when the coldness of the weather requires it; they are supplied with the musical instruments of their country; they are encouraged to be cheerful, to sing and to dance, and they do both; the women are supplied with beads to ornament themselves; they are kept clean shaved; and every attention paid to their heads that there be no vermin lodged there; they are secured with fetters on their legs, two and two together; and if a turbulent disposition appears, with another on the wrist; their apartments are clean washed, and fumigated with the fumes of tar and frankincense, and sprinkled with vinegar, &c. As an extenuation of the crimes laid to the charge of the agents for the merchants, who are accustomed to this traffic, it has been mentioned with some degree of triumph, that they were treated on board with all manner of luxurious indulgence. The luxury alluded to was this – the song and the dance were promoted; the women were employed in weaving ornaments for the hair, and the utmost attention was observed to keep up their spirits.

'To hear a recital of these facts would make people shudder'

The truth of this observation was evidently the very reverse, and if it were possible to cast a film over the eyes of mankind, so as to deprive them of sight by a total blindness, the prevaricating mode of mentioning the transactions, could not be depicted in a more absurd point of view. The poor wretches were in such a deplorable state and unparalleled torment, and suffering such torture, that the surgeon who visited them, when bound two and two, could not pass without having his legs bitten by the slaves. Sir George Yonge affirms, that the stench was so intolerable as to be past all sufferance; and that in the article of water there was a miserable allowance. It was extremely worthy of observation to explain how the songs and dances were promoted. It was not a scene of freedom or spontaneous joy; for one man was employed to dance the men, and another to dance the women. If they found themselves inclined not to undergo the fatigue, certain persons were ordered to whip them into a compliance. To hear a recital of these facts would make people shudder; and the tear of sympathy would communicate from one man to another with congenial celerity. There was one captain who declared that his feelings revolted at such measures. He applauded highly the

1807
Parliament abolishes the British slave trade in the Atlantic, and the USA follows suit.

1808
The British West Africa Squadron is established to prevent illegal slaving by intercepting ships; Sierra Leone is founded as a crown colony and destination for freed slaves.

1833
The Abolition of Slavery Act ends slavery in the West Indies.

1838
Emancipation occurs in British territories worldwide.

1865
Slavery is abolished in the USA after a civil war fought partly on the issue.

1888
Brazil, which over several hundred years has absorbed 40 per cent of all transatlantic slaves, finally abolishes slavery.

sensations of this man, who had made such a concession in defiance of the barbarous practises already described. But DEATH, which on every occasion levels all distinctions, gave the unhappy victims that freedom from persecution and torture which other wise they could not have received.

When first I heard, Sir, of these iniquities, I considered them as exaggerations, and could not believe it possible, that men had determined to live by exerting themselves for the torture and misery of their fellow-creatures. I have taken great pains to make myself master of the subject, and can declare, that such scenes of barbarity are enough to rouse the indignation and horror of the most callous of mankind. Upon making an average of the loss sustained in the cargo of the Guinea ships, it appears, that one-eighth of the whole generally suffered. Upon examining the Jamaica Report, another essential loss was discovered, numbers died by the attempt of seasoning the slaves, that is, changing them from one climate to another – sometimes the loss appeared by death to be 4 1-half per cent. – at other times 17 per cent. the last of which calculation is generally admitted by the best writers. In every common cargo, it has been observed, that about 50 or 60 perish. From the windward coast about Sierra Leona, the general average of mortality was not found more than three per cent. From Bonny [in the Niger Delta region], the number of slaves was not recollected that died on the voyage. From Benin, nine were buried out of 300 in the course of three months. But the general average of mortality from Benin, Bonny, New Calabar, Old Calabar, Cameroon, and Gaboon, was much greater. That the slaves are subject to the following disorders: the small pox, measles, dysentery, fluxes, and fevers. They are rendered more sickly by laying up in land rivers. They generally lie longer on the coast than a slave ship does. An epidemical disorder on the coast prevails sometimes to a very great degree. – Mr Jones had a ship, in which a fever broke out before she had purchased twenty slaves. This distemper carried off a great number of the crew in the course of a month. From every consideration I shall deal frankly with the House, by declaring, that no act of policy whatever will make me swerve from my duty and oblige me to abandon a measure which I think will be an honour to humanity. Mr Wilberforce then mentioned, that he intended to submit to the consideration of the House, several resolutions, upon which a General Motion should be found for the TOTAL ABOLITION of the SLAVE TRADE.

'Sympathy is the great source of humanity'

When, says he, I was persuaded of the frequent commission of the crimes mentioned, I found myself impelled to go boldly forward; and had before I had time to reflect, proceeded so far that I could not recede; but had I deserted the great and important undertaking, I should have considered myself wanting in that necessary portion of duty which I owed to my constituents and to my country. There is no accusation made against the gentlemen of the West India trade; but, by bringing forward the consideration of such a mighty object, we unite with the person of sensibility, that the measure is necessary, as founded in rectitude and universal benevolence. The great cause, it has been stated, of mortality in the West Indies is, that the slaves are very profligate and dissolute in their manners; but the principal cause, however, is their ill treatment; for the agents squeeze as much as possible from their exertions. Here the Divine Doctrine is contradicted by the reverse action – That sympathy is the great source of humanity.

'The *pure principles of toleration*'

House of Commons, London, 11 May 1792

Charles James Fox
on the need for religious liberty

The dissolute son of a dissolute father (Henry Fox, the first Lord Holland, had at an early age lost his fortune gambling), Charles James Fox (1749–1806) was one of the founding fathers of modern liberalism, and spent much of his political career in a famous rivalry with William Pitt the Younger. A friend of Dr Johnson, and hated by George III (though a friend of his son, the Prince of Wales), Fox made a name for himself first by his flamboyance, but also through his espousal of progressive causes. He took the side of the American colonists against the crown, rejoiced at the French Revolution, and championed the Prince of Wales, the future George IV, against his reactionary father, campaigning for the former to be made regent.

Fox also upheld freedom of speech, in campaigning for the libel laws to be made less restrictive. His defence of religious liberty, the subject of the following speech, is a natural concomitant of such a philosophy – as was his campaign for freedom of association and public meetings. He particularly wished for the repeal of the Test and Corporation Acts, passed in the reigns of Charles II and Queen Anne, which effectively banned Catholics from public positions. In his philosophy can be discerned the foundations not only of the early 19th-century Whig creed, but also of the attitudes of later Liberals such as W. E. Gladstone and John Morley. 'Disabilities', as the impediments were known, for Roman Catholics were removed by 1829, though, ironically, by a Tory government under the supposedly arch-reactionary Duke of Wellington.

It has been said by some persons that, although toleration is of itself abstractedly a matter of justice, yet, that in political speculation it should never be allowed to intrench upon, or endanger existing establishments. The converse of this appears to me to be the true policy, and that no defence of any establishment whatever should be built on principles repugnant to toleration. Toleration is not to be regarded as a thing convenient and useful to a state, but a thing in itself essentially right and just. I, therefore, lay it down as my principle, that those who live in a state where there is an establishment of religion [i.e. the Established Church] can fairly be bound only by that part of the establishment which is consistent with the pure principles of toleration. What are those principles? On what were they founded? On the fundamental, unalienable rights of man. It is true there are some rights which man should give up for the sake of securing others in a state of society. But it is true also that he should give up but a portion of his material rights in order that he may have a government for the protection of the remainder. But to call on man to give up his religious rights is to call on him to do that which is impossible. I will say that no state can compel it; no state ought to require it, because it is not in the power of man to comply with that requisition.

'For us there is no excuse for persecution'

But there are those who say, though a man could not help his opinions, yet that, unless under certain restrictions, they ought not to be made public; for that whatever a man naturally has,

CATHOLIC EMANCIPATION

1778
A Relief Act improves Catholic rights of land inheritance and ownership.

1780
The Gordon Riots see a reaction against liberalisation for Catholics.

1791–3
Further Relief Acts give qualifying Irish Catholics the right to vote and remove many civil disabilities for English Catholics.

1800
Union with Ireland means the loss of a separate Irish Parliament.

1801
Pitt the Younger resigns prime ministership (and Lord Castlereagh the Irish secretaryship) because of George III's opposition to Irish Catholic representation at Westminster.

1807
The administration of Lord Grenville resigns after George III opposes army commissions for Catholics.

1810
The radical MP for Westminster, Sir Francis Burdett, is arrested for a pro-toleration newspaper article, prompting riots in support of him in London.

1813–25
Several further Catholic Relief bills falter in Parliament.

1828
Daniel O'Connell, leader of the Irish Catholic Association, is elected MP for County Clare but is barred from attending Westminster on account of his religion.

1829
Fears of a crisis in Ireland help passage of the Roman Catholic Relief Bill, sponsored by Sir Robert Peel, and Catholics can henceforth take their place in Parliament.

---

he gives them all up when he comes into society, and therefore religious liberty, among the rest, must be modified for the good of society; so that by the liberty of man is meant nothing more than that which is convenient to the State in which he lives, and under this idea penalties on religion are deemed expedient. This I take to be a radical error, and for the reason I have assigned already – that it is not in the power of man to surrender his opinion, and therefore the society which demands him to make this sacrifice demands an impossibility. What, then, does this lead to? That no man shall be deprived of any part of his liberty, with respect to his opinions, unless his actions derived from such opinions are clearly prejudicial to the state.

There are three different situations in which a man may be placed in regard to religion – a total indifference to it, as was the case with the pagan world before Christianity was known, and also with those who do not now believe it. Upon this I refer the House to the History of the Decline and Fall of the Roman Empire, written by an hon. gentleman♥ who was once a member of this House; he said that persecution in the pagans was less criminal than in Christians, because the pagans had not the same doctrines that the Christians have to teach them the principles of toleration. Another situation that diminished the cruelty of persecution, or rather rendered it less criminal, was a state of popery; for these deluded persons, in the time of bigotry, thought that, by persecuting those who differed from them, they were serving the cause of truth and justice; that God had inspired them with the true religion, and that they were serving him while they were destroying their fellow beings: although these practices were deplorable, yet, as they were the mere effects of ignorance, the principle on which they proceeded diminished the criminality of persecution. The third state is that in which we now are. The people of this country are neither indifferent about religion, nor are they blindly attached to any particular faith; they are not pagans, nor popish bigots. For us there is no excuse for persecution. We know full well that religion is founded on a principle that should not, cannot, be subject to any human power. There is a maxim which has been a thousand and a thousand times repeated, and yet by some as often forgotten, although there are not two opinions as to its propriety and justice, 'Do as you would be done by'. Will the members of the establishment be tried by this maxim? Will they submit to be governed by principles which they themselves inculcate; or will they proudly and impiously say that they are sure theirs is the only true religion, and that all who deviate from it are devoted to eternal torment?

In this country we are governed by King, Lords, and Commons. No man will contend that any of these powers is infallible? Then why do the members of the established church proceed as if they are infallible? For so they do, if they claim exclusive privileges and enforced penalties on those who differ from them. Upon what principle is an establishment to be maintained at all? It is upon the principle of its being agreeable to the opinion of the majority of the people, and not, surely, upon the slightest pretence of infallibility. The members of the establishment should say to those who differ from them:

You who differ from, as well as you who agree with us, are equal in rights, and have an equal title to enjoyments. We are neither pagans nor Papists. We have learned to do as we would be done by. If we were to persecute you for your opinions, we should, for aught we know to the contrary, be persecuting truth instead of falsehood. Come, then, let us each enjoy the freedom of our own mind, and equally participate of all social enjoyments.

Persecution is a word so odious, and toleration a word so generally embraced, that two opinions are not entered on either; and yet, strange to tell, much difference has arisen upon the application of them. The question, then, seems first to be, what really is to be understood by toleration? I think that, in defining this word, and conveying the ideas which I annex to it, I ought to go much farther than proving that it means the total absence of persecution, and that to refuse to any man any civil right, and an equal participation of civil advantage, on account of his religious opinions, is in itself, persecution.

'The question now is, what is, and what is not toleration'

On these general principles I trust that it is not necessary to dilate farther. The question now is, what is, and what is not toleration. In my own opinion toleration ought to go beyond abstinence from persecution; but on my own opinion alone I do not rely. I will quote the sentiments of a very eminent man, Archdeacon Paley*, who had declared himself to be a friend to complete toleration of all Dissenters. The reverend divine, however, meant more than it is my intention at present to propose. My motion I confess to be limited. A future and a fitter period may be found to introduce a measure whose verge would be more ample, more extensive, and consequently more complete.

Many persons opposed unlimited toleration from an apprehension that it might prove injurious to the state. To such I beg leave to say that they ought first to be well convinced that it really would produce that effect. The most moderate and the most enlightened men in this country, and those, too, members of the establishment, are friends to general toleration. Indeed, the right hon. the chancellor of the exchequer [Pitt the Younger] himself last year stood pledged to support the principle of general toleration, and has said that it is a matter not of favour, but of right, and that whether it should be granted is only a question of justice.

What is the principle of persecution? The condemnation of a man before he has committed a breach of the law. A principle which compels us to live in a constant state of hypocrisy towards God and man; for it calls on those who do not believe in the doctrines of the Church of England to give a constant attendance at divine service, and subscribe to the ceremonies of the church. This is commanding hypocrisy by authority. It is ordaining by law that a man shall pursue that form of religion here which, in his mind, is to insure his eternal damnation hereafter. By this we say to a father – 'You shall not teach your son that religion which in your soul you believe is to secure his eternal happiness. You are to choose, either to teach him no religion at all, or to teach him that by which you believe he will be damned to eternity.' This is the true spirit of persecution. And is it the fact? Most unquestionably it is the case in the law with regard to Catholics. In the opinion of some there once was an occasion for these states; in my opinion, there never was, nor would they have been adequate to the end proposed if there had; but now there is not the shadow of excuse, for it has ceased. The most dangerous periods, the reigns of Elizabeth and James, did not justify even one of the penal statutes that exist. If such times, therefore, did not justify them, what argument can be used for their existence now?

'We have no right to construe what actions are to follow opinions'

Sometimes attempts are made to defend the principle of persecution by considering it as a mode of preventing the mischief that may arise from a propagation of erroneous religious opinions; it is alleged that it is the business of a statesman to consider the effect of any religious opinion, and in that view, whatever appears to him as dangerous to the state, he ought to prevent. The first part of this doctrine, namely, that of assuming any mode of religion to be wrong, is begging the question; but I must protest against the whole of this mode of argument. We have no right to construe what actions are to follow opinions. We should weigh actions before we pretend to judge of them at all. In order that we may guess what actions are likely to follow opinions, we should ourselves first have entertained those opinions; or, if we guess at all, we ought to guess on the favourable side. But, it is said, there are no commands in the church which may not safely be obeyed; or at least the Church of England is the safeguard of the state. Is it the fact? Is it possible for a man to become a very bad citizen, even by implicitly obeying the doctrine of the Church of England itself? Most unquestionably it is; for the Church of England teaches us that we are to make no resistance to the commands of the magistrate, although they should be unlawful, or even unnatural; the doctrine is passive obedience and non-resistance, and consequences were to be left to a future state; this is the doctrine of James II; this, it is true, is not now the law, but it is still the doctrine of the church, and thus, by being a good churchman, a person may become a bad citizen. What is the result of all this? That, as in the established church there is so much error that it cannot be obeyed totally without breach of moral obligation and even of positive law (for a man may be punished for obedience to the illegal commands of a legal master), it is the essence of injustice to persecute any person for omitting to conform to this established religion.

♥ The historian Edward Gibbon (1737–94) had twice been an MP, in the 1770s and 1780s.
♦ William Paley (1743–1805), Archdeacon of Carlisle and author of *Evidences of Christianity*.

'I stand up to defend Thomas Paine'

Court of King's Bench, London, 18 December 1792

Thomas Erskine

defends *The Rights of Man* against charges of 'sedition'

Thomas Erskine (1750–1823) was the youngest son of the 10th Earl of Buchan. Born in Edinburgh and educated at St Andrew's Grammar School, he became a midshipman in the Navy aged 14, then on the death of his father and aged 18 he bought himself a commission in the Army. In 1775, having been attracted to the idea of the law, he sold his commission and went up to Cambridge University the following year. Shortly after he began to practise he made an instant reputation in a case against Lord Sandwich, the First Lord of the Admiralty, who was accused of corruption in respect of the hospital at Greenwich.

Erskine soon had a large and remunerative practice, becoming a King's Counsel when aged only 33 – and after only five years' experience – and earning the then stupendous sum of £10,000 a year by 1791. He became MP for Portsmouth, was a friend of Charles James Fox and Richard Brinsley Sheridan (sharing their progressive Whig views) and, had George, Prince of Wales, become regent in 1789 when the king was incapacitated, Erskine would have been made attorney-general. When in 1792 the radical Tom Paine (1737–1809) was prosecuted in absentia for treason for his attacks on the royal family in his book *The Rights of Man* (a riposte to Edmund Burke's *Reflections on the Revolution in France*), Erskine defended him, despite many of his friends, including the Prince of Wales, urging him not to accept the brief.

The same day that Erskine made this impassioned speech in defence of freedom of speech, the jury found Paine guilty without even bothering to retire. On William Pitt the Younger's death in 1806, Erskine became lord chancellor and was widely condemned for accepting the post, since he had little knowledge of some quite substantial areas of the civil law. As can be judged from this speech, however, he had an advanced idea of the importance of liberty of expression.

'Gentlemen, it is now my duty to address myself without digression to the defence.

The first thing which presents itself in the discussion of any subject is to state distinctly, and with precision, what the question is, and, where prejudice and misrepresentation have been exerted, to distinguish it accurately from what it is NOT. The question, then, is NOT whether the constitution of our fathers – under which we live, under which I present myself before you, and under which alone you have any jurisdiction to hear me – be or be not preferable to the constitution of America or France, or any other human constitution. For upon what principle can a court, constituted by the authority of any government, and administering a positive system of law under it, pronounce a decision against the constitution which creates its authority, or the rule of action which its jurisdiction is to enforce? The common sense of the most uninformed person must revolt at such an absurd supposition.

I have no difficulty, therefore, in admitting that, if by accident some or all of you were alienated in opinion and affection from the forms and principles of the English government, and were impressed with the value of that unmixed representative constitution which this work recommends and inculcates, you could not, on that account acquit the defendant. Nay, to speak out plainly, I freely admit that even if you were avowed enemies to monarchy, and devoted to republicanism, you would be nevertheless bound by your oaths, as a jury sworn to administer justice according to the English law, to convict the author of *The Rights of Man*, if it were brought home to your consciences that he had exceeded those widely extended bounds which the ancient wisdom and liberal policy of the English constitution have allotted to the range of a free press. I freely concede this, because you have no jurisdiction to judge either the author or the work by any rule but that of English law, which is the source of your authority. But having made this large concession, it follows, by a consequence so inevitable as to be invulnerable to all argument or artifice, that if, on the other hand, you should be impressed (which I know you to be) not only with a dutiful regard, but with an enthusiasm, for the whole form and substance of your own government; and though you should think that this work, in its circulation amongst classes of men unequal to political researches, may tend to alienate opinion; still you cannot, upon such grounds, without a similar breach of duty, convict the defendant of a libel – unless he has clearly stepped beyond that extended range of communication which the same ancient wisdom and liberal policy of the British constitution has allotted for the liberty of the press ...

'I come to defend his having written this book'

What crime is it that the defendant comes to answer for to-day? – what is the notice that I, who am his counsel, have from this parchment of the crime alleged against him? I come to defend his having written this book. The record states nothing else:– the general charge of sedition in the introduction is notoriously paper and packthread; because the innuendoes cannot enlarge the sense or natural construction of the text. The record does not state any one extrinsic fact or circumstance to render the work criminal at one time more than another; it states no peculiarity of time or season or intention, not provable from the writing itself, which is the naked charge upon record. There is nothing, therefore, which gives you any jurisdiction beyond the construction of the work itself; and you cannot be justified in finding it criminal because published at this time, unless it would have been a criminal publication under any circumstances, or at any other time.

The law of England, then, both in its forms and substance, being the only rule by which the author or the work can be justified or condemned, and the charge upon the record being the

THE CAREER OF THOMAS PAINE

1774
Emigrates to the American colonies after pursuing various jobs, as corset-maker, teacher and excise collector, and acquires increasingly radical ideas.

1776
Begins publishing pamphlets in support of American

independence and joins the (American) Continental Army.

1777–9
Serves as secretary of foreign affairs for the Congress Committee.

1781
Travels to Revolutionary France.

naked charge of a libel, the cause resolves itself into a question of the deepest importance to us all – THE NATURE AND EXTENT OF THE LIBERTY OF THE ENGLISH PRESS.

The proposition which I mean to maintain as the basis of the liberty of the press, and without which it is an empty sound, is this: that every man, not intending to mislead, but seeking to enlighten others with what his own reason and conscience, however erroneously, have dictated to him as truth, may address himself to the universal reason of a whole nation, either upon the subject of governments in general, or upon that of our own particular country: that he may analyse the principles of its constitution, point out its errors and defects, examine and publish its corruptions, warn his fellow-citizens against their ruinous consequences, and exert his whole faculties in pointing out the most advantageous changes in establishments which he considers to be radically defective, or sliding from their object by abuse. All this every subject of this country has a right to do, if he contemplates only what he thinks would be for its advantage, and but seeks to change the public mind by the conviction which flows from reasonings dictated by conscience.

If, indeed, he writes what he does not think; if, contemplating the misery of others, he wickedly condemns what his own understanding approves; or, even admitting his real disgust against the government or its corruptions, if he calumniates living magistrates, or holds out to individuals that they have a right to run before the public mind in their conduct; that they may oppose by contumacy or force what private reason only disapproves; that they may disobey the law, because their judgment condemns it; or resist the public will, because they honestly wish to change it – he is then a criminal upon every principle of rational policy, as well as upon the immemorial precedents of English justice; because such a person seeks to disunite individuals from their duty to the whole, and excites to overt acts of misconduct in a part of the community, instead of endeavouring to change, by the impulse of reason, that universal assent which, in this and in every country, constitutes the law for all.

'These are undoubtedly the rights of man'

I have, therefore, no difficulty in admitting that if, upon an attentive perusal of this work, it shall be found that the defendant has promulgated any doctrines which excite individuals to withdraw from their subjection to the law by which the whole nation consents to be governed; if his book shall be found to have warranted or excited that unfortunate criminal who appeared here yesterday to endeavour to relieve himself from imprisonment by the

1786
Publishes his *Dissertation on Government*.

1787
Returns to Britain.

1791–2
Publishes the anti-monarchical *The Rights of Man*, the second part of which is labelled 'seditious'.

1792
Flees to France, thus escaping trial *in absentia*, and serves briefly as a deputy in the French National Assembly.

1794
Publishes *The Age of Reason*, but is imprisoned in France for opposing the execution of King Louis XVI.

1795
Is released from prison on claiming American citizenship.

1802
Leaves France for USA, where he spends his last years obscurely in New York State, his ideas considered too radical for the young American republic.

destruction of a prison, or dictated to him the language of defiance which ran through the whole of his defence; if, throughout the work there shall be found any syllable or letter which strikes at the security of property; or which hints that anything less than the whole nation can constitute the law, or that the law, be it what it may, is not the inexorable rule of action for every individual, I willingly yield him up to the justice of the court.

Gentlemen, I say, in the name of Thomas Paine, and in his words as author of *The Rights of Man*, as written in the very volume that is charged with seeking the destruction of property:

The end of all political associations is the preservation of the rights of man, which rights are liberty, property, and security; that the nation is the source of all sovereignty derived from it; the right of property being secured and inviolable, no one ought to be deprived of it, except in cases of evident public necessity, legally ascertained, and on condition of a previous just indemnity.

These are undoubtedly the rights of man – the rights for which all governments are established – and the only rights Mr Paine contends for; but which he thinks (no matter whether right or wrong) are better to be secured by a republican constitution than by the forms of the English government. He instructs me to admit that, when government is once constituted, no individuals, without rebellion, can withdraw their obedience from it; that all attempts to excite them to it are highly criminal for the most obvious reasons of policy and justice; that nothing short of the will of a whole people can change or affect the rule by which a nation is to be governed; and that no private opinion, however honestly inimical to the forms or substance of the law, can justify resistance to its authority, while it remains in force. The author of *The Rights of Man* not only admits the truth of all this doctrine, but he consents to be convicted, and I also consent for him, unless his work shall be found studiously and painfully to inculcate those great principles of government which it is charged to have been written to destroy.

'This freedom has alone made our government what it is'

Let me not, therefore, be suspected to be contending that it is lawful to write a book pointing out defects in the English government, and exciting individuals to destroy its sanctions, and to refuse obedience. But, on the other hand, I do contend that it is lawful to address the English nation as their momentous subjects; for had it not been for this inalienable right (thanks be to God and our fathers for establishing it!), how should we have had this constitution which we so loudly boast of? If, in the march of the human mind, no man could have gone before the establishments of the time he lived in, how could our establishment, by reiterated changes, have become what it is? If no man could have awakened the public mind to errors and abuses in our government, how could it have passed on from stage to stage, through reformation and revolution, so as to have arrived from barbarism to such a pitch of happiness and perfection, that the attorney-general considers it as profanation to touch it further, or to look for any further amendment?

In this manner power has reasoned in every age; government, in its own estimation, has been at all times a system of perfection; but a free press has examined and detected its errors, and the people have from time to time reformed them. This freedom has alone made our government what it is; this freedom alone can preserve it; and therefore, under the banners of that freedom, today I stand up to defend Thomas Paine.

'*Man has the fundamental right to state his opinion*'

House of Commons, London, 22 May 1797

Charles James Fox
on the freedoms of speech and association

The existence of an international emergency is a ready excuse for politicians to seek to restrict the liberties of the people in the interests of preserving national security. The Treasonable Practices and Seditious Meetings bills had been passed in 1795, despite a ferocious campaign against them by the progressive Whig Charles James Fox. He said they would be a death-blow to the constitution, and said in the Commons that he would advise civil disobedience to prevent the enforcement of the new laws – a statement that drew heavy criticism. Even some of his natural supporters felt he was using the national crisis as an opportunity to gain party advantage, which also reflected badly upon him.

Fox suggests in this speech, made later in the course of the war with Revolutionary France, that recent international reverses, which had led to calls for the dismissal of Pitt's government, had been the cause of decisions by various local officials to restrict the right of public assembly. William Pitt (the Younger) had spent much of the previous year unsuccessfully seeking to negotiate a peace with France. On Christmas Day 1796 he had been spared the calamity of a French invasion of Ireland only by the force of the gales in Bantry Bay. In the weeks before Fox made this speech, the Navy had mutinied at Spithead, with further mutinies in succeeding weeks at other main naval stations.

Fox must have known that he stood little chance of securing his aim of having the Treason and Sedition Acts repealed. His aim was to embarrass the government, which he succeeded in doing; but in the course of doing so he set out clearly another, consistent tenet of his liberal philosophy that would, within a few decades, become the accepted norm, and he registered another step along the path to proper liberty of the subject being a recognised part of the English constitution.

Failing to get his way, Fox stopped attending Parliament from 1797 to 1802. He died in 1806 of 'dropsy', and despite never having held the highest office was buried in Westminster Abbey, near the grave of his rival Pitt, who predeceased him by eight months.

This act for the outlawing of seditious meetings is outrageous, because it throws difficulties in the way of the exercise of the right, and enables sheriffs to prevent meetings; and it has been proved, that since the passing of this act more refusals have been given by magistrates than in any former period. This has been particularly the case since recent calamities have disposed the country to assemble so generally to petition for the dismission of ministers. Very extraordinary reasons have been assigned by some of them for refusing to convoke meetings. The sheriff of Suffolk refused, because the subject had been debated in Parliament, and because he was going to London. Another magistrate refused, though called upon by a numerous body of persons, because he would not disturb the unanimity of the county. The power of dispersing meetings is as obnoxious as the refusal to convoke them. In the county in which I live, the sheriff, after putting the question, said there was a visible majority of votes, but because he did not know whether they were all freeholders that were present, he refused to sign the proceedings, and give validity to the record. Another person on this capricious objection could not take the chair, because the sheriff had the power to disperse the meeting; and thus an attempt was made to defeat the petition in the county of Surrey, even under the colour of complying with the statute. In many other cases difficulties have been found that make it vexatious, and almost impossible, to exercise this right under the provisions of this act.

It requires so much trouble to comply with all the provisions of the act, where the meeting is not called by the regular magistrate, that it is next to an impossibility to carry the exercise of the right generally into effect. In some instances, where zeal and perseverance had conquered every obstacle, inconveniences were suffered that would deter men on ordinary occasions from assembling. In Westminster, for instance, where the meeting was called in strict conformity to the act, the day of meeting was most unfavourable in point of weather, but it was found inconvenient to adjourn, because they must have renewed all the formalities required by the statute.

And what is the benefit expected to be derived from all this? Are provisions like these likely to alter the minds of men? Are they calculated to prevent communication, and stifle the opinions and discontents of a people? If it were a new and an abstract question, there might, perhaps, be a difference of opinion upon the subject; but unfortunately, a book is laid open to us, in which we may read, in most legible characters, the true character and consequences of such a measure – that book is the kingdom of Ireland. In the year 1794 a Convention Bill was passed in Ireland to prevent meetings of the people. What was the consequence? Ministers boasted of the success of the measure: they flattered themselves they had succeeded in preventing meetings; but I have now the authority of the Parliament of Ireland for saying that what they had prevented publicly had been done in private; and that ever since the year 1791 meetings of the people had been held, which, up to the year 1795, were small and insignificant – small, because up to that time they still had the power of meeting in public, and discussing their grievances openly, and without reserve. Up to the year 1794, then, they were small and harmless – but then comes the Convention Bill, that forces them into clandestine and secret meetings by midnight; then comes correspondence with the foreign enemy, and all the terrifying and alarming plots which the report of the House of Lords of Ireland has ascribed to the people of that distracted country.

'What deplorable ignorance of the human heart'

What deplorable ignorance of the human heart to think that, by a mere Convention Bill to prevent the meetings without redressing grievances, they could make men forget by making them silent? What criminal ignorance to conceive that, by damming up a torrent, it would not force its way in another direction? But it seems that, as our act has not yet produced the same effects in England, we must not go for instruction to the sister kingdom. I see no sense in any such argument: human nature is the same in all countries; if you prevent a man who feels himself aggrieved from declaring his sentiments, you force him to other expedients for redress. Do you think that you gain a proselyte when you silence a disclaimer? No; you have only, by preventing the declaration of grievances in a constitutional way, forced men to more pernicious modes of coming at relief. In proportion as opinions are open, they are innocent and harmless.

Opinions become dangerous to a state only when persecution makes it necessary for the people to communicate their ideas under the bond of secrecy. Do you believe it possible that the calamity which now rages in Ireland would have come to its present height, if the people had been allowed to meet and divulge their grievances? Publicity makes it impossible for artifice to succeed, and designs of a hostile nature lose their danger by the certainty of exposure.

But it is said that these bills will expire in a few years; that they will expire when we shall have peace and tranquillity restored to us. What a sentiment to inculcate! You tell the people, that when every thing goes well, when they are happy and comfortable, then they meet freely, to recognise their happiness, and pass eulogiums on their government; but that in a moment of war and calamity of distrust and misconduct, it is not permitted them to meet together, because then, instead of eulogising, they might think proper to condemn ministers. What a

WAR AND CIVIL LIBERTY
1790–6

1790
In Parliament, Charles James Fox and Edmund Burke respectively support and oppose the revolutionary developments in France (Feb.).

1791
Pitt attempts neutrality as continental powers manoeuvre against France; in Belfast, Wolfe Tone founds the United Irishmen to campaign for Irish rights (Oct.).

1792
Austria and Prussia are now at war with France, which repels invasion forces and in turn invades German lands and occupies the Spanish Netherlands; Louis XVI and his family are imprisoned, and a French republic is declared; Part 2 of Thomas Paine's pro-republican *The Rights of Man* earns him a trial for treason (verdict: guilty), but he has already fled to France.

1793
France declares war on Britain and Holland, executes its king (Jan.) and queen (Marie-Antoinette, Oct.), and faces royalist rebellions and internecine revolutionary struggles that result in the 'Terror'; Britain enters alliance with other powers, besieging Toulon; the British goverment suspends the Habeus Corpus Act (March).

1794
The radical Thomas Hardy, founder of the pro-Reform London Corresponding Society, is tried for treason but acquitted (May–Nov.); the United Irishmen are declared illegal (May); in France, the toppling of Robespierre and St-Just finally ends the Terror (July).

1795
France defeats Holland and makes peace with Prussia; British forces fight in Brittany, attack Dutch colonies, and enter a triple alliance with Russia and Austria; George III's carriage is stoned in London by crowds who want an end to war and more food (Oct.); the Treasonable Practices and Seditious Meetings bills are passed (Nov.).

1796
George III and Queen Charlotte are again attacked with stones by protestors demanding bread (Jan.); an Insurrection Act is introduced in Ireland; Spain, now under French sway, declares war on Britain (Oct.); a French invasion of Ireland, aided by Wolfe Tone, is prevented only by bad weather in Bantry Bay (Dec.).

mockery is this! What an insult to say that this is preserving to the people the right of petition! To tell them that they shall have a right to applaud, a right to rejoice, a right to meet when they are happy, but not a right to condemn, not a right to deplore their misfortunes, not a right to suggest a remedy! I hate those insidious modes of undermining and libelling the constitution of the country. If you mean to say that the mixed and balanced government of England is good only for holidays and sunshine, but that it is inapplicable to a day of distress and difficulty, say so. If you mean that freedom is not as conducive to order and strength as it is to happiness, say so; and I will enter the lists with you, and contend that, among all the other advantages arising from liberty, are the advantages of order and strength in a super-eminent degree, and that too, in the moment when they are most wanted. Liberty is order. Liberty is strength. Good God, Sir, am I, on this day, to be called upon to illustrate the glorious and soothing doctrine? Look round the world and admire, as you must, the instructive spectacle! You will see that liberty not only is power and order, but that it is power and order predominant and invincible; that it derides all other sources of strength; that the heart of man has no impulse, and can have none that dares to stand in competition with it; and if, as Englishmen, we know how to respect its value, surely the present is the moment of all others, when we ought to secure its invigorating alliance.

'Embodying all the love of liberty'

Whether we look at our relative situation with regard to foreign powers, with regard to the situation of the sister kingdom, and with regard to our own internal affairs, there never was a moment when national strength was so much demanded, and when it was so incumbent upon us to call forth and embody all the vigour of the nation, by rousing, animating, and embodying all the love of liberty that used to characterise the country, and which, I trust, is not yet totally extinct. Is this a moment to diminish our strength, by indisposing all that part of the nation whose hearts glow with ardour for their original rights, but who feel with indignation that they are trampled upon and overthrown? Is not this a moment when, in addition to every other emotion, freedom should be roused as an ally, a supplementary force, and a substitute for all the other weak and inefficient levies that have been suggested in its stead? Have we not been nearly reduced to a situation, when it was too perilous, perhaps, to take the right course? May we not be again called upon for exertions that will demand the union of every hand and every heart in the kingdom? What might not this House do, if this House had the opinion of the country with it? Do not let us say, then, that we are to increase the force of the country by stifling opinion. It is only by promoting it, by giving facility to its expression, by meeting it with open hearts, by incorporating ourselves with the sense of the nation, that we can again revive that firm and compact power of British strength, that sprung out of British liberty.

'The deliverance of Europe'

House of Commons, London, 7 June 1799

William Pitt, the Younger
on the need to resist French expansionism

Even though William Pitt the Younger (1759–1806) was only 46 when he died, he had spent nearly 19 years as prime minister, 17 of them continuously between 1783 and 1801. His father, Pitt the Elder, 1st Earl of Chatham, had himself been prime minister from 1766 to 1768, and his son was brought up in the business of politics. Pitt the Younger was elected to the Commons at the age of 21. Within 18 months he was chancellor of the exchequer and within three years was prime minister. His great achievement in office was financial reform, but he was much less sure-footed when it came to leading Britain in the war against France. He left office when he fell out with George III over his policy of union with Ireland, which Pitt wished to accompany with a degree of Catholic emancipation. He returned as prime minister in 1804, attempting to put together an international alliance to fight Napoleon's France, but he was to die without realising that aim.

Pitt had attempted with varying degrees of success to put together an alliance when France had declared war on Britain on 1 February 1793. This speech, made six years into the war, argues for a subvention to the Russian tsar, Paul I, in the hope of bringing Russia in on the fight against France. In the speech, Pitt argues that until the French are driven back to within the boundaries of France there will be no 'deliverance' for Europe, nor any security for Britain. While Pitt is on the defensive to some extent about his policy, he also demonstrates his fierce patriotism and determination to defend Britain, and his fine oratorical skills.

The 'honourable gentleman' to whom Pitt refers at the start of this extract is George Tierney, the radical MP for Southwark, who on 27 May the previous year had fought Pitt in a duel on Putney Heath: both escaped unharmed.

'The honourable gentleman [Mr Tierney] says he wishes for peace, and that he approved more of what I said on this subject towards the close of my speech, than of the opening. Now what I said was, that if by powerfully seconding the efforts of our allies, we could only look for peace with any prospect of realising our hopes, whatever would enable us to do so promptly and effectually would be true economy. I must, indeed, be much misunderstood, if generally it was not perceived that I meant, that whether the period which is to carry us to peace be shorter or longer, what we have to look to is not so much when we make peace, as whether we shall derive from it complete and solid security; and that whatever other nations may do, whether they shall persevere in the contest, or untimely abandon it, we have to look to ourselves for the means of defence, we are to look to the means to secure our constitution, preserve our character, and maintain our independence, in the virtue and perseverance of the people. There is a high-spirited pride, an elevated loyalty, a generous warmth of heart, a nobleness of spirit, a hearty, manly gaiety, which distinguish our nation, in which we are to look for the best pledges of general safety, and of that security against an aggressing usurpation, which other nations in their weakness or in their folly have yet nowhere found. With respect to that which appears so much to embarrass certain gentlemen – the deliverance of Europe – I will not say particularly what it is.

Whether it is to be its deliverance from that under which it suffers, or that from which it is in danger; whether from the infection of false principles, the corroding cares of a period of distraction and dismay, or that dissolution of all governments, and that death of religion and social order which are to signalise the triumph of the French republic, if unfortunately for mankind she should, in spite of all opposition, prevail in the contest; – from whichsoever of these Europe is to be delivered, it will not be difficult to prove, that what she suffers, and what is her danger, are the power and existence of the French government. If any man says that the government is not a tyranny, he miserably mistakes the character of that body. It is an insupportable and odious tyranny, holding within its grasp the lives, the characters, and the fortunes of all who are forced to own its sway, and only holding these that it may at will measure out of each the portion, which from time to time it sacrifices to its avarice, its cruelty, and injustice. The French republic is dyked and fenced round with crime, and owes much of its present security to its being regarded with a horror which appals men in their approaches to its impious battlements.

'Some of the nations of Europe have shamefully crouched to that power'

The honourable gentleman says, that he does not know whether the emperor of Russia understands what we mean by the deliverance of Europe. I do not think it proper here to dwell much at length on this curious doubt. But whatever may be the meaning which that august personage attaches to our phrase 'the deliverance of Europe,' at least he has shown that he is no stranger to the condition of the world, that whatever be the specific object of the contest, he has learnt rightly to consider the character of the common enemy, and shows by his public proceedings that he is determined to take measures of more than ordinary precaution against the common disturbers of Europe, and the common enemy of man. Will the honourable gentleman continue in his state of doubt? Let him look to the conduct of that prince during what has passed of the present campaign. If in such conduct be not unfolded some solicitude for the deliverance of Europe from the tyranny of France, I know not, sir, in what we are to look for it. But the honourable gentleman seems to think no alliance can long be preserved against France. I do not deny that unfortunately some of the nations of Europe have shamefully crouched to that power, and receded from the common cause, at a moment

NAPOLEON IN THE 1790s

1793
Defeats the British forces at Toulon and is promoted to general (Dec.).

1794
Defends the Revolutionary government in Paris through the threat of force against rioters, the so-called 'whiff of grapeshot' (Oct.); the *Directoire* of five men now rules France (until 1799).

1796
Marries Josephine, the widow of a French aristocrat (March); commands French forces to defeat the Austrians (Battle of Millesimo) and the Piedmontese (Battle of Modovi), giving the French effective control of Lombardy.

when it was due to their own dignity, to what they owed to that civilised community of which they are still a part, to persevere in the struggle, to reanimate their legions with that spirit of just detestation and vengeance which such inhumanity and cruelty might so well provoke. I do not say that the powers of Europe have not acted improperly in many other instances; and Russia in her turn; for, during a period of infinite peril to this country, she saw our danger advance upon us, and four different treaties entered into of offensive alliance against us, without comment, and without a single expression of its disapprobation. This was the conduct of that power in former times. The conduct of His present Majesty [Tsar Paul I] raises quite other emotions, and excites altogether a different interest.

'Misery, and nakedness, to the unhappy victims of its power'

His Majesty, since his accession, has unequivocally declared his attachment to Great Britain, and, abandoning those projects of ambition which formed the occupation of his predecessor, he chose rather to join in the cause of religion and order against France, than to pursue the plan marked out for him to humble and destroy a power, which he was taught to consider as his common enemy. He turned aside from all hostility against the Ottoman Porte [Ottoman empire], and united his force to the power of that prince, the more effectually to check the progress of the common enemy. Will, then, gentlemen continue to regard with suspicion the conduct of that prince? Has he not sufficiently shown his devotion to the cause in which we are engaged, by the kind, and number, and value of his sacrifices, ultimately to prevail in the struggle against a tyranny which, in changing our point of vision, we everywhere find accompanied in its desolating progress by degradation. Misery, and nakedness, to the unhappy victims of its power – a tyranny which has magnified and strengthened its powers to do mischief, in the proportion that the legitimate and venerable fabrics of civilised and polished society have declined from the meridian of their glory, and lost the power of doing good – a tyranny which strides across the ill-fated domain of France, its foot armed with the scythe of oppression and indiscriminate proscription, that touches only to blight, and rests only to destroy; the reproach and the curse of the infatuated people who still continue to acknowledge it. When we consider that it is against this monster the emperor of Russia has sent down his legions, shall we say that he is not entitled to our confidence?

1797
Defeats the Austrians again, at the Battle of Rivoli, Italy (Jan.).

1798
Leads French forces in the occupation of Rome (Feb.), causing the pope to leave for exile; leads the French invasion of Egypt (May), but is cut off by Nelson's destruction of his fleet (Battle of the Nile, 1 Aug.).

1799
Returning to France, and already the country's outstanding general, stages a coup with others, becoming 'first consul', effectively sole ruler, under a new constitution. By now, France has subordinated Holland, Spain, the Austrian Netherlands and much of northern and central Italy, has seen off Prussia, and has forced Russia (Sept.) to withdraw from the war.

But what is the constitutional state of the question? It is competent, undoubtedly, to any gentleman to make the character of an ally the subject of consideration; but in this case it is not to the emperor of Russia we vote a subsidy, but to His Majesty. The question, therefore, is, whether His Majesty's government affix any undue object to the message, whether they draw any undue inference from the deliverance of Europe. The honourable gentleman has told us, that his deliverance of Europe is the driving of France within her ancient limits – that he is not indifferent to the restoration of the other states of Europe to independence, as connected with the independence of this country; but it is assumed by the honourable gentleman, that we are not content with wishing to drive France within her ancient limits, that, on the contrary, we seek to overthrow the government of France; and he would make us say, that we never will treat with it as a republic. Now I neither meant anything like this, nor expressed myself so as to lead to such inferences. Whatever I may in the abstract think of the kind of government called a republic, whatever may be its fitness to the nation where it prevails, there may be times when it would not be dangerous to exist in its vicinity. But while the spirit of France remains what at present it is, its government despotic, vindictive, unjust, with a temper untamed, a character unchanged, if its power to do wrong at all remains, there does not exist any security for this country or Europe. In my view of security, every object of ambition and aggrandisement is abandoned. Our simple object is security, just security, with a little mixture of indemnification. These are the legitimate objects of war at all times; and when we have attained that end, we are in a condition to derive from peace its beneficent advantages; but until then, our duty and our interest require that we should persevere unappalled in the struggle to which we were provoked. We shall not be satisfied with a false security. War, with all its evils, is better than a peace in which there is nothing to be seen but usurpation and injustice, dwelling with savage delight on the humble, prostrate condition of some timid suppliant people. It is not to be dissembled, that in the changes and chances to which the fortunes of individuals, as well as of states, are continually subject, we may have the misfortune, and great it would be, of seeing our allies decline the contest. I hope this will not happen. I hope it is not reserved for us to behold the mortifying spectacle of two mighty nations abandoning a contest, in which they have sacrificed so much, and made such brilliant progress.

'That mighty mass of iniquity'

In the application of this principle, I have no doubt but the honourable gentleman admits the security of the country to be the legitimate object of the contest; and I must think I am sufficiently intelligible on this topic. But wishing to be fully understood, I answer the honourable gentleman when he asks, 'Does the right honourable gentleman mean to prosecute the war until the French republic is overthrown? Is it his determination not to treat with France while it continues a republic?' – I answer, I do not confine my views to the territorial limits of France; I contemplate the principles, character, and conduct of France; I consider what these are; I see in them the issues of distraction, of infamy and ruin, to every state in her alliance; and therefore I say, that until the aspect of that mighty mass of iniquity and folly is entirely changed;– until the character of the government is totally reversed; until, by the common consent of the general voice of all men, I can with truth tell Parliament, France is no longer terrible for her contempt of the rights of every other nation – she no longer avows schemes of universal empire – she has settled into a state whose government can maintain those relations in their integrity, in which alone civilised communities are to find their security, and from which they are to derive their distinction and their glory; – until in the situation of

France we have exhibited to us those features of a wise, a just, and a liberal policy, I cannot treat with her.

'I earnestly pray that all the powers engaged in the contest may think as I do'

The time to come to the discussion of a peace can only be the time when you can look with confidence to an honourable issue; to such a peace as shall at once restore to Europe her settled and balanced constitution of general polity, and to every negotiating power in particular, that weight in the scale of general empire which has ever been found the best guarantee and pledge of local independence and general security. Such are my sentiments. I am not afraid to avow them. I commit them to the thinking part of mankind; and if they have not been poisoned by the stream of French sophistry, and prejudiced by her falsehood, I am sure they will approve of the determination I have avowed, for those grave and mature reasons on which I found it. I earnestly pray that all the powers engaged in the contest may think as I do, and particularly the emperor of Russia, which, indeed, I do not doubt; and therefore I do contend, that with that power it is fit that the house should enter into the engagement recommended in His Majesty's message.

'The arduous and most desperate struggle'

House of Commons, London, 22 July 1803

William Pitt, the Younger
on the need for strong defences against possible invasion

The Peace of Amiens, concluded in 1802, had marked a truce in the wars between Britain and France. However, it was soon clear that Napoleon was amassing a huge invasion force near Boulogne – estimated at 130,000 men – and on 18 May 1803 Britain declared war on France again. Pitt the Younger had resigned as prime minister in March 1801, following his failure, in the teeth of royal opposition, to advance the cause of Catholic emancipation. After the declaration of war he returned to the House of Commons from a self-imposed exile at Walmer, Kent, to give support to the ministry of his successor, Henry Addington, when he felt the measures being proposed were sufficient, and in order to oppose those he regarded as too weak.

Pitt made this speech on the third reading of the Defence Act Amendment Bill, one of the measures instituted to ensure the proper defence of the realm, which included building better coastal defences such as the Martello towers that would eventually appear along the southeast and east coasts. On 10 May 1804 he became First Lord of the treasury once more, though his health was already broken. His friends thought that the news of Napoleon's victory at Austerlitz in December 1805 dealt him his death-blow, countering as it did the hopeful news of Nelson's triumph at Trafalgar six weeks earlier. He died at Putney on 23 January 1806 after uttering the last words 'Oh, my country! How I leave my country!'

I am ready to admit to the honourable officer*, that our regular army is not quite so great as we could wish in this country, but we have provided means for augmenting it to a degree much greater than was ever known in this country; and in addition to all this, we are now providing an immense irregular force, the advantages to be derived from which are admitted and confirmed by the honourable officer himself, being indeed too obvious to be disputed by any one. As far, therefore, as relates to the description and to the extent of our force, Parliament has provided means, which to the honourable officer himself (cautious, honourably cautious, and anxious as he is for the safety of his country) appear sufficient to place this country in a state of absolute safety. All this is undoubtedly matter of great consolation; but at the same time it will not justify us in diminishing our anxiety, or in relaxing our efforts, for its completion, because there must remain some interval before all these plans are completely arranged and organised and brought to that state of perfection at which I hope they will, however, soon arrive; but even supposing that all the measures which I have stated were brought to perfection, still it would not dispense us from the necessity of adopting other means of defence, particularly in two points of view.

Suppose all the objects attained at this moment, yet the foundation of our security would not be these objects, however completely attained. Against the arduous and most desperate struggle in which we may be engaged, all these kinds of strength can only give us this kind of security, that if we are not wanting to ourselves, if we have not forgotten our national character, but remember who we are, and what we are contending for, the contest will be glorious to us and must terminate in the complete discomfiture of the enemy and ultimate security to this kingdom. But if there remain any measure, by the adoption of which our safety may be yet rendered, not the only more certain, perhaps, but more easy; by which our defence can be secured with less effusion of blood, less anxiety of mind, less interruption of the industry of the nation, less, I will not say of alarm, but of the evils, the inconveniences, the agitation that necessarily belong to a great struggle of this kind, however short, or however certain its issue may be; – in a contest of such a nature it certainly would be most unwise to run any hazard of protracting it, or to neglect any means of shortening it still more if possible; – if, upon these grounds, I say, it can be pointed out to me that there are any means by which our regular army could be immediately increased and all our regiments completed, I should say that, although we are safe without it, yet our interest, our prosperity, and every object that can influence us, would require that such a measure should be adopted.

'The proud despot of France'

... I know very well that the manly feelings and, if I may say so, the obstinate courage of my right honourable friend*, will not let him believe that the French would offer us such an insult as to come over here to fight us for our capital. I am sure I shall not be suspected of depreciating or of not placing due confidence in the Army, in the Navy, or in the courage of the people of England; on the contrary, I am firmly convinced that the enemy will find us to be invincible. But it must be admitted that in war there are accidents depending sometimes upon a day or an hour, in which, with the bravest and most numerous army, the enemy, by hazarding an operation for which in any other service a general would be broke or shot, but which a French general would attempt, because he knows he would be broke or shot if he did not, might obtain an advantage, the consequences of which might be most serious if some such measure as that recommended by the honourable officer was not adopted. We unfortunately know that attempts of this kind may be made, however rash or desperate, for those who will make them know that they will not appear so to Bonaparte. The proud despot of France will, however, have reason to tremble on his usurped throne, when the people of France find that they have sacrificed hundreds of thousands of men to gratify his ambition and his revenge. With respect to that despot himself, he would, I am sure, feel as little hesitation in sacrificing a hundred thousand Frenchmen, as he would millions of Englishmen if he had them within his grasp.

In arranging, therefore, the plan of national defence, we ought not to estimate upon probabilities merely. It is not enough for us to say that if he is eccentric and mad, he will pay the price of his madness and folly; we must take care that we do not pay for it first; we must not now disdain to adopt precautions which were formerly thought unnecessary. I cannot, therefore, agree with the short and decisive opinion of my right honourable friend, who, when the honourable officer recommended it to government to fortify London, replied, 'I say, do not fortify it'. I must enter my protest against such language. He says, he would not affront the people of England by supposing that, while they have 80,000 seamen on board their fleet and have such an army as is now on foot, it could be necessary to fortify the capital. Why, sir, in the first place as to the Navy, we must remember, that although we have 80,000 seamen, a great part of them are detached on service in different quarters of the world, and consequently could not in any degree prevent an invasion at home. I am certainly not denying that the enemy would find great difficulty and danger in transporting his army to this country, but it is by running desperate risks that he can alone hope for success. We may have a proud Navy of ships of the line and frigates – I will not now stop to inquire whether that Navy might not have been in readiness sooner – but I can conceive a case in which ships of that kind would not be sufficient to meet an innumerable flotilla of boats issuing from all the ports, harbours, and creeks on the opposite coast of France, and covering the Channel for several miles in length. Whether, in order to meet a force of this kind, it would not be wise to multiply the smaller sort of our naval force and to mount them with guns of heavy metal and with carronades, I do not know; I hope something of this kind has been done already. It is admitted, indeed, that our Navy, great and powerful as it is, cannot be relied on with absolute certainty to prevent an invasion; because if it could, there would be no occasion for all the precautions which we are adopting.

But it is said, we ought not to fortify London because our ancestors did not fortify it. Why, Sir, that is no argument, unless you can show me that our ancestors were in the same situation that we are. Look back to the days when the genius, the wisdom, and the fortitude of Elizabeth defeated the proud and invincible Armada, fitted out by Spain to conquer us – and I trust that the invincible battalion from France will meet with the same fate – we must admit that not only the situation of this country, but of all Europe, is changed; and it is absurd to say that, when the circumstances are changed, the means of defence should be precisely the same. We might as well be told that, because our ancestors fought with arrows and with lances, we ought to use them now, and that we ought to consider shields and corslets as affording a secure defence against musketry and artillery.

... Englishmen must look to this as a species of contest from which, by the extraordinary favour of Divine

'It is for everything dear and valuable to man'

Providence, we have been for a long series of years exempted. If we are now at length called upon to take our share in it, we must meet it with just gratitude for the exemptions we have hitherto enjoyed, and with a firm determination to support it with courage and resolution. We must show ourselves worthy, by our conduct on this occasion, of the happiness which we have hitherto enjoyed and which, by the blessing of God, I hope we shall continue to enjoy. We ought to have a due sense of the magnitude of the danger with

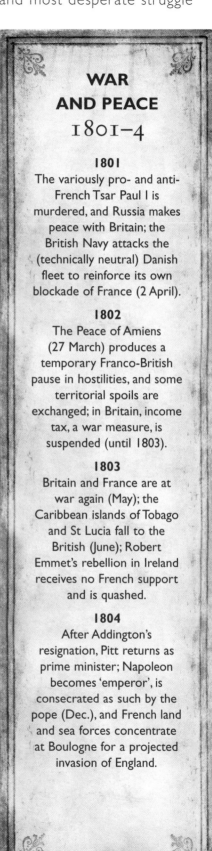

WAR AND PEACE 1801–4

1801
The variously pro- and anti-French Tsar Paul I is murdered, and Russia makes peace with Britain; the British Navy attacks the (technically neutral) Danish fleet to reinforce its own blockade of France (2 April).

1802
The Peace of Amiens (27 March) produces a temporary Franco-British pause in hostilities, and some territorial spoils are exchanged; in Britain, income tax, a war measure, is suspended (until 1803).

1803
Britain and France are at war again (May); the Caribbean islands of Tobago and St Lucia fall to the British (June); Robert Emmet's rebellion in Ireland receives no French support and is quashed.

1804
After Addington's resignation, Pitt returns as prime minister; Napoleon becomes 'emperor', is consecrated as such by the pope (Dec.), and French land and sea forces concentrate at Boulogne for a projected invasion of England.

which we are threatened; we ought to meet it in that temper of mind which produces just confidence, which neither despises nor dreads the enemy; and while on the one hand we accurately estimate the danger with which we are threatened at this awful crisis, we must recollect on the other hand what it is we have at stake, what it is we have to contend for. It is for our property, it is for our liberty, it is for our independence, nay, for our existence as a nation; it is for our character, it is for everything dear and valuable to man on this side of the grave.

'The eternal glory of this country'

Parliament has now provided ample means for our defence; it remains for the executive government to employ them to the best advantage. The regular army must be augmented to that point to which the means are now given to raise it; the militia must be kept high in numbers and unbroken in spirit; the auxiliary force must be as promptly raised and disciplined as the nature of things will admit; nothing must be omitted that military skill can suggest to render the contest certain as to its success and short in its duration. If government show the same determination to apply all those means that Parliament has shown in providing them; if the people follow up the example which the legislature has set them, we are safe. Then I may say, without being too sanguine, that the result of this great contest will ensure the permanent security, the eternal glory of this country; that it will terminate in the confusion, the dismay, and the shame of our vaunting enemy; that it will afford the means of animating the spirits, of rousing the courage, of breaking the lethargy of the surrounding nations of Europe; and I trust that, if after being driven from our coasts, it will find the people of Europe reviving in spirits and anxious to retaliate upon France all the wrongs, all the oppressions, they have suffered from her; and that we shall at length see that wicked fabric destroyed which was raised upon the prostitution of liberty, and which has caused more miseries, more horrors to France and to the surrounding nations, than are to be paralleled in any part of the annals of mankind.

♥ Lieutenant-Colonel Robert Craufurd (1764–1812), MP for East Retford, who died as a result of wounds sustained in the siege of Ciudad Rodrigo during the Peninsular Wars.
♦ Charles Yorke (1764–1834), secretary at war '1801–3'.

'Armed with the liberty of the press'

House of Commons, London, 6 February 1810

Richard Brinsley Sheridan

on the freedom of the press

Richard Brinsley Sheridan (1751–1816) was born in Dublin, the son of a famous actor and grandson of a famous headmaster. He went to Harrow school and settled with his widowed father in Bath in 1770. He determined to be a dramatist and, shortly after his marriage in 1773, he set to work on a comedy, which was produced at the Covent Garden Theatre, London, in January 1775. The play – *The Rivals* – was critically lambasted, but Sheridan withdrew it, revised it, put it on again, and since that time it has been one of the most acclaimed comedies in the English language. Another of similar repute, *The School for Scandal*, soon followed it into the canon. Sheridan became wealthy, took a part share in the Drury Lane Theatre, and soon acquired many friends in politics. One was Charles James Fox, whose broadly liberal and reforming aims Sheridan shared.

In 1780 Sheridan became MP for Stafford and quickly made a name for himself as one of the finest orators in the Commons. In the Duke of Portland's ministry in 1783 Sheridan held office as secretary to the treasury. During the long years of opposition during Pitt the Younger's administration, Sheridan became, as did Fox, a confidant of the Prince of Wales and lobbied for him to be made regent without the approval of Parliament in 1788. He took a leading role in the impeachment of Warren Hastings, making on 7 February 1787 what was said to be one of the most memorable speeches ever heard in the Commons: nearly six hours long, no reliable text exists of it, but it was met with what the official history of Parliament calls 'a tumult of applause'.

The *Dictionary of National Biography*, however, records that 'none of the many effective speeches which Sheridan delivered in the house did him more honour, or has given him more deserved credit, than those relating to the public press'. This is one such, made towards the end of his long parliamentary career. In it, Sheridan takes not merely the accepted Whig view of such liberties, but also outlines a philosophy that, within a few years, would be common to all sides of the political debate.

Sheridan lost a fortune when the Drury Lane Theatre burned down in 1809, and he was briefly imprisoned for debt in 1813. He died, however, heaped with honour, being buried in Westminster Abbey, and with the contemporary estimate that only Shakespeare had exceeded him as a writer for the stage, and that no finer orator had ever been heard in the House of Commons.

My right hon. friend**ᵛ** has called me a counsel for the Press … I am proud of the appellation. But I confess that I was a good deal surprised when he put in his claim to a share of the distinction. He has, by implication, questioned the use of the liberty of the press! Can he have been serious? Give me but the liberty of the press, and I will give to the minister a venal House of Peers – I will give him a corrupt and servile House of Commons – I will give him the whole host of ministerial influence – I will give him all the power that place can confer upon him to purchase up submission and overawe resistance; and yet, armed with the liberty of the press, I will go forth to meet him undismayed; I will attack the mighty fabric he has reared with that mightier engine; I will

THE EMERGING PRESS

1774
Luke Hansard begins publishing reports of parliamentary proceedings.

1788
The *Daily Universal Register* (founded 1785) is renamed *The Times*.

1791
The Observer, a Sunday newspaper, is founded.

1792
In Belfast, the *Northern Star*, supporting Wolfe Tone and the United Irishmen's cause, begins publication; in London, sedition laws are tested by the trial of Thomas Paine's *The Rights of Man* (Paine is found guilty *in absentia*).

1798
Pitt's budget bans the import of foreign newspapers.

1802
William Cobbett founds the (initially Tory) *Weekly Political Register*, before his politics move towards radicalism around 1804; Francis Jeffrey begins the new Whig publication, *Edinburgh Review*.

1806
Cobbett begins publication of *Parliamentary Debates*, which is acquired by Hansard.

1808
Leigh Hunt edits the new radical *Examiner*.

1809
The Tory *Quarterly Review* is founded.

1810
A pro-Reform article by radical MP Sir Francis Burdett earns him a spell in the Tower of London and prompts supportive riots in London.

shake down from its height corruption, and bury it beneath the ruins of the abuses it was meant to shelter.

My only object in the motion which I have submitted to the House is, not to prevent any individual member from clearing the gallery, but to require that, after he had done so, he should condescend to give some reason for the step. The right hon. gentleman opposite said it was his humour. That is the very thing of which I complain. If, after the exclusion of strangers, the House should acquiesce in the propriety of the motives for that exclusion, the public would then be satisfied.

'All this I can attribute to the liberty of the press alone'

To some of the opinions of my right hon. friend I have listened with the greatest regret, and even horror. For the first time in my life I have almost wished that the public had been excluded from hearing his opinions ... He has asserted a broad general principle that the publication of the proceedings of Parliament is injurious to the country. He has declared that, when the doors of the gallery of this House are closed, the country has done well. I am not one of those who think or speak despondingly of the situation, or degradingly of the character of the country. On the contrary, I am of opinion that Great Britain stands on a proud eminence, struggling as she is, and successfully struggling as I hope she will be, for the liberties of the world. To what is it owing that she is able to maintain such a contest, and bid defiance to that powerful enemy [France], who has already overthrown every power against which he has directed his victorious arms, and trampled upon the rights and independence of the prostrate nations of Europe? All this I can attribute to the liberty of the press alone, and most particularly and emphatically to the unrestrained publication of the debates and proceedings of Parliament.

'In former times, when the press was bound in fetters'

My right hon. friend has asked how such publication can produce any public benefit, or conduce to the well-being or happiness of the nation? To that I would answer, by shewing to the people the grounds upon which public measures are resorted to, and particularly by convincing them of their necessity; thus inducing the public to submit with patience to the heaviest burdens that have ever been imposed upon a nation. He has adverted to the state of the country in former times, when the press was bound in fetters, and the terrors of the Court of Star Chamber♦ blighted every germ of freedom. But I would tell him that publicity given to all public measures, and especially to great measures of finance, in modern times, has been the principal, if not the sole means of reconciling the nation to a weight of taxes, which in these boasted periods of former excellence would neither have been thought of, nor supposed likely to be borne or endured by the country.

I am sorry to hear my right hon. friend resorting to a topic, which I must be allowed to denominate the old bugbear, when I find him gravely asserting that the practice of reporting the proceedings of this House, which has grown up of late, is likely to encourage revolutionary doctrines, or lead to a revolution. Can it for a moment be supposed that the people of this country, possessing the blessings of freedom, and in the enjoyment of all the benefits of their constitution, can, by reading the debates in this House, be induced to get rid of these blessings and this constitution? Yet he has thought proper to state that the freedom of the press, as acted upon in latter times, would, in all probability, reduce this country to the same dreadful state of convulsion and disorder in which France was involved during the period of her late sanguinary revolution. Is it, I ask, the liberty of the Press that brought France into that dreadful state of anarchy and ruin, which characterised the revolution? Is it not, on the contrary, the suppression of all liberty of discussion – the prohibition of all publications not sanctioned by the permission of authority – the prevention of that rational and temperate consideration of public interests and measures, which alone can excite and nourish patriotic feelings and public spirit, that has caused all the mischiefs which attended that revolution? What is it that has caused the downfall of all the nations of Europe? Is it the liberty of the press? No: it is the want of that salutary control upon their governments, that animating source of public spirit and national exertion. If the liberty of the Press had existed in France before or since the revolution – if it had existed in Austria – if in Prussia – if in Spain, Bonaparte would not now find himself in the situation to dictate to Europe, and filling the throne of nearly an universal monarch.

♥ William Windham MP, secretary of state for war and for the colonies in Grenville's administration from 1806.
♦ The royal council sitting as a court, established by Cardinal Wolsey in Henry VIII's reign. It acquired a reputation for severity.

'To blast the name of an English queen!'

House of Lords, London, 4 October 1820

Henry Brougham
defends the reputation of Queen Caroline

enry Peter Brougham (1778–1868), later 1st Baron Brougham and Vaux, had a long and distinguished career in the law and in politics that culminated in his becoming lord chancellor. Born into a family of Westmorland squires and educated in Edinburgh, Brougham was called to the Scottish bar in 1800. Two years later he helped launch the *Edinburgh Review*, and wrote for it prodigiously. He moved to London in 1804 and sought a political career, becoming the MP for Camelford, in Cornwall, in 1810. Most significantly, he acted from 1812 as the legal adviser to Princess Caroline, the estranged wife of the prince regent and mother of the prince's heir, Princess Charlotte. When in 1819 the prince was agitiating for a divorce, Brougham conducted the negotiations on the princess's behalf with the government. When George III died in 1820, Caroline determined to claim her place as queen. To try to prevent this the government brought a bill of Pains and Penalties against her, and Brougham, who was sworn in as the queen's attorney-general, represented her in the trial in the House of Lords.

The *Dictionary of National Biography* describes his speech, which lasted two days, as 'brilliant, ridiculing the evidence against the queen, cooley analysing the issues, and passionately appealing to their lordships' consciences'. The Lords gave the bill a second reading, but the government dropped it; the queen died the following year. In 1830, after some manoeuvring, Brougham became lord chancellor in Lord Grey's Whig administration. Later on in his career Brougham, a Whig until the age of 63, broke with his old Party and supported Peel.

Space permits only an extract from his speech at Queen Caroline's trial, but it is one that demonstrates the full force of Brougham's oratory and logic, as well as the manner in which he sought to play the House of Lords like the proverbial violin. Having spent the best part of two days outlining the evidence against the queen of her various alleged adulteries, and ridiculing it, this was Brougham's peroration.

Such then, my lords, is this case. And again let me call on you, even at the risk of repetition, never to dismiss for a moment from your minds, the two great points upon which I rest my attack upon the evidence; first, that the accusers have not proved the facts by the good witnesses who were within their reach, whom they had no shadow of pretext for not calling; and secondly, that the witnesses whom they have ventured to call are, every one of them, irreparably damaged in their credit. How, I again ask, is a plot ever to be discovered, except by the means of these two principles? Nay, there are instances, in which plots have been discovered, through the medium of the second principle, when the first had happened to fail. When venerable witnesses have been seen brought forward, when persons above all suspicion have lent themselves for a season to impure plans, when no escape for the guiltless seemed open, no chance of safety to remain, they have almost providentially escaped from the snare by the second of those two principles; by the evidence breaking-down where it was not expected to be sifted; by a weak point being found, where no provision, from the attack being unforeseen, had been made to support it.

Your lordships recollect that great passage – I say great, for it is poetically just and eloquent, even were it not inspired in the sacred writings, where the Elders* had joined themselves in a plot which had appeared to have succeeded, for that, as the Book says, they had hardened their hearts, and had turned away their eyes, that they might not look at Heaven, and that they might do the purposes of unjust judgments. But they, though giving a clear, consistent, uncontradicted story, were disappointed, and their victim was rescued from their gripe, by the trifling circumstance of a contradiction about a tamarisk tree. Let not man call those contradictions or those falsehoods which false witnesses swear to from needless and heed less falsehood, such as Sacchi˅ about his changing his name or such as Demont about her letters or such as Majocchi about the bankers clerk or such as all the other contradictions and falsehoods not going to the main body of the case, but to the main body of the credit of the witnesses let not man rashly and blindly, call these things accidents. They are just rather than merciful dispensations of that Providence, which wills not that the guilty should triumph, and which favourably protects the innocent!

'Save the country, my lords'

Such, my lords, is the case now before you! Such is the evidence in support of this measure, evidence inadequate to prove a debt, impotent to deprive of a civil right, ridiculous to convict of the lowest offence, scandalous if brought forward to support a charge of the highest nature, which the law knows monstrous to ruin the honour, to blast the name of an English queen! What shall I say, then, if this is the proof by which an act of judicial legislation, a parliamentary sentence, an ex post facto law, is sought to be passed against this defenceless woman? My lords, I pray you to pause. I do earnestly beseech you to take heed! You are standing upon the brink of a precipice, then beware! It will go

THE LIFE OF CAROLINE OF BRUNSWICK

1768
Born in Brunswick, the daughter of the Duke of Brunswick-Wolfenbüttel and Amelia, sister to George III.

1795
Marries George, Prince of Wales, who is her first cousin, at St James's Palace, London.

1796
Gives birth to their only child, Charlotte (who dies in 1817).

1799
Estranged from George, is sent to live at a residence in Blackheath, south of London, where several alleged infidelities occur.

1806
After rumours that a four-year-old boy in her entourage is her son by a footman, a so-called 'delicate investigation' of her behaviour is launched, but no proofs are discovered.

1814–20
Lives on the Continent.

1820
On the death of George III, returns to England to claim her title as queen, refusing offers of money to stay abroad and renounce title (June); House of Lords launches the Pains and Penalties Bill against her, on grounds of her 'licentious' lifestyle (July), but eventually abandons it in the face of popular support for Caroline.

1821
Dies (7 Aug.), having been refused entry to the king's coronation (21 July).

forth your judgment, if sentence shall go against the queen. But it will be the only judgment you ever pronounced, which, instead of reaching its object, will return and bound back upon those who give it. Save the country, my lords, from the horrors of this catastrophe, save yourselves from this peril, rescue that country, of which you are the ornaments, but in which you can flourish no longer, when severed from the people, than the blossom when cut off from the roots and the stem of the tree. Save that country, that you may continue to adorn it, save the crown, which is in jeopardy, the aristocracy which is shaken, save the altar, which must stagger with the blow that rends its kindred throne! You have said, my lords, you have willed the church, and the king have willed that the queen should be deprived of its solemn service. She has instead of that solemnity, the heartfelt prayers of the people. She wants no prayers of mine. But I do here pour forth my humble supplications at the throne of mercy, that that mercy may be poured down upon the people, in a larger measure than the merits of its rulers may deserve, and that your hearts may be turned to justice!

♥ Sacchi, Demont and Majocchi were attendants and servants of the queen during her Italian travels, called as witnesses to blacken her character.

'Worship of a hero'

London, 5 May 1840

Thomas Carlyle

lectures on the role of 'great men' in history

Thomas Carlyle (1795–1881) was the towering figure of the Victorian literary world. Eccentric, irascible, tortured and driven, he was nonetheless the centre of an artistic and intellectual circle that included Charles Dickens, Leigh Hunt, John Forster, Harriet Martineau, John Stuart Mill (from whom he later became estranged), his biographer James Anthony Froude and his disciple-in-chief John Ruskin. Carlyle had come from humble origins in the village of Ecclefechan in Dumfriesshire to make a name for himself as a regular writer for the influential literary reviews of the 1820s and 1830s. He had also had the good fortune to marry, somewhat above his station, Jane Baillie Welsh, who supported him in his often epic and infuriating literary endeavours.

Carlyle had attracted what would now be termed a cult following after the publication in 1833–4 in *Fraser's Magazine* of his allegorical-philosophical work *Sartor Resartus*; and he had come to the notice of a much wider public in 1837 with his dramatic *History of the French Revolution*. Urged to give lectures – he was a formidable monologuist – these came to fruition in the spring of 1840 with a series of talks entitled 'On Heroes, Hero-Worship and the Heroic in History'. These extracts from the first lecture, 'The Hero as Divinity', not only give a flavour of Carlyle's superb rhetorical gifts, but also show the sweep of his erudition and the outlines of his philosophy, which was that history depended on the role of the strong man. It is easy to see from such powerful oratory how he had such enormous influence on a generation of writers: not only Dickens, but also George Eliot, Charles Kingsley and even, in his role as a novelist, Disraeli. Carlyle went on to set himself up in opposition to what he saw as the weak-minded sentimentality of contemporary thought and politicians, which estranged him from many of his friends (notably Mill) and left his voice unheard for much of the 20th century.

We have undertaken to discourse here for a little on great men, their manner of appearance in our world's business, how they have shaped themselves in the world's history, what ideas men formed of them, what work they did; – on heroes, namely, and on their reception and performance; what I call hero-worship and the heroic in human affairs. Too evidently this is a large topic; deserving quite other treatment than we can expect to give it at present. A large topic; indeed an illimitable one; wide as universal history itself. For, as I take it, universal history, the history of what man has accomplished in this world, is at bottom the history of the great men who have worked here. They were the leaders of men, these great ones; the modellers, patterns, and in a wide sense creators, of whatsoever the general mass of men contrived to do or to attain; all things that we see standing accomplished in the world are properly the outer material result, the practical realisation and embodiment, of thoughts that dwelt in the great men sent into the world: the soul of the whole world's history, it may justly be considered, were the history of these. Too clearly it is a topic we shall do no justice to in this place!

One comfort is, that great men, taken up in any way, are profitable company. We cannot look, however imperfectly, upon a great man, without gaining something by him. He is the living light-fountain, which it is good and pleasant to be near. The light which enlightens, which has enlightened the darkness of the world; and this not as a kindled lamp only, but rather as a natural luminary shining by the gift of heaven; a flowing light-fountain, as I say, of native original insight, of manhood and heroic nobleness; – in whose radiance all souls feel that it is well with them. On any terms whatsoever, you will not grudge to wander in such neighbourhood for a while. These six classes of heroes, chosen out of widely distant countries and epochs, and in mere external figure differing altogether, ought, if we look faithfully at them, to illustrate several things for us. Could we see them well, we should get some glimpses into the very marrow of the world's history. How happy, could I but, in any measure, in such times as these, make manifest to you the meanings of heroism; the divine revelation (for I may well call it such) which in all times unites a great man to other men; and thus, as it were, not exhaust my subject, but so much as break ground on it! At all events, I must make the attempt …

Transcendent admiration of a great man

The young generations of the world, who had in them the freshness of young children, and yet the depth of the earnest men, who did not think that they had finished-off all things in heaven and earth by merely giving them scientific names, but had to gaze direct at them there, with awe and wonder: they felt better what of divinity is in man and Nature; – they, without being mad, could worship Nature, and man more than anything else in Nature. Worship, that is, as I said above, admire without limit: this, in the full use of their faculties, with all sincerity of heart, they could do. I consider hero-worship to be the grand modifying element in that ancient system of thought. What I called the perplexed jungle of paganism sprang, we may say, out of many roots: every admiration, adoration of a star or natural object, was a root or fibre of a root, from which in a great degree all the rest were nourished and grown.

THE CAREER OF THOMAS CARLYLE

1820s
Having studied German literature, publishes a biography of Schiller and translations of Goethe and other German writers.

1833–4
Publishes *Sartor Resartus*.

1834
Moves with his wife Jane to Chelsea, London.

1837
Establishes himself with his *History of the French Revolution*.

1840–1
Gives the high-profile lectures that he then publishes as *On Heroes, Hero-Worship and the Heroic in History*.

1843
Publishes *Past and Present*, containing his thoughts on medieval life and feudalism.

1845
Edits the letters and speeches of Oliver Cromwell, whom he admires.

1850
Publishes *Latter-day Pamphlets*, expressing his general disapprobation of democratic ideas.

1858–65
Issues his six-volume biography of another 'great man' in history, Frederick the Great of Prussia.

1866
Becomes a widower; his *Reminiscences* of his life and relationships are published in 1881.

And now if worship even of a star had some meaning in it, how much more might that of a hero! Worship of a hero is transcendent admiration of a great man. I say great men are still admirable; I say there is, at bottom, nothing else admirable! No nobler feeling than this of admiration for one higher than himself dwells in the breast of man. It is to this hour, and at all hours, the vivifying influence in man's life. Religion I find stands upon it; not paganism only, but far higher and truer religions, – all religion hitherto known. Hero-worship, heartfelt prostrate admiration, submission, burning, boundless, for a noblest godlike form of man, – is not that the germ of Christianity itself? The greatest of all heroes is One – whom we do not name here! Let sacred silence meditate that sacred matter; you will find it the ultimate perfection of a principle extant throughout man's whole history on earth.

'Faith is loyalty to some inspired teacher, some spiritual hero'

Or coming into lower, less unspeakable provinces, is not all Loyalty akin to religious Faith also? Faith is loyalty to some inspired teacher, some spiritual hero. And what therefore is loyalty proper, the life-breath of all society, but an effluence of hero-worship, submissive admiration for the truly great? Society is founded on hero-worship. All dignities of rank, on which human association rests, are what we may call a heroarchy (government of heroes), – or a hierarchy, for it is 'sacred' enough withal! The duke means dux, leader; king is Kon-ning, Kan-ning, man that knows or cans (*sic*). Society everywhere is some representation, not insupportably inaccurate, of a graduated worship of heroes; – reverence and obedience done to men really great and wise. Not insupportably inaccurate, I say! They are all as bank-notes, these social dignitaries, all representing gold; – and several of them, alas, always are forged notes. We can do with some forged false notes; with a good many even; but not with all, or the most of them forged! No: there have to come revolutions then; cries of democracy, liberty and equality, and I know not what:– the notes being all false, and no gold to be had for them, people take to crying in their despair that there is no gold, that there never was any! – 'Gold', hero-worship, is nevertheless, as it was always and everywhere, and cannot cease till man himself ceases.

I am well aware that in these days hero-worship, the thing I call hero-worship, professes to have gone out, and finally ceased. This, for reasons which it will be worthwhile some time to inquire into, is an age that as it were denies the existence of great men; denies the desirableness of great men. Show our critics a great man, a Luther for example, they begin to what they call 'account' for him; not to worship, but take the dimensions of him, – and bring him out to be a little kind of man! He was the 'creature of the time,' they say; the time called him forth, the time did everything, he nothing – but what we the little critic could have done too! This seems to me but melancholy work, the time call forth? Alas, we have known times call loudly enough for their great man; but not find him when they called! He was not there; Providence had not sent him; the time calling its loudest, had to go down to confusion and wreck because he would not come when called.

For if we will think of it, no Time need have gone to ruin, could it have found a man great enough, a man wise and good enough: wisdom to discern truly what the time wanted, valour to lead it on the right road thither; these are the salvation of any time. But I liken common languid times, with their unbelief, distress, perplexity, with their languid doubting characters and embarrassed circumstances, impotently crumbling-down into ever worse distress towards final ruin; – all this I liken to dry dead fuel, waiting for the lightning out of heaven that shall kindle it. The great man, with his free force direct out of God's own hand, is the lightning.

'Such general blindness to the spiritual lightning'

His word is the wise healing word which all can believe in. All blazes round him now, when he has once struck on it, into fire like his own. The dry mouldering sticks are thought to have called him forth. They did want him greatly; but as to calling him forth! – Those critics are critics of small vision, I think, who cry: 'See, is it not the sticks that made the fire?' No sadder proof can be given by a man of his own littleness than disbelief in great men. There is no sadder symptom of a generation than such general blindness to the spiritual lightning, with faith only in the heap of barren dead fuel. It is the last consummation of unbelief. In all epochs of the world's history, we shall find the great man to have been the indispensable saviour of his epoch; – the lightning, without which the fuel never would have burnt. The history of the world, I said already, was the biography of great men.

PARLIAMENT STREET

R. PEEL. BAKER.

DOWN AGAIN GREAT FALL IN BREAD

THIS SHOP WILL OPEN TO SUPPLY THE BRITISH PUBLIC WITH CHEAP BREAD

NO CONNECTION WITH A PERSON OF THE NAME OF RUSSELL

PEEL'S CHEAP BREAD SHOP,

'The immediate suspension of the law'

House of Commons, London, 16 February 1846

Sir Robert Peel

on the need to repeal the Corn Laws

When Sir Robert Peel (1788–1850) became prime minister for the second time, after the 1841 general election, he found that his pledge to sustain the Corn Laws – the system by which the price of grain was maintained at an artificially high level through protection from cheaper exports – was increasingly unsustainable. The potato blight of 1845, which was at its worst in Ireland, leading to the Great Famine and serious civil unrest, gave Peel the practical excuse he needed to act on what had become his convictions about the importance of free trade and the wrongness of protectionism. The Tory Party's main supporters in the landed interest, whose income the 1815 Corn Law Act had been passed to protect, were appalled by what they regarded as his betrayal of them and of their Party's principles.

In this speech, advocating a second reading for the repeal of the Corn Laws, Peel attempted to persuade the landed interest that they would be the victims of insurrection if the country were allowed to starve because of restrictions on the importation of grain. He spoke, in the moments before the start of this extract, of his hopes that the impending food crisis, already evident in Ireland, might be the cause of political unity in trying to head off the problem; but it was not to be. One of his loudest opponents was fellow Tory Benjamin Disraeli, who had begged him for office not long before. Peel's spirited defence in this speech helped secure the repeal, but did his career no good. Defeated in June on a measure to ameliorate conditions in Ireland, he was forced to leave office four days later.

The Tory Party did not finally shake off its love affair with protectionism until well into the 20th century, and the issue was one of the reasons for the disintegration of the Balfour government in 1905.

There have been times before the present when there has been the apprehension of scarcity in this country; what has been the remedy? What has been the remedy that the heart of every man suggested? What has been the remedy that legislative wisdom took? Why, in every case, without exception, the removal for a time of the duties upon foreign corn. (*Cheers*) (*An hon. Member: 'What was done at the end of the time?'*) I will come to that immediately. I rejoice in the cheer which I received from that quarter (*looking to the Protection benches*); what is it but an assent – apparently a unanimous assent – ('*No*') at any rate, a very general assent – that at a period of impending famine, the proper precaution to be taken is to encourage the free importation of food? I have a right to infer, that if that had been the proposal, namely, that existing duties upon corn and other articles of provision should be suspended for a time that proposal would have met with general assent. Then, if that be so, I ask you to expedite the passing of this bill: either do that, or move as an Amendment that the duties upon all articles of provision shall forthwith be suspended.

I will not omit the other consideration – the course to be taken after you have suspended the law; I am trying now to convince you that I should have been unfaithful and treacherous to the landed interest, and to the party that protect the landed interest, if I had concealed the real pressure of this Irish case, and had called forth party cheers by talking about 'hoisting the flag of protection' – or 'rousing the British lion' – or 'adhering to the true blue colour' or steadfast maintenance of the Corn Laws 'in all their integrity'. I am trying to convince you, by fair reasoning, that that is a course which would not have been consistent either with the public interest, or with the credit of the landed aristocracy. That is all I am asking you now to admit. If you answer me, 'We will readily consent to suspend this law until next harvest', I am rejoiced to have that admission from three fourths of those by whom I shall be opposed, that it would but be wise to stipulate that for the present no alteration should be made in the Corn Law, that no maize should be admitted, at a reduced rate of duty, and that the duty upon wheat should be maintained at 17s; I am rejoiced that I have established, to the satisfaction of the great majority, that that would not have been a prudent or a defensible course, I say it would not, because at all periods of our history the natural precaution that has been taken has been the admission, free of duty, of foreign corn in times of scarcity. I must quote some of those instances.

> *'I believe that course would have involved the government and the Parliament in the greatest discredit'*

In 1756, there was the apprehension of famine: Parliament was assembled: the first step taken was to prohibit, unwisely, in my opinion, the exportation of corn; the second was, to permit importation duty free. In 1767, you were again threatened with scarcity: the first act of the Parliament was, to admit provisions duty free. In 1791, Parliament altered the Corn Laws – they established a new Corn Law; in 1793, there was the apprehension of scarcity; notwithstanding the new Corn Law, one of the very first acts upon the statute book of 1793 is to remove, for a time, all duties upon the importation of foreign corn. In 1795, there was an apprehension, not of famine, but of scarcity, severely pressing upon some classes of the

THE CORN LAWS

1791
A Corn Law imposes duty on imported grain should the price of domestic corn fall to 50 shillings or less per quarter (1 quarter = 8 bushels).

1790s–1815
The import of foreign corn is hampered by European turmoil during the French Revolutionary and Napoleonic Wars.

1815
At resumption of grain imports, a new law imposes punitive duty should the domestic price fall to 80 shillings per quarter; the law, regarded as serving the landed interest, is deeply resented in other sectors of society and in the urban centres.

1816
Britain experiences a very poor harvest, leading to social unrest.

1832
The Great Reform Act results in a

community; and in that year, and again in 1796, the same remedy was adopted – the removal of all duty upon foreign corn. In 1799, the same course was pursued, and free importation allowed. Why then, I ask, with all these precedents – when the danger, in the case of some at least, was less than it is at present – would it have been wise for a government to counsel that we should pursue a different course, refuse facilities for importation, and determine upon maintaining the existing law? Sir, I believe that course would have involved the government and the Parliament in the greatest discredit; and so far from assisting us in maintaining the existing law, my firm belief is, that that law would have been encumbered with a degree of odium which would have made the defence of it impossible. It was upon these grounds that I acted …

'The question is, what shall we do now?'

We advised, therefore – at least I advised, and three of my colleagues concurred with me – the immediate suspension of the law. The question is, what shall we do now? The law is not suspended – Parliament is sitting. It would be disrespectful towards Parliament for the executive to take any step; it is impossible for the executive, by an Order of Council, to do that which might have been done by an extreme exercise of authority, when Parliament was not sitting; it would not be constitutional to do it. It may be true that the best time has passed away; that the 1st of November was a better period for doing this than the present. Yes, but admitting that, the necessity for acting with decision on the 16th February is only increased. True, the supplies of foreign corn might have been more ample, had the ports been opened on the 1st November; but you have six months yet before you – and what course do you suggest? If any one dissents from that course which we propose, let him propose another. You must make your choice. You must either maintain the existing law, or make some proposal for increasing the facilities of procuring foreign articles of food …

After the suspension of the existing law, and the admission of foreign importation for a period of several months, how do you propose to deal with the existing Corn Laws? That is the question which a Minister was bound to consider who advised the suspension of the Corn Laws. Now, my conviction is so strong that it would be utterly impossible, after establishing perfect freedom of trade in corn for a period of seven or eight months, to give a guarantee that

greater number of MPs from towns and cities, effectively reducing the influence in the Commons of the landed interest.

1839
The businessman Richard Cobden and others form the national Anti-Corn Law League, which is joined by the firebrand John Bright.

1840–2
There is economic depression in Britain.

1842
Cobden is elected MP for Stockport.

1845
The failure of the Irish potato harvest, due to blight, creates conditions for mass starvation and the threat of serious unrest throughout the British Isles.

1846
Prime Minister Peel, through cross-Party alliances with Whigs under Lord Russell, Irish MPs and peers under the sway of the Duke of Wellington, passes legislation reducing import duty to a minimal amount, effectively freeing up the market.

1870
The last vestiges of tariffs on grain are removed by W.E. Gladstone.

the existing Corn Law should come into operation at the end of that period, that I could not encourage the delusive hope of such a result. I know it may be said, that after a temporary suspension of the law, the law itself would revive by its own operation, that there would be no necessity for any special enactment to restore its vigour. But I think it is an utter misapprehension of the state of public opinion to suppose it possible that after this country, for eight months, should have tasted of freedom in the trade in corn, you could revive, either by the tacit operation of the law itself, or by new and special enactment, the existing Corn Law. Surely, the fact of suspension would be a condemnation of the law. It would demonstrate that the law, which professed by the total reduction of duty on corn when it had reached a certain price to provide security against scarcity, has failed in one of its essential parts. Yet you insist on the revival of this law.

'Public feeling cannot safely be disregarded'

Now let me ask, would you revive the existing Corn Law in all its provisions? Would you refuse the admission of maize at lower duties? – at present the duty on maize is almost prohibitory. Do not suppose that those who advised suspension overlooked the consideration of the consequences of suspension – of the bearing it would have upon the state of the Corn Laws, and the question of future protection. At the expiration of suspension will you revive the existing law, or will you propose a new and modified Corn Law? If the existing law, every manifest defect must be preserved. By that law, the duty on maize varies inversely not with the price of maize, but with the price of barley. We want maize – the price of barley is falling, but we can get no maize, because there is a prohibitory duty on maize in consequence of the low price of barley. Oh, say some, we will have a little alteration of the law, we will provide for the case of maize. Now, do not disregard public feeling in matters of this kind. It is not right that mere feeling should overbear the deliberate conviction of reason; but depend upon it, that when questions of food are concerned, public feeling cannot safely be disregarded. In the course of last Session notice was given that maize should be imported duty free, because it was for the interest of the farmer to have maize for food for cattle. Do you think it possible to devise a new Corn Law, the leading principle of which should be that maize should come in duty free, because the admission of that article would enable the farmer to feed his cattle and pigs with it, but that there are certain other articles used for consumption by human beings – and in respect to them the law shall be maintained in all its force? Do you advise me to commit you to fight that battle? I am assuming now that the necessity for the suspension of the law has been established; that suspension having taken place, would you deliberately advise the Government, for the sake of the public interests, or for the sake of Party interests, to give a pledge either that the existing Corn Law, at the expiration of that suspension should be revived unaltered – or that there should be some trumpery modification of it, for the special benefit of the feeders of pigs and cattle? Are you insensible to the real state of public opinion on this question? Are you insensible to the altered convictions of many of your own Party? Could I safely rely upon your cordial and unanimous support, as a Party, for the redemption of that pledge? Look to the change of opinion, not among politicians, which you are apt to attribute to some interested or corrupt motives; but look to the opinions that have been expressed – to the sincerity of which conclusive proofs have been given by some of the most honourable men that ever sat upon these benches …

This night, then – if on this night the debate shall close – you will have to decide what are the principles by which your commercial policy is to be regulated. Most earnestly, from a deep conviction, founded not upon the limited experience of three years alone, but upon the experience of the results of every relaxation of restriction and prohibition, I counsel you to set the example of liberality to other countries. Act thus, and it will be in perfect consistency with the course you have hitherto taken. Act thus, and you will provide an additional guarantee for the continued contentment, and happiness, and well being of the great body of the people. Act thus, and you will have done whatever human sagacity can do for the promotion of commercial prosperity.

You may fail. Your precautions may be unavailing. They may give no certain assurance that mercantile and manufacturing prosperity will continue without interruption. It seems to be incident to great prosperity that there shall be a reverse – that the time of depression shall follow the season of excitement and success. That time of depression must perhaps return; and its return may be coincident with scarcity caused by unfavourable seasons. Gloomy winters, like those of 1841 and 1842, may again set in. Are those winters effaced from your memory? From mine they never can be. Surely you cannot have forgotten with what earnestness and sincerity you re echoed the deep feelings of a gracious queen, when at the opening and at the close of each session, She expressed the warmest sympathy with the sufferings of Her people, and the warmest admiration of their heroic fortitude.

These sad times may recur. 'The years of plenteousness may have ended', and 'the years of dearth may have come'; and again you may have to offer the unavailing expressions of sympathy, and the urgent exhortations to patient resignation.

'The free circulation of the Creator's bounty'

Commune with your own hearts and answer me this question: will your assurances of sympathy be less consolatory – will your exhortations to patience be less impressive – if, with your willing consent, the Corn Laws shall have then ceased to exist? Will it be no satisfaction to you to reflect, that by your own act, you have been relieved from the grievous responsibility of regulating the supply of food? Will you not then cherish with delight the reflection that, in this the present hour of comparative prosperity, yielding to no clamour, impelled by no fear – except, indeed, that provident fear, which is the mother of safety – you had anticipated the evil day, and, long before its advent, had trampled on every impediment to the free circulation of the Creator's bounty?

When you are again exhorting a suffering people to fortitude under their privations, when you are telling them, 'These are the chastenings of an all wise and merciful Providence, sent for some inscrutable but just and beneficial purpose – it may be, to humble our pride, or to punish our unfaithfulness, or to impress us with the sense of our own nothingness and dependence on His mercy' when you are thus addressing your suffering fellow subjects, and encouraging them to bear without repining the dispensations of Providence, may God grant that by your decision of this night you may have laid in store for yourselves the consolation of reflecting that such calamities are, in truth, the dispensations of Providence – that they have not been caused, they have not been aggravated by laws of man restricting, in the hour of scarcity, the supply of food!

'*Civis Romanus sum ...*
the strong arm of England'

House of Commons, London, 25 June 1850

Lord Palmerston
on defending British citizens and
British honour abroad

Henry John Temple, 3rd Viscount Palmerston (1784–1865) held an Irish peerage that did not qualify him to sit in the House of Lords; but he sat (initially as a Tory) in the Commons from the age of 23. At 25 he was a privy counsellor, and served for almost 20 years as secretary at war. In 1830 Lord Grey appointed him foreign secretary, and it was in that office that he made his name as a statesman. While diplomatically skilful, he soon acquired a reputation for adamantly standing up for British interests abroad, and he was the father of 'gunboat diplomacy'.

Perhaps the most notorious example of this came in 1850, when Palmerston once more held the foreign office in the ministry of Lord John Russell, a Whig. Two British subjects, Dr George Finlay and David Pacifico, a Jewish Gibraltarian of doubtful reputation, had been denied compensation by the Greek government for injuries allegedly suffered at the hands of Greek nationals. Pacifico's house had been plundered by a mob. France offered her good offices to sort the matter out, but instead Palmerston sent a ship to blockade Piraeus. The discourtesy this implied towards the French was felt to have risked war with that country. The House of Lords censured Palmerston, and a Whig member, Roebuck, put down the motion that: 'the principles which hitherto have regulated the foreign policy of Her Majesty's government are such as were required to preserve untarnished the honour and dignity of this country, and in times of unexampled difficulty the best qualified to maintain peace between England and various nations of the world'. It was passed by 46 votes, after a speech of four hours by Palmerston in which, according to the *Dictionary of National Biography*, he 'vindicated his whole foreign policy with a breadth of view, a tenacity of logical argument, a moderation of tone, and a height of eloquence which the house listened to with rapture and interrupted with volleys of cheers. It was the greatest speech he ever made.' Palmerston was later twice prime minister, and he died in office two days before his 81st birthday.

> The rights of a man depend on the merits of the particular case; and it is an abuse of argument to say, that you are not to give redress to a man, because in some former transaction he may have done something which is questionable'. Punish him if you will, punish him if he is guilty, but don't pursue him as a pariah through life.

What happened in this case? In the middle of the town of Athens, in a house which I must be allowed to say is not a wretched hovel, as some people have described it; but it does not matter what it is, for whether a man's home be a palace or a cabin, the owner has a right to be there safe from injury – well, in a house which is not a wretched hovel, but which in the early days of King Otho was, I am told, the residence of the Count Armansperg, the Chief of the Regency – a house as good as the generality of those which existed in Athens before the sovereign ascended the throne – M. Pacifico, living in this house, within forty yards of the great street, within a few minutes' walk of a guard-house, where soldiers were stationed, was attacked by a mob. Fearing injury, when the mob began to assemble, he sent an intimation to the British minister, who immediately informed the authorities. Application was made to the

Greek government for protection. No protection was afforded. The mob, in which were soldiers and gens-d'armes, who, even if officers were not with them, ought, from a sense of duty, to have interfered and to have prevented plunder – that mob, headed by the sons of the minister of war, not children of eight or ten years old, but older – that mob, for nearly two hours, employed themselves in gutting the house of an unoffending man, carrying away or destroying every single thing the house contained, and left it a perfect wreck.

Is not that a case in which a man is entitled to redress from somebody? I venture to think it is. I think that there is no civilised country where a man subjected to such grievous wrong, not to speak of insults and injuries to the members of his family, would not justly expect redress from some quarter or other. Where was he to apply for redress at Athens? The Greek government neglected its duty, and did not pursue judicial inquiries, or institute legal prosecutions as it might have done for the purpose of finding out and punishing some of the culprits. The sons of the minister of war were pointed out to the government as actors in the outrage. The Greek government were told to 'search a particular house; and that some part of M. Pacifico's jewels would be found there'. They declined to prosecute the minister's sons, or to search the house. But, it is said, M. Pacifico should have applied to a court of law for redress. What was he to do? Was he to prosecute a mob of five hundred persons? Was he to prosecute them criminally, or in order to make them pay the value of his loss? Where was he to find his witnesses? Why, he and his family were hiding or flying, during the pillage, to avoid the personal outrages with which they were threatened. He states, that his own life was saved by the help of an English friend. It was impossible, if he could have identified the leaders, to have prosecuted them with success.

'He wanted redress, not revenge'

But what satisfaction would it have been to M. Pacifico to have succeeded in a criminal prosecution against the ringleaders of that assault? Would that have restored to him his property? He wanted redress, not revenge. A criminal prosecution was out of the question, to say nothing of the chances, if not the certainty, of failure in a country where the tribunals are at the mercy of the advisers of the crown, the judges being liable to be removed, and being often actually removed upon grounds of private interest and personal feeling. Was he to prosecute for damages? His action would have lain against individuals, and not, as in this country, against the hundred. Suppose he had been able to prove that one particular man had carried off one particular thing, or destroyed one particular article of furniture; what redress could he anticipate by a lawsuit, which, as his legal advisers told him, it would be vain for him to undertake? M. Pacifico truly said, 'if the man I prosecute is rich, he is sure to be acquitted; if he is poor, he has nothing out of which to afford me compensation if he is condemned.'

The Greek government having neglected to give the protection they were bound to extend, and having abstained from taking means to afford redress, this was a case in which we were justified in calling on the Greek government for compensation for the losses, whatever they might be, which M. Pacifico had suffered. I think that claim was founded in justice. The amount we did not pretend to fix. If the Greek government had admitted the principle of the claim, and had objected to the account sent in by M. Pacifico – if they had said, 'This is too much, and we think a less sum sufficient', that would have been a question open to discussion, and which our ministers, Sir E. Lyons at first, or Mr Wyse afterwards, would have been ready to have gone into, and no doubt some satisfactory arrangement might thus have been effected with the Greek government. But the Greek government denied altogether the principle of the claim ...

M. Pacifico having, from year to year, been treated either with answers wholly unsatisfactory, or with a positive refusal, or with pertinacious silence, it came at last to this, either that his demand was to be abandoned altogether, or that, in pursuance of the notice we had given the Greek government a year or two before, we were to proceed to use our own means of enforcing the claim. 'Oh! but', it is said, 'what an ungenerous proceeding to employ so large a force against so small a Power!' Does the smallness of a country justify the magnitude of its evil acts? Is it to be held that if your subjects suffer violence, outrage, plunder in a country which is small and weak, you are to tell them when they apply for redress, that the country is so weak and so small that we cannot ask it for compensation? Their answer would be, that the weakness and smallness of the country make it so much the more easy to obtain redress.

THE CAREER OF LORD PALMERSTON

1807
Enters Commons as MP for Newport, Isle of Wight.

1811
Becomes MP for Cambridge University (until 1831).

1809–27
Secretary at war under successive Tory administrations.

1818
Is shot and wounded by an ex-soldier with a grievance over pension reductions.

1828
Resigns from administration of Duke of Wellington, eventually joining Whig Party.

1830–41
Serves as foreign secretary almost continuously; helps establish Belgian independence, new monarchies in Spain and Portugal, and works to contain Russian global influence.

1841–6
Is out of office after the victory of the Tories under Sir Robert Peel.

1846
Returns as foreign secretary under Lord Russell.

1850
A House of Lords censure motion for his actions over the Pacifico affair loses in the Commons.

1851
Is dismissed from office for his unauthorised private support of Napoleon III's coup in France.

1854
Having caused Russell's administration to collapse after defeat in a vote (1852), becomes home secretary under coalition administration of Lord Aberdeen.

1855
Becomes prime minister, supporting the Crimean War (which concludes in 1856).

1857
Wins a general election and increases majority, following a Commons censure motion over his support of belligerency against China.

1858
Resigns as prime minister.

1859–65
Having co-founded the Liberal Party with Russell and others, is reappointed prime minister; enforces treaty obligations on China through joint military pressure with France, and tacitly supports American Confederate states.

1865
Having won a general election, dies before taking office (18 Oct.).

'No,' it is said, 'generosity is to be the rule'. We are to be generous to those who have been ungenerous to you; and we cannot give you redress because we have such ample and easy means of procuring it.

'The honour and dignity of the government'

Well, then, was there anything so uncourteous in sending, to back our demands, a force which should make it manifest to all the world that resistance was out of the question? Why, it seems to me, on the contrary, that it was more consistent with the honour and dignity of the government on whom we made those demands, that there should be placed before their eyes a force, which it would be vain to resist, and before which it would be no indignity to yield.

I believe I have now gone through all the heads of the charges which have been brought against me in this debate. I think I have shown that the foreign policy of the government, in all the transactions with respect to which its conduct has been impugned, has throughout been guided by those principles which, according to the resolution of the honourable and learned gentleman the Member for Sheffield, ought to regulate the conduct of the government of England in the management of our foreign affairs. I believe that the principles on which we have acted are those which are held by the great mass of the people of this country. I am convinced these principles are calculated, so far as the influence of England may properly be exercised with respect to the destinies of other countries, to conduce to the maintenance of peace, to the advancement of civilisation, to the welfare and happiness of mankind.

I do not complain of the conduct of those who have made these matters the means of attack upon Her Majesty's ministers. The government of a great country like this, is undoubtedly an object of fair and legitimate ambition to men of all shades of opinion. It is a noble thing to be allowed to guide the policy and to influence the destinies of such a country; and, if ever it was an object of honourable ambition, more than ever must it be so at the moment at which I am speaking. For while we have seen, as stated by the right Baronet the Member for Ripon* the political earthquake rocking Europe from side to side – while we have seen thrones shaken, shattered, levelled; institutions overthrown and destroyed – while in almost every country of Europe the conflict of civil war has deluged the land with blood, from the Atlantic to the Black Sea, from the Baltic to the Mediterranean; this country has presented a spectacle honourable to the people of England, and worthy of the admiration of mankind.

'Civis Romanus sum'

We have shown that liberty is compatible with order; that individual freedom is reconcilable with obedience to the law. We have shown the example of a nation, in which every class of society accepts with cheerfulness the lot which Providence has assigned to it; while at the same time every individual of each class is constantly striving to raise himself in the social scale – not by injustice and wrong, not by violence and illegality – but by persevering good conduct, and by the steady and energetic exertion of the moral and intellectual faculties with which his Creator has endowed him. To govern such a people as this, is indeed an object worthy of the ambition of the noblest man who lives in the land; and therefore I find no fault with those who may think any opportunity a fair one, for endeavouring to place themselves in so distinguished and honourable a position. But I contend that we have not in our foreign policy done anything to forfeit the confidence of the country. We may not, perhaps, in this matter or in that, have acted precisely up to the opinions of one person or of another – and hard indeed it is, as we all know by our individual and private experience, to find any number of men agreeing entirely in any matter, on which they may not be equally possessed of the details of the facts, and circumstances, and reasons, and conditions which led to action. But, making allowance for those differences of opinion which may fairly and honourably arise among those who concur in general views, I maintain that the principles which can be traced through all our foreign transactions, as the guiding rule and directing spirit of our proceedings, are such as deserve approbation. I therefore fearlessly challenge the verdict which this House, as representing a political, a commercial, a constitutional country, is to give on the question now brought before it; whether the principles on which the foreign policy of Her Majesty's government has been conducted, and the sense of duty which has led us to think ourselves bound to afford protection to our fellow subjects abroad, are proper and fitting guides for those who are charged with the government of England; and whether, as the Roman, in days of old, held himself free from indignity, when he could say *Civis Romanus sum*; so also a British subject, in whatever land he may be, shall feel confident that the watchful eye and the strong arm of England, will protect him against injustice and wrong.

♥ A reference to the 'imputations on the character' of Pacifico.
♦ Sir James Graham (1792–1861), home secretary in Peel's second administration.

'The Angel of Death has been abroad'

House of Commons, London, 23 February 1855

John Bright
on the sufferings in the Crimean War

On the day before John Bright (1811–89) made this speech, four senior ministers in Lord Palmerston's administration – W.E. Gladstone (chancellor of the exchequer), Sidney Herbert (colonial secretary), Lord Cardwell (president of the board of trade) and Sir James Graham (First Lord of the Admiralty) had resigned from the government. They had inferred censure upon them because of the establishment of a committee of inquiry into the decision by the previous administration of Lord Aberdeen to go to war against Russia in the Crimea. All four had been prominent members of that coalition administration.

Bright was a radical from Lancashire who entered Parliament in 1843 claiming that he was a free-trader and, therefore, the representative of the working classes. Together with Richard Cobden he was one of the cornerstones of Manchester liberalism. Bright was prominent in the Anti-Corn Law League (founded 1839) and the movement for electoral reform. Although his opponents in the Tory press had long branded Bright a demagogue, he carefully avoided joining the wave of public enthusiasm for war with Russia towards the end of 1853. He argued against the war from before its outset, together with Cobden and other radicals, and this brought them, initially, great unpopularity.

This speech, widely regarded as his masterpiece, and with a poetic turn of phrase as resonant now as then, could not have been predicted. Bright offered to support the newly peace-mongering Palmerston in his attempt to secure peace by negotiation in a conference at Vienna, at which Lord John Russell was the British representative. The negotiations failed, for which Bright later, and vociferously, blamed Palmerston. The atmosphere he evoked of senseless death prefigures the far more widespread carnage of World War I and its effect on the British people.

‘I am one of those forming the majority of the House, I suspect, who are disposed to look upon our present position as one of more than ordinary gravity. I am one, also, of those, not probably constituting so great a majority of the House, who regret extremely the circumstances which have obliged the right hon. Gentlemen who are now upon this bench to secede from the government of the noble lord the Member for Tiverton [Lord Palmerston]. I do not take upon me for a moment to condemn them; because I think, if there be anything in which a man must judge for himself, it is whether he should take office if it be offered to him, whether he should secede from office, whether he should serve under a particular leader, or engage in the service of the crown, or retain office in a particular emergency. In such cases I think that the decision must be left to his own conscience and his own judgment; and I should be the last person to condemn any one for the decision to which he might come. I think, however, that the speech of the right honourable gentleman is one which the House cannot have listened to without being convinced that he and his retiring colleagues have been moved to the course which they have taken by a deliberate judgment upon this question, which, whether it be right or wrong, is fully explained, and is honest to the House and to the country.

'We are at war with the greatest military power'

… The House knows well, and nobody knows better than the noble lord, that I have never been one of his ardent and enthusiastic supporters. I have often disapproved of his policy both at home and abroad; but I hope that I do not bear to him, as I can honestly say that I do not bear to any man in this House – for from all I have received unnumbered courtesies – any feeling that takes even the tinge of a personal animosity; and even if I did, at a moment so grave as this, no feeling of a personal character whatever should prevent me from doing that which I think now, of all times, we are called upon to do – that which we honestly and conscientiously believe to be for the permanent interests of the country. We are in this position, that for a month past, at least, there has been a chaos in the regions of the administration. Nothing can be more embarrassing – I had almost said nothing can be more humiliating – than the position which we offer to the country; and I am afraid that the knowledge of our position is not confined to the limits of these islands.

It will be admitted that we want a government; that if the country is to be saved from the breakers which now surround it, there must be a government; and it devolves upon the House of Commons to rise to the gravity of the occasion, and to support any man who is conscious of his responsibility, and who is honestly offering and endeavouring to deliver the country from the embarrassment in which we now find it. We are at war, and I shall not say one single sentence with regard to the policy of the war or its origin, and I know not that I shall say a single sentence with regard to the conduct of it; but the fact is that we are at war with the greatest military power, probably, of the world, and that we are carrying on our operations at a distance of 3,000 miles from home, and in the neighbourhood of the strongest fortifications of that great military empire. I will not stop to criticise – though it really invites me – the fact that some who have told us that we were in danger from the aggressions of that empire, at the same time told us that that empire was powerless for aggression, and also that it was impregnable to attack. By some means, however, the public have been alarmed as if that aggressive power were unbounded, and they have been induced to undertake an expedition, as if the invasion of an impregnable country were a matter of holiday-making rather than of war.

THE CRIMEAN WAR

1853

Lord Aberdeen's coalition administration attempts to prevent Russo-Turkish tensions escalating into war, but fails: the Ottoman empire declares war, but Russia destroys the Ottoman fleet at Sinope.

1854

The Treaty of Constantinople (March) binds Britain, France and Turkey together; Anglo-French expeditionary forces land in the Crimea, and the Russians are defeated at Alma (20 Sept.); the siege of Sebastopol begins (Oct.); at the Battle of Balaclava (25 Oct.) the allies win, but with

... Now, there are some gentlemen not far from me – there are men who write in the public press – there are thousands of persons in the United Kingdom at this moment – and I learn with astonishment and dismay that there are persons even in that grave assembly which we are not allowed to specify by a name in this House [i.e. 'another place', the House of Lords] – who have entertained dreams – impracticable theories – expectations of vast European and Asiatic changes, of revived nationalities, and of a new map of Europe, if not of the world, as a result or an object of this war. And it is from those gentlemen that we hear continually, addressed to the noble lord the Member for Tiverton, language which I cannot well understand. They call upon him to act, to carry on the war with vigour, and to prosecute enterprises which neither his government nor any other government has ever seriously entertained; but I would appeal to those gentlemen whether it does not become us – regarding the true interests and the true honour of the country – if our government have offered terms of peace to Russia, not to draw back from those terms, not to cause any unnecessary delay, not to adopt any subterfuge to prevent those terms being accepted, not to attempt shuffles of any kind, not to endeavour to insist upon harder terms, and thus make the approach of peace even still more distant than it is at present?

'The sufferings and agonies of our soldiers in the Crimea'

Whatever may be said about the honour of the country in any other relation involved in this affair, this, at least, I expect every man who hears me to admit – that if terms of peace have been offered they have been offered in good faith, and shall be in honour and good faith adhered to; so that if, unfortunately for Europe and humanity, there should be any failure at Vienna, no man should point to the English government and to the authorities and rulers of this Christian country, and say that we have prolonged the war and the infinite calamities of which it is the cause.

I have said that I was anxious that the government of the noble lord should not be overthrown. Will the House allow me to say why I am so? The noble lord at the head of the government has long been a great authority with many persons in this country upon foreign

large losses, including during the Charge of the Light Brigade; Florence Nightingale and her nursing staff arrive in the region (Nov.); the allies win at Inkerman (5 Nov.).

1855
MP Arthur Roebuck proposes official investigation of the conditions affecting the Army, and Aberdeen resigns

(Jan.) to be replaced by Palmerston; Lord Russell attends Vienna Conference to seek peace, but fails (March–April); after heavy losses during assaults over the year, the allies finally break into Sebastopol (Sept.).

1856
At the prospect of Austria's entry on the allies' side,

Russia puts out peace feelers, resulting in Paris Conference and treaties (Feb.–April): the Black Sea to remain neutral, a future independent Romania is proposed, and Britain, France and Austria guarantee to uphold the weak Ottoman empire.

policy. His late colleague, and present envoy to Vienna, has long been a great authority with a large portion of the people of this country upon almost all political questions. With the exception of that unhappy selection of an ambassador at Constantinople, I hold that there are no men in this country more truly responsible for our present position in this war than the noble lord who now fills the highest office in the state and the noble lord who is now, I trust, rapidly approaching the scene of his labours in Vienna. I do not say this now to throw blame upon those noble lords, because their policy, which I hold to be wrong, they, without doubt, as firmly believe to be right; but I am only stating facts. It has been their policy that they have entered into war for certain objects, and I am sure that neither the noble lord at the head of the government nor his late colleague the noble lord the Member for London will shrink from the responsibility which attaches to them. Well, sir, now we have those noble lords in a position which is, in my humble opinion, favourable to the termination of the troubles which exist. I think that the noble lord at the head of the government himself would have more influence in stilling whatever may exist of clamour in this country than any other Member of this House. I think, also, that the noble lord the Member for London would not have undertaken the mission to Vienna if he had not entertained some strong belief that, by so doing, he might bring the war to an end. Nobody gains reputation by a failure in negotiation, and as that noble lord is well acquainted with the whole question from beginning to end, I entertain a hope – I will not say a sanguine hope – that the result of that mission to Vienna will be to bring about a peace, to extricate this country from some of those difficulties inseparable from a state of war.

'A bitter and angry feeling'

There is one subject upon which I should like to put a question to the noble lord at the head of the government. I shall not say one word here about the state of the Army in the Crimea, or one word about its numbers or its condition. Every Member of this House, every inhabitant of this country, has been sufficiently harrowed with details regarding it. To my solemn belief, thousands – nay, scores of thousands of persons – have retired to rest, night after night, whose slumbers have been disturbed or whose dreams have been based upon the sufferings and agonies of our soldiers in the Crimea. I should like to ask the noble lord at the head of the government – although I am not sure if he will feel that he can or ought to answer the question – whether the noble lord the Member for London has power, after discussions have commenced, and as soon as there shall be established good grounds for believing that the negotiations for peace will prove successful, to enter into any armistice? (*'No! No!'*)

I know not, sir, who it is that says 'No, no', but I should like to see any man get up and say that the destruction of 200,000 human lives lost on all sides during the course of this unhappy conflict is not a sufficient sacrifice. You are not pretending to conquer territory – you are not pretending to hold fortified or unfortified towns; you have offered terms of peace which, as I understand them, I do not say are not moderate; and breathes there a man in this House or in this country whose appetite for blood is so insatiable that, even when terms of peace have been offered and accepted, he pines for that assault in which of Russian, Turk, French and English, as sure as one man dies, 20,000 corpses will strew the streets of Sebastopol? I say I should like to ask the noble lord – and I am sure that he will feel, and that this House will feel, that I am speaking in no unfriendly manner towards the government of which he is at the head – I should like to know, and I venture to hope that it is so, if the noble lord the Member for London has power, at the earliest stage of these proceedings at Vienna, at which it can properly be done – and I should think that it might properly be done at a very early stage – to adopt a course by which all further waste of human life may be put an end to, and further animosity between three great nations be, as far as possible, prevented?

'The Angel of Death has been abroad'

I appeal to the noble lord at the head of the government and to this House; I am not now complaining of the war – I am not now complaining of the terms of peace, nor, indeed, of anything that has been done – but I wish to suggest to this House what, I believe, thousands and tens of thousands of the most educated and of the most Christian portion of the people of this country are feeling upon this subject, although, indeed, in the midst of a certain clamour in the country, they do not give public expression to their feelings. Your country is not in an advantageous state at this moment; from one end of the kingdom to the other there is a general collapse of industry. Those Members of this House not intimately acquainted with the trade and commerce of the country do not fully comprehend our position as to the diminution of employment and the lessening of wages. An increase in the cost of living is finding its way to the homes and hearts of a vast number of the labouring population.

At the same time there is growing up – and, notwithstanding what some hon. Members of this House may think of me, no man regrets it more than I do – a bitter and angry feeling against that class which has for a long period conducted the public affairs of this country. I like political changes when such changes are made as the result, not of passion, but of deliberation and reason. Changes so made are safe, but changes made under the influence of violent exaggeration, or of the violent passions of public meetings, are not changes usually approved by this House or advantageous to the country. I cannot but notice, in speaking to gentlemen who sit on either side of this House, or in speaking to any one I meet between this House and any of those localities we frequent when this House is up – I cannot, I say, but notice that an uneasy feeling exists as to the news which may arrive by the very next mail from the East. I do not suppose that your troops are to be beaten in actual conflict with the foe, or that they will be driven into the sea; but I am certain that many homes in England in which there now exists a fond hope that the distant one may return – many such homes may be rendered desolate when the next mail shall arrive. The Angel of Death has been abroad throughout the land; you may almost hear the beating of his wings. There is no one, as when the first-born were slain of old, to sprinkle with blood the lintel and the two sideposts of our doors, that he may spare and pass on; he takes his victims from the castle of the noble, the mansion of the wealthy, and the cottage of the poor and the lowly, and it is on behalf of all these classes that I make this solemn appeal.

'The indescribable calamities of war'

I tell the noble lord, that if he be ready honestly and frankly to endeavour, by the negotiations about to be opened at Vienna, to put an end to this war, no word of mine, no vote of mine, will be given to shake his power for one single moment, or to change his position in this

House. I am sure that the noble lord is not inaccessible to appeals made to him from honest motives and with no unfriendly feeling. The noble lord has been for more than forty years a Member of this House. Before I was born, he sat upon the treasury bench, and he has spent his life in the service of his country. He is no longer young, and his life has extended almost to the term allotted to man. I would ask, I would entreat the noble lord to take a course which, when he looks back upon his whole political career – whatever he may therein find to be pleased with, whatever to regret – cannot but be a source of gratification to him. By adopting that course he would have the satisfaction of reflecting that, having obtained the object of his laudable ambition – having become the foremost subject of the crown, the director of, it may be, the destinies of his country, and the presiding genius in her councils – he had achieved a still higher and nobler ambition: that he had returned the sword to the scabbard – that at his word torrents of blood had ceased to flow – that he had restored tranquillity to Europe, and saved this country from the indescribable calamities of war.

*'The noblest government
in the world'*

Manchester, 3 April 1872

Benjamin Disraeli

on the virtues of monarchy and the
House of Lords

Benjamin Disraeli (1804–81) had been prime minister for nine months in 1868, and would hold the office again from 1874 to 1880. He had had a colourful early career, making his name as a novelist, and using one of his novels, *Sybil, or the Two Nations* (1845), to set a template for progressive, reforming Conservatism that has helped him remain a hero to centre-left Tories to this day – and from which the progressive One Nation group took, by inference, its name when it was formed in 1950.

Disraeli was not always accurate with the facts – when Sir Robert Peel, under attack from him during the debate on repeal of the Corn Laws, accused him (truthfully) of having touted for office under him, Disraeli flatly denied it. He ruthlessly manoeuvred to achieve office and was successful, becoming chancellor of the exchequer under Lord Derby in 1852. A favourite of Queen Victoria, whom (as in this speech) he flattered relentlessly, he sought to maintain the institutions of the British nation while, through reforming acts aimed at ameliorating the lot of what the Victorians called 'the submerged tenth', removing the provocation for the poorer classes to become revolutionary. His espousal of the 2nd Reform Act under Lord Derby in 1867 brought him the wrath of the reactionary Right, notably of Thomas Carlyle, who branded him a 'superlative Hebrew conjuror' (impugning Disraeli's Jewish origins). During the six years of opposition between Disraeli's terms as prime minister he not only revamped the organisation of the Conservative Party but also set out a programme of audacious reform aimed at capturing the public's imagination and the support, in particular, of the newly enfranchised who had supported W.E. Gladstone so strongly in 1868. He was successful in this, the Conservatives winning a majority of 49 in the general election of January 1874, and in this speech at Manchester, two years before, he had set out both the tone, and some of the detail, of his programme.

Disraeli's paternalist Toryism was to start a current running through the Party for the next century, its spell only broken by Thatcherism with its – paradoxically – Manchester liberal roots. Disraeli also confronts head-on a strain of republicanism then emerging in the Liberal Party, championed by the young radical MP Sir Charles Dilke.

6The Conservative Party are accused of having no programme of policy. If by a programme is meant a plan to despoil churches and plunder landlords, I admit we have no programme. If by a programme is meant a policy which assails or menaces every institution and every interest, every class and every calling in the country, I admit we have no programme. But if to have a policy with distinct ends, and these such as most deeply interest the great body of the nation, be a becoming programme for a political party, then, I contend, we have an adequate programme, and one which, here or elsewhere, I shall always be prepared to assert and to vindicate.

Gentlemen, the programme of the Conservative Party is to maintain the constitution of the country. I have not come down to Manchester to deliver an essay on the English constitution;

but when the banner of republicanism is unfurled – when the fundamental principles of our institutions are controverted – I think, perhaps, it may not be inconvenient that I should make some few practical remarks upon the character of our constitution – upon that monarchy, limited by the coordinate authority of estates of the realm, which, under the title of Queen, Lords and Commons, has contributed so greatly to the prosperity of this country, and with the maintenance of which I believe that prosperity is bound up.

Gentlemen, since the settlement of that constitution, now nearly two centuries ago, England has never experienced a revolution, though there is no country in which there has been so continuous and such considerable change. How is this? Because the wisdom of your forefathers placed the prize of supreme power without the sphere of human passions. Whatever the struggle of parties, whatever the strife of factions, whatever the excitement and exaltation of the public mind, there has always been something in this country round which all classes and parties could rally, representing the majesty of the law, the administration of justice, and involving, at the same time, the security for every man's rights and the fountain of honour. Now, gentlemen, it is well clearly to comprehend what is meant by a country not having a revolution for two centuries. It means, for that space, the unbroken exercise and enjoyment of the ingenuity of man. It means, for that space, the continuous application of the discoveries of science to his comfort and convenience. It means the accumulation of capital, the elevation of labour, the establishment of those admirable factories which cover your district; the unwearied improvement of the cultivation of the land, which has extracted from a somewhat churlish soil harvests more exuberant than those furnished by lands nearer to the sun. It means the continuous order which is the only parent of personel liberty and political right. And you owe all these, gentlemen, to the throne

'An intelligence superior to all Party'

There is another powerful and most beneficial influence which is also exercised by the crown. Gentlemen, I am a Party man. I believe that, without Party, parliamentary government is impossible. I look upon parliamentary government as the noblest government in the world, and certainly the most suited to England. But without the discipline of political connection, animated by the principle of private honour, I feel certain that a popular assembly would sink, before the power or the corruption of a minister. Yet, gentlemen, I am not blind to the faults of Party government. It has one great defect. Party has a tendency to warp the intelligence, and there is no minister, however resolved he may be in treating a great public question, who does not find some difficulty in emancipating himself from the traditionary prejudice on which he has long acted. It is, therefore, a great merit in our constitution that before a minister introduces a measure to Parliament, he must submit it to an intelligence superior to all Party, and entirely free from influences of that character.

I know it will be said, gentlemen, that, however beautiful in theory, the personal influence of the sovereign is now absorbed in the responsibility of the minister. Gentlemen, I think you will find there is great fallacy in this view. The principles of the English constitution do not contemplate the absence of personal influence on the part of the sovereign; and if they did, the principles of human nature would prevent the fulfilment of such a theory. Gentlemen, I need not tell you that I am now making on this subject abstract observations of general application to our institutions and our history. But take the case of a sovereign of England who accedes to his throne at the earliest age the law permits and who enjoys a long reign – take an instance like that of George III. From the earliest moment of his accession that sovereign is placed in constant communication with the most able statesmen of the period, and of all parties. Even with average ability it is impossible not to perceive that such a sovereign must soon attain a great mass of political information and political experience. Information and experience, gentlemen, whether they are possessed by a sovereign or by the humblest of his subjects, are irresistible in life. No man with the vast responsibility that devolves upon an English minister can afford to treat with indifference a suggestion that has not occurred to him, or information with which he had not been previously supplied. But, gentlemen, pursue this view of the subject. The longer the reign, the influence of that sovereign must proportionately increase. All the illustrious statesmen who served his youth disappear. A new generation of public servants rises up. There is a critical conjuncture in affairs – a moment of perplexity and peril. Then it is that the sovereign can appeal to a similar state of affairs that occurred perhaps thirty years before. When all are in doubt among his servants he can quote the advice that was given by the illustrious men of his early years, and though he may maintain himself within the strictest limits of the constitution, who can suppose when such information and such suggestions are made by the most exalted person in the country that they can be without effect? No, gentlemen; a minister who could venture to treat such influence with indifference would not be a constitutional minister, but an arrogant idiot.

'Here the home is revered and the hearth is sacred'

Gentlemen, the influence of the crown is not confined merely to political affairs. England is a domestic country. Here the home is revered and the hearth is sacred. The nation is represented by a family – the royal family; and if that family is educated with a sense of responsibility and a sentiment of public duty, it is difficult to exaggerate the salutary influence they may exercise over a nation. It is not merely an influence upon manners; it is not merely that they are a model for refinement and for good taste – they affect the heart as well as the intelligence of the people; and in the hour of public adversity, or in the anxious conjuncture of public affairs, the nation rallies round the family and the throne, and its spirit is animated and sustained by the expression of public affection.

DISRAELI'S POLITICAL CAREER

1837
Is elected Tory MP for Maidstone.

1842
Becomes leader of the Tories in the 'Young England' group.

1846
Opposes fellow-Tory Sir Robert Peel's repeal of Corn Laws, helping to end Peel's premiership.

1852
Under Lord Derby becomes chancellor of the exchequer and rejects his former protectionist stance as regards tariffs.

1866–7
After seven years in Opposition, returns as chancellor under Lord Derby and carries the second Reform Bill.

1868
Prime minister (Feb.–Dec.).

... I would say something on the subject of the House of Lords. It is not merely the authority of the Throne that is now disputed, but the character and influence of the House of Lords that are held up by some to public disregard. Gentlemen, I shall not stop for a moment to offer you any proofs of the advantage of a second chamber; and for this reason. That subject has been discussed now for a century, ever since the establishment of the government of the United States, and all great authorities, American, German, French, Italian, have agreed in this, that a representative government is impossible without a second chamber. And it has been, especially of late, maintained by great political writers in all countries that the repeated failure of what is called the French Republic is mainly to be ascribed to its not having a second chamber.

But, gentlemen, however anxious foreign countries have been to enjoy this advantage, that anxiety has only been equalled by the difficulty which they have found in fulfilling their object. How is a second chamber to be constituted? By nominees of the sovereign power? Are they to be bound by popular election? In what manner are they to be elected? If by the same constituency as the popular body, what claim have they, under such circumstances, to criticise or to control the decisions of that body? If they are to be elected by a more select body, qualified by a higher franchise, there immediately occurs the objection, why should the majority be governed by the minority? The United States of America were fortunate in finding a solution of this difficulty; but the United States of America had elements to deal with which never occurred before, and never probably will occur again, because they formed their illustrious Senate from the materials that were offered them by the thirty-seven States. We, gentlemen, have the House of Lords, an assembly which has historically developed and periodically adapted itself to the wants and necessities of the times.

'He will never see a Cumberland man ill-treated'

What, gentlemen, is the first quality which is required in a second chamber? Without doubt, independence. What is the best foundation of independence? Without doubt, property. The prime minister of England [Gladstone] has only recently told you, and I believe he spoke quite

1874	created Earl of	1878	1880
After six years in Opposition, returns as prime minister.	Beaconsfield and enters House of Lords; his perceived indifference in the face of the Ottoman suppression of the Bulgarian uprising earns the scorn of W.E. Gladstone and of much of the popular opinion.	At the Congress of Berlin, following Russo-Turkish war, negotiates a treaty with Russia that respects mutual interests, divides up Bulgaria, and by which Britain acquires Cyprus.	Following the annihilation of the Conservatives in the general election, begins a withdrawal from political life, returning to his literary endeavours.
1875 Espouses Anglo-French ownership of the Suez Canal.			
1876 Creates Queen Victoria 'Empress of India', and is himself			

accurately, that the average income of the members of the House of Lords is £20,000 per annum. Of course there are some who have more and some who have less; but the influence of a public assembly, so far as property is concerned, depends upon its aggregate property, which, in the present case, is a revenue of £9,000,000 a year. But, gentlemen, you must look to the nature of this property. It is visible property, and therefore it is responsible property, which every ratepayer in the room knows to his cost. But, gentlemen, it is not only visible property; it is, generally speaking, territorial property; and one of the elements of territorial property is that it is representative. Now, for illustration, suppose – which God forbid – there was no House of Commons, and any Englishman – I will take him from either end of the island – a Cumberland or a Cornish man, finds himself aggrieved. The Cumbrian says, 'This conduct I experience is most unjust. I know a Cumberland man in the House of Lords, the Earl of Carlisle or the Earl of Lonsdale; I will go to him; he will never see a Cumberland man ill-treated.' The Cornish man will say, 'I will go to the Lord of Port Eliot; his family have sacrificed themselves before this for the liberties of Englishmen, and he will get justice done me.'

'The charge against the House of Lords is that the dignities are hereditary'

But, gentlemen, the charge against the House of Lords is that the dignities are hereditary, and we are told that if we have a House of Peers they should be peers for life. There are great authorities in favour of this, and even my noble friend [Lord Derby] near me the other day gave in his adhesion to a limited application of this principle. Now, gentlemen, in the first place let me observe that every peer is a peer for life, as he cannot be a peer after his death; but some peers for life are succeeded in their dignities by their children. The question arises, who is most responsible – a peer for life whose dignities are not descendible, or a peer for life whose dignities are hereditary? Now, gentlemen, a peer for life is in a very strong position. He says, 'Here I am; I have got power and I will exercise it.' I have no doubt that, on the whole, a peer for life would exercise it for what he deemed was the public good. Let us hope that. But, after all, he might and could exercise it according to his own will. Nobody can call him to account; he is independent of everybody. But a peer for life whose dignities descend is in a very different position. He has every inducement to study public opinion, and, when he believes it just, to yield; because he naturally feels that if the order to which he belongs is in constant collision with public opinion, the chances are that his dignities will not descend to his posterity.

Therefore, gentlemen, I am not prepared myself to believe that a solution of any difficulties in the public mind on this subject is to be found by creating peers for life. I know there are some philosophers who believe that the best substitute for the House of Lords would be an assembly formed of ex-governors of colonies. I have not sufficient experience on that subject to give a decided opinion upon it. When the Muse of Comedy threw her frolic grace over society, a retired governor was generally one of the characters in every comedy; and the last of our great actors – who, by the by, was a great favourite at Manchester – Mr Fairen, was celebrated for his delineation of the character in question. Whether it be the recollection of that performance or not, I confess I am inclined to believe that an English gentleman – born to business, managing his own estate, administering the affairs of his county, mixing with all classes of his fellow-men, now in the hunting field, now in the Railway Direction, unaffected, unostentatious, proud of his ancestors, if they have contributed to the greatness of our common country is, on the whole, more likely to form a senator agreeable to English opinion and English taste than any substitute that has yet been produced.

'Thank God, there is the House of Lords'

Gentlemen, let me make one observation more, on the subject of the House of Lords, before I conclude. There is some advantage in political experience. I remember the time when there was a similar outcry against the House of Lords, but much more intense and powerful; and, gentlemen, it arose from the same cause. A Liberal government had been installed in office, with an immense Liberal majority. They proposed some violent measures. The House of Lords modified some, delayed others, and some they threw out. Instantly there was a cry to abolish or to reform the House of Lords, and the greatest popular orator [Daniel O'Connell] that probably ever existed was sent on a pilgrimage over England to excite the people in favour of this opinion. What happened? That happened, gentlemen, which may happen to-morrow. There was a dissolution of Parliament. The great Liberal majority vanished. The balance of parties was restored. It was discovered that the House of Lords had behind them at least half of the English people. We heard no more cries for their abolition or their reform, and before two years more passed England was really governed by the House of Lords, under the wise influence of the Duke of Wellington and the commanding eloquence of Lyndhurst♥; and such was the enthusiasm of the nation in favour of the Second Chamber that at every public meeting its health was drunk, with the additional sentiment, for which we are indebted to one of the most distinguished members that ever represented the House of Commons, 'Thank God, there is the House of Lords.'

Gentlemen, you will perhaps not be surprised that, having made some remarks upon the Monarchy and the House of Lords, I should say something respecting that House in which I have literally passed the greater part of my life and to which I am devotedly attached. It is not likely, therefore, that I should say anything to depreciate the legitimate position and influence of the House of Commons. Gentlemen it is said that the diminished power of the throne and the assailed authority of the House of Lords are owing to the increased power of the House of Commons, and the new position which of late years, and especially during the last forty years, it has assumed in the English constitution. Gentlemen, the main power of the House of Commons depends upon its command over the public purse and its control of the public expenditure; and if that power is possessed by a party which has a large majority in the House of Commons, the influence of the House of Commons is proportionately increased, and, under some circumstances, becomes more predominant. But, gentlemen, this power of the House of Commons is not a power which has been created by any Reform Act, from the days of Lord Grey in 1832 to 1867. It is the power which the House of Commons has enjoyed for centuries – which it has frequently asserted and sometimes even tyrannically exercised. Gentlemen, the House of Commons represents the constituencies of England, and I am here to show you that no addition to the elements of that constituency has placed the House of Commons in a different position with regard to the throne and the House of Lords from that it has always constitutionally occupied.

♥ John Singleton Copley (1772–1863), 1st Baron Lyndhurst, three times lord chancellor in the 1820s–40s.

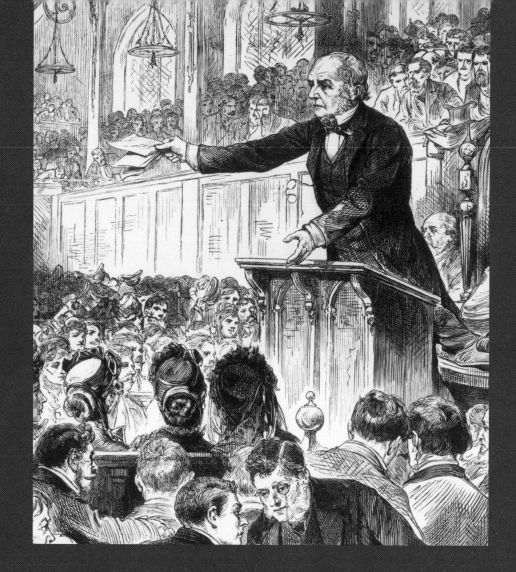

'It is his duty to protest'

Edinburgh, 25 November 1879

William Ewart Gladstone
on Disraeli's foreign policy and the
Eastern Question

William Ewart Gladstone (1809–98) was, arguably, the titanic figure of 19th-century politics. He entered Parliament in 1832 as a Tory, and only ceased to be an MP at the general election of 1895, having transferred to the Liberal Party in 1859: he was chancellor of the exchequer in governments formed by both parties. He was four times prime minister (1868–74, 1880–5, Feb.–July 1886, and 1892–4). A staunch Anglican, he was married for nearly 60 years, though he is remembered today also for his desire to 'save' fallen women: he would go out at night and talk to prostitutes, and flagellate himself afterwards. As well as seriously developing the administration of the public finances during his time as chancellor, he took up the cause of Ireland, realising – correctly, as it turned out – the scope of a rebellious nation to undermine the United Kingdom. He was also a passionate advocate of parliamentary reform. After the Liberal Party's defeat at the 1874 election Gladstone retired – temporarily – as leader of the Party.

His spell without this responsibility saw the publication of a famous pamphlet, on the atrocities committed by Bulgaria's Ottoman rulers in 1874 against its nationalist rebels, which contained a savage attack on the foreign policy of Disraeli's Conservative administration. He came to loathe Disraeli, and this stirred him, in the months before the 1880 election, to wage what came to be known as 'the Midlothian campaign', as he prepared to fight the seat of Edinburghshire. He delivered five major speeches in public halls, and a number of other shorter speeches on the stump, denouncing the policies of the outgoing government. It was extremely rare at this time for politicians of Gladstone's standing to engage in such electioneering, and his activities were all the more powerful since they were motivated quite clearly by moral indignation and not by personal ambition. Reported widely as they were, these speeches had a decisive effect on mobilising public opinion against Disraeli (who had, in 1876, been created Earl of Beaconsfield). When the Liberals won the ensuing election, Queen Victoria, who seriously disliked Gladstone, sought to persuade the Marquess of Hartington – heir to the dukedom of Devonshire – to form a government. He refused, recognising the overwhelming popularity of Gladstone in the country, and with some reluctance Victoria was persuaded to send for Gladstone to take up, once more, the office of prime minister.

In this speech, which opened that campaign, Gladstone explained why, as an outsider to Edinburgh, he felt qualified to represent its people in Parliament; but also, in a ferocious forensic attack to which he brought all his high-minded and intellectual qualities, he explained why he deplored Disraeli's foreign policy. Gladstone was especially outraged that (after the Congress of Berlin the previous year) Disraeli had connived in the partial return of Bulgaria, with its large Christian population, to the control of the Turks in return for Turkey's support against Russia. This was also the year of disastrous Afghan and Zulu wars, and Gladstone capitalised on all these setbacks. He would be hoist with his own petard in 1885, however, when he was widely perceived – not least by the queen – to have failed to save the life of General Gordon at Khartoum.

I really have but one great anxiety. This is a self-governing country. Let us bring home to the minds of the people the state of the facts they have to deal with, and in Heaven's name let them determine whether or not this is the way in which they like to be governed. Do not let us suppose this is like the old question between Whig and Tory. It is nothing of the kind. It is not now as if we were disputing about some secondary matter – it is not even as if we were disputing about the Irish Church, which no doubt was a very important affair. What we are disputing about is a whole system of government, and to make good that proposition that it is a whole system of government will be my great object in any addresses that I may deliver in this country. If it is acceptable, if it is liked by the people – they are the masters – it is for them to have it. It is not particularly pleasant for any man, I suppose, to spend the closing years of his life in vain and unavailing protest; but as long as he thinks his protest may avail, as long as he feels that the people have not yet had their fair chance and opportunity, it is his duty to protest, and it is to perform that duty, gentlemen, that I come here.

'The rights of the Christian subjects'

I have spoken, gentlemen, of the inheritance given over to the present government by their predecessors, and of the inheritance that they will give over to those who succeed them. Now, our condition is not only, in my judgment, a condition of embarrassment, but it is one of embarrassment we have made for ourselves; and before I close, although I have already detained you too long, I must give a single illustration of the manner in which we have been making our own embarrassments. Why did we quarrel with the present government about Turkey? I have shown that we were extremely slow in doing it. I believe we were too slow, and that, perhaps, if we had begun sooner our exertions might have availed more; but it was from a good motive. Why did we quarrel? What was the point upon which we quarrelled?

The point upon which we quarrelled was this: Whether coercion was under any circumstances to be applied to Turkey to bring about the better government of that country … The foundation of the policy of the present government was that coercion was not to be applied to Turkey.

THE 'BULGARIAN HORRORS' 1876

APRIL
Bulgarians of the 'Revolutionary Central Committee' lead a nationalist uprising, but over 10,000 Bulgarians are killed in retaliation by forces loyal to Bulgaria's Ottoman rulers.

MAY
A British fleet sails to the Dardanelles as a precautionary measure in case of a wider crisis in the region.

JUNE
The British press reports atrocities in Bulgaria, which are subsequently dismissed by Disraeli, the prime minister.

Here is what Lord Cranbrook*, who stated the case of the government in the House of Commons, said: 'We have proclaimed, and I proclaim again, in the strongest language, that we should be wrong in every sense of the word if we were to endeavour to apply material coercion against Turkey'; that was what Lord Cranbrook said on the 15th February 1877, nor had he repented in April, for in April he said: 'Above all, we feel that we, who have engaged ourselves by treaty, at least in former times, who have had no personal wrong done to us, have no right and no commission, either as a country, or, as I may say, from Heaven, to take upon ourselves the vindication by violence of the rights of the Christian subjects of the Porte [the Ottoman empire], however much we may feel for them.' Higher authority, of course, still than Lord Cranbrook, but in perfect conformity with him, was Lord Beaconsfield himself, who, on the 20th February 1877, after a speech of Lord Granville's*, said this: 'The noble Lord and his friends are of opinion that we should have coerced the Porte into the acceptation of the policy which we recommended. That is not a course which we can conscientiously profess or promote, and I think therefore, when an issue so broad is brought before the House, it really is the duty of noble Lords to give us an opportunity to clear the mind of the country by letting it know what is the opinion of Parliament upon policies so distinct, and which in their consequences must be so different.' Now, you see plainly that coercion in the extreme case that had arisen was recommended by the Liberal Party. Coercion was objected to on the highest grounds by the Tory Party; and Lord Beaconsfield virtually said, 'Such is the profound difference between these policies that I challenge you to make a motion in Parliament, and to take the opinion of Parliament in order that we may know which way we are to move.' That was not all, for after the English government had disclaimed coercion, and after that terribly calamitous Russo-Turkish war had been begun and ended, Lord Beaconsfield declared that if the government had been entirely consistent, they would not have rested satisfied with protesting against the action of Russia, so sacred was this principle of non-coercion in their eyes, but that they ought to have warned Russia that if she acted she must be prepared to encounter the opposition of England.

I will read a very short passage from a letter of Sir Henry Layard♦ which refers to that declaration. Sir Henry Layard, on the 18th April 1879, wrote or spoke as follows, I am not quite sure which; I quote it from an unexceptionable authority, the *Daily Telegraph* of April 19; 'I agree with the remark of Lord Beaconsfield when he returned from the Berlin Congress, that if England had shown firmness in the first instance the late war might have been avoided.

SEPTEMBER
Gladstone emerges from political retirement with his pamphlet *The Bulgarian Horrors and the Question of the East*; three days later he resumes political speech-making, on this issue, his views reflecting a public outcry throughout Western Europe.

NOVEMBER
With Russia eager to use the Bulgarian crisis to further its regional goals, Disraeli proposes an international conference to be held in Constantinople.

DECEMBER
At the conference, Russia and Britain disagree on the size of a future independent Bulgaria, and ultimately Ottoman/ British interests prevent agreement; partial Bulgarian independence must wait until Ottoman defeat in the Russo-Turkish War of 1877–8 and the subsequent Treaty of Berlin, orchestrated by Germany's Otto von Bismarck and Disraeli.

That is my conviction, and everything I have seen tends to confirm it.' If England had shown firmness – that is to say, if she had threatened Russia. There is no other meaning applicable to the words. I have shown you, therefore, gentlemen, what it is upon which we went to issue – whether Turkey should be coerced, or whether she should not.

'Coercion by the united authority of Europe'

But there is an important limitation. We had never given countenance to single-handed attempts to coerce Turkey. We felt that single-handed attempts to coerce Turkey would probably lead to immediate bloodshed and calamity, with great uncertainty as to the issue. The coercion we recommended was coercion by the united authority of Europe, and we always contended that in the case where the united authority of Europe was brought into action, there was no fear of having to proceed to actual coercion. The Turk knew very well how to measure strength on one side and the other, and he would have yielded to that authority. But no, there must be no coercion under any circumstances.

Such was the issue, gentlemen. Well, where do we stand now? We know what has taken place in the interval. We know that a great work of liberation has been done, in which we have had no part whatever. With the traditions of liberty which we think we cherish, with the recollection that you Scotchmen entertain of the struggles in which you have engaged to establish your own liberties here, a great work of emancipation has been going on in the world, and you have been prevented by your government from any share in it whatever. But bitter as is the mortification with which I for one reflect upon that exclusion, I thank God that the work has been done. It has been done in one sense, perhaps, by the most inappropriate of instruments; but I rejoice in the result, that six or seven millions of people who were in partial subjection have been brought into total independence, and many millions more who were in absolute subjection to the Ottoman rule have been brought into a state which, if not one of total independence, yet is one of practical liberation actually attained, or very shortly to be realised – practical liberation from the worst of the evils which they suffered.

But what happens now? Why, it appears the Turk is going to be coerced after all. But is not it a most astounding fact that the government, who said they would on no consideration coerce the Turk, and who said that if Europe attempted to coerce the Turk nothing but misery could result, now expects to coerce the Turk by sending an order to Admiral Hornby* at Malta, and desiring him to sail with his fleet into the east of the Mediterranean? Now, gentlemen, neither you nor I are acquainted with the whole of the circumstances attendant upon these measures. We don't know the reasons of State that have brought about this extraordinary result. But what I have pointed out to you is this, that Her Majesty's government have in matter of fact come round to the very principle upon which they compelled the Liberals to join issue with them two or three years ago – the very principle which they then declared to be totally inadmissible, and for urging which upon them, their agents and organs through the country have been incessantly maintaining that nothing but the spirit of faction could have induced us to do anything so monstrous. That which nothing but the spirit of faction could have induced us to do, is embraced in principle by Her Majesty's government. But is it embraced in the same form? No. We said: Let coercion be applied by the united authority of Europe – that is to say, for it is not an exaggeration so to put it, by the united authority of the civilised world applicable to this case. Our American friends have too remote an interest in it to take part. God forbid I should exclude them from the civilised world; but it was by the united authority of Europe that we demanded it. It is now attempted by the single authority and by the single hand of England. Will it succeed? All I can say is this, if it be directed to good and honest ends, to practical improvement, with all my heart I hope it may; but it may not, and then where is the responsibility? Where is the responsibility of those who refused to allow all Europe to act in unison, and who then took upon themselves this single-handed action? If it fails, they incur an immense responsibility. If it succeeds, it only becomes the more plain that had they but acceded to the advice which was at first so humbly tendered by the Liberal Party, and which only after a long time was vigorously pressed – had they then acceded to the view of the Liberal Party, and allowed Turkey to be dealt with as she ought to have been dealt with at the close of the Constantinople Conference, Turkey would have given way at once. The power which yields to one state would still more readily have yielded to the united voice of the six great states. The concessions to be made by her would then have been made, and the horrors and the bloodshed, the loss of life and treasure, the heartburnings, the difficulties, the confusion, and the anarchy that have followed, would all of them have been saved.

'The terrible penalties of an almost immeasurable bloodshed'

Therefore, gentlemen, I say that our present embarrassments are of our own creation. It would be a very cruel thing to hold the present government responsible for the existence of an Eastern Question that from time to time troubles Europe. I have not held them so responsible. I hold them responsible for having interrupted that concerted action which, it is as evident as considerations of sense and policy can make it – which could not have failed to attain its effect; and for now being driven to make the same effort, with diminished resources, in greater difficulties, and after the terrible penalties of an almost immeasurable bloodshed had been paid.

Now, gentlemen, all this, and a great deal more than this, has to be said, which cannot be said now. Neither your patience nor my strength could enable me to say it. I have detained you at great length. I have only opened, as it were, these questions. I have not even touched the great number of important subjects in which you naturally, as men of Scotland and men of Midlothian, feel very special interest. I will, however, gentlemen, for this day bid you farewell. But I shall say one word in closing, and it is this. It is constantly said by the government, and it is a fair claim on their part, that they have been supported by large majorities in the House of Commons. It is a very fair claim, indeed, for a certain purpose. I should, indeed, have something to say upon the other side – viz. this, that you will find in no instance that I am aware of in history, neither in the American War nor in the great Revolutionary War, nor at any period known to me, has objection been taken, persistently and increasingly taken, by such large fractions of the House of Commons – not less, at any rate, than two-fifths of the House, sometimes more – to the foreign policy of the government, as during this great controversy. The fact is, gentlemen, that in matters of foreign policy it does require, and it ought to require, very great errors and very great misdeeds on the part of the government to drive a large portion of Parliament into opposition. It is most important to maintain our national unity in the face of the world. I, for my part, have always admitted, and admit now, that our responsibility in opposing the government has been immense, but their responsibility in refusing to do right has been still greater. Still they are right in alleging that they have been supported by large majorities. Pray, consider what that means. That is a most important proposition; it is a proposition that ought to come home to the mind of every one here. It means this, that though I have been obliged all through this discourse to attack the government, I am really attacking the majority of the House of Commons. Please to consider that you might, if you like, strike out of my speech all reference to the government, all reference to any name, all reference to the body.

'The majority of the House of Commons has completely acquitted the government'

It is no longer the government with which you have to deal. You have to deal with the majority of the House of Commons. The majority of the House of Commons has completely acquitted the government. Upon every occasion when the government has appealed to it, the majority of the House of Commons has been ready to answer to the call. Hardly a man has ever hesitated to grant the confidence that was desired, however outrageous in our view the nature of the demand might be. Completely and bodily, the majority of the House of Commons has taken on itself the responsibility of the government – and not only the collective majority of the House of Commons, gentlemen. If you had got to deal with them by a vote of censure on that majority in the lump, that would be a very ineffective method of dealing. They must be dealt with individually. That majority is made up of units. It is the unit with which you have got to deal. And let me tell you that the occasion is a solemn one; for as I am the first to aver that now fully and bodily the majority of the House of Commons has, in the face of the country, by a multitude of repeated and deliberate acts, made itself wholly and absolutely responsible in the whole of these transactions that I have been commenting upon, and in many more; and as the House of Commons has done that, so upon the coming general election will it have to be determined whether that responsibility, so shifted from an Administration to a Parliament, shall again be shifted from a Parliament to a nation. As yet the nation has had no opportunity. Nay, as I pointed out early in these remarks, the government do not seem disposed to give them the opportunity. To the last moment, so far as we are informed by the best authorities, they intend to withhold it. The nation, therefore, is not yet responsible.

'If the name of England has been discredited'

If faith has been broken, if blood has been needlessly shed, if the name of England has been discredited and lowered from that lofty standard which it ought to exhibit to the whole world, if the country has been needlessly distressed, if finance has been thrown into confusion, if the foundations of the Indian Empire have been impaired, all these things as yet are the work of an Administration and a Parliament; but the day is coming, and is near at hand, when that event will take place which will lead the historian to declare whether or not they are the work, not of an Administration and not of a Parliament, but the work of a great and a free people. If this great and free and powerful people is disposed to associate itself with such transactions, if it is disposed to assume upon itself what some of us would call the guilt, and many of us must declare to be the heavy burden, of all those events that have been passing before our eyes, it rests with them to do it. But, gentlemen, let every one of us resolve in his inner conscience, before God and before man – let him resolve that he at least will have no share in such a proceeding; that he will do his best to exempt himself; that he will exempt himself from every participation in what he believes to be mischievous and ruinous misdeeds; that, so far as his exertions can avail, no trifling, no secondary consideration shall stand in the way of them, or abate them; that he will do what in him lies to dissuade his countrymen from arriving at a resolution so full of mischief, of peril, and of shame.

Gentlemen, this is the issue which the people of this country will have to try. Our minds are made up. You and they have got to speak. I for my part have done and will do the little that rests with me to make clear the nature of the great controversy that is to be decided; and I say from the bottom of my soul, 'God speed the right'.

♥ Gathorne Gathorne-Hardy (1814–1906), secretary for war 1874–8, ennobled as Viscount Cranbrook in 1878, subsequently secretary of state for India.
♦ Granville George Leveson-Gower, 2nd Earl Granville (1815–91), Liberal leader in the House of Lords, colonial secretary 1868–70 and 1886, foreign secretary 1870–4 and 1880–5.
♣ Austen Henry Layard (1817–94), archaeologist and art historian, former MP, ambassador to Constantinople 1877–80.
♠ Sir Geoffrey Thomas Phipps Hornby (1825–95), later Admiral of the Fleet, commander-in-chief, Mediterranean, 1877–80.

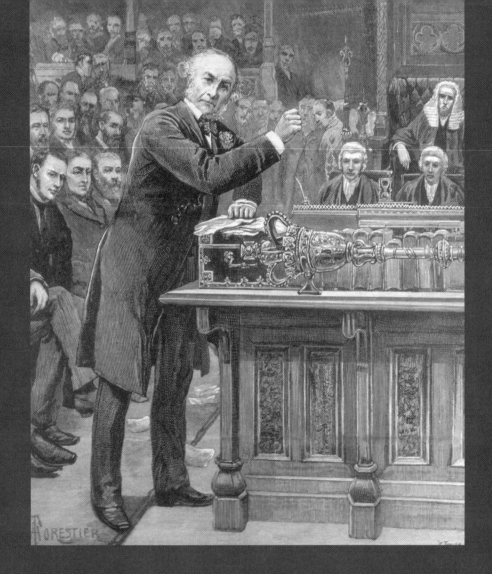

'Ireland stands at your bar expectant'

House of Commons, London, 7 June 1886

William Ewart Gladstone
on the need for Home Rule in Ireland

Agitation for Irish Home Rule had been mounting since its more extreme manisfestation in the Fenian Brotherhood stepped up its activities in the 1860s. Although extremists had resorted to acts of terrorism to secure their ends – notably the murders in Dublin's Phoenix Park in 1882 of the chief secretary for Ireland, Lord Frederick Cavendish (who happened to be Gladstone's nephew) and Thomas Henry Burke, the permanent under-secretary – there was also enormous pressure from constitutional politicians, notably the charismatic but flawed Charles Stewart Parnell, to give Ireland self-government. Gladstone had long been alert to the need to redress Irish grievances, and had as prime minister sponsored the Disestablishment Act of 1869 and the Land Act of 1881. In proposing this far-sighted Home Rule Bill, he recognised the impossibility of imposing authority on Ireland by force without the likelihood of serious bloodshed, in which point of view he was right.

His speech displays a magisterial command of history and of logic, and draws not merely on Gladstone's experience as an orator, but also on what was by then more than half a century's experience of politics at the highest level. Despite his persuasive powers, more than 90 of his followers broke with him on the issue and became 'Liberal Unionists', and the day after this speech they helped defeat him on the second reading of the bill. The Conservatives won the ensuing general election and Gladstone was out of office for six years. The consequences of the rejection of Home Rule are still being felt in Ireland to this day.

'I hear constantly used the terms unionists and separatists. But what I want to know is, who are the unionists? I want to know who are the separatists? I see this bill described in newspapers of great circulation, and elsewhere, as a Separation Bill. Several gentlemen opposite adopt and make that style of description their own. Speaking of that description, I say that it is the merest slang of vulgar controversy. Do you think this bill will tend to separation? (*'Hear, hear!'*) Well, your arguments, and even your prejudices, are worthy of all consideration and respect; but is it a fair and rational mode of conducting a controversy to attach these hard names to measures on which you wish to argue, and on which, I suppose, you desire to convince by argument? Let me illustrate. I go back to the Reform Act of Lord Grey. When that Reform Bill was introduced, it was conscientiously and honestly believed by great masses of men, and intelligent men, too, that the bill absolutely involved the destruction of the monarchy. The Duke of Wellington propounded a doctrine very much to this effect; but I do not think that any of those gentlemen, nor the newspapers that supported them, ever descended so low in their choice of weapons as to call the measure 'the Monarchy Destruction Bill'. Such language is a mere begging of the question. Now, I must make a large demand on your patience and your indulgence – we conscientiously believe that there are unionists and disunionists; but that it is our policy that leads to union and yours to separation. This involves a very large and deep historical question. Let us try, for a few moments, to look at it historically.

The arguments used on the other side of the House appear to me to rest in principle and in the main upon one of two suppositions. One of them, which I will not now discuss, is the

IRISH HOME RULE
1880–6

1880
Sixty-one Home Rule MPs are returned to Westminster in the general election, and Charles Stewart Parnell is elected chairman of the Commons' Irish Party.

1881
Against increasing agitation for reform of land laws in Ireland, the government suspends Habeas Corpus (March) and introduces the Peace Preservation Act (March); an attempt at reforming rents and tenancies, the Irish Land Act, comes into force (Aug.), but activist Irish Land League is declared illegal (Dec.).

1882
The Kilmainham 'treaty' offers Parnell an amnesty from criminal charges if he stops supporting Irish extremists (Jan.); the so-called Phoenix Park murders shock Britain and bring Irish issues to the fore (May); the Irish Crime Prevention Act abolishes jury trial and extends police powers (July).

1885
Explosions caused by Irish extremists hit Parliament and the Tower of London (Jan.); the Irish Party moves its support to the Conservatives after they make sympathetic noises about Home Rule, thereby toppling Gladstone and propping up Lord Salisbury's minority government after general election (Nov.).

1886
The Irish Party withdraws support from Conservatives, leading to return of Gladstone (Feb.); the Home Rule Bill is defeated in the Commons, as 93 Liberal 'Unionist' MPs vote against it.

profound incompetency of the Irish people; but there is another, and it is this. It is, I believe, the conscientious conviction of honourable gentlemen opposite that when two or more countries, associated but not incorporated together, are in disturbed relations with each other, the remedy is to create an absolute legislative incorporation. On the other hand, they believe that the dissolution of such an incorporation is clearly the mode to bring about the dissolution of the political relations of those countries. I do not deny that there may be cases in which legislative incorporation may have been the means of constituting a great country, as in the case of France. But we believe, as proved by history, that where there are those disturbed relations between countries associated, but not incorporated, the true principle is to make ample provision for local independence, subject to imperial unity. These are propositions of the greatest interest and importance. Gentlemen speak of tightening the ties between England and Ireland as if tightening the tie were always the means to be adopted. Tightening the tie is frequently the means of making it burst, whilst relaxing the tie is very frequently the way to provide for its durability, and to enable it to stand a stronger strain; so that it is true, as was said by the honourable Member for Newcastle [Joseph Cowen], that the separation of legislatures is often the union of countries, and the union of legislatures is often the severance of countries.

'The weakness of the tie which binds'

... It has been asked in this debate, why have we put aside all the other business of Parliament, and why have we thrown the country into all this agitation for the sake of the Irish Question? (*'Hear, hear!'*) That cheer is the echo that I wanted. Well, sir, the first reason is this – because in Ireland the primary purposes of government are not attained. What said the honourable Member for Newcastle in his eloquent speech? That in a considerable part of Ireland distress was chronic, disaffection was perpetual, and insurrection was smouldering. What is implied by those who speak of the dreadful murder that lately took place in Kerry? And I must quote the Belfast outrage along with it; not as being precisely of the same character, but as a significant proof of the weakness of the tie which binds the people to the law. Sir, it is that you have not got that respect for the law, that sympathy with the law on the part of the people without which real civilisation cannot exist. That is our first reason. I will not go back at this time on the dreadful story of the Union; but that, too, must be unfolded in all its hideous features if this controversy is to be prolonged – that Union of which I ought to say that, without qualifying in the least any epithet I have used, I do not believe that that Union can or ought to be repealed, for it has made marks upon history that cannot be effaced. But I go on to another pious belief which prevails on the other side of the House, or which is often professed in controversies on the Irish Question. It is supposed that all the abuses of English power in Ireland relate to a remote period of history, and that from the year 1800 onwards from the time of the Union there has been a period of steady redress of grievances. Sir, I am sorry to say that there has been nothing of the kind. There has been a period when grievances have been redressed under compulsion, as in 1829, when Catholic emancipation was granted to avoid civil war. There have been grievances mixed up with the most terrible evidence of the general failure of government, as was exhibited by the Devon Commission in the year 1843. On a former night I made a quotation from the Report which spoke of the labourer. Now I have a corresponding quotation which is more important, and which speaks of the cottier. What was the proportion of the population which more than 40 years after the Union was described by the Devon Report as being in a condition worse and more disgraceful than any population in Europe? Mr O'Connell⁕ has estimated it in this House at 5,000,000 out of 7,000,000; and Sir James Graham, in debate with him, declined to admit that it was 5,000,000, but did admit that it was 3,500,000. Well, sir, in 1815 Parliament passed an act of Irish legislation. What was the purpose of that act? The act declared that, from the state of the law in Ireland, the old intertangled usages and provisions containing effectual protection for the tenant against the landlord could not avail. These intertangled usages, which had replaced in an imperfect manner the tribal usages on which the tenure of land in Ireland was founded – Parliament swept them away and did everything to expose the tenant to the action of the landlord, but nothing to relieve or to deal with, by any amendment, of the law, the terrible distress which was finally disclosed by the Devon Commission.

'Ireland wants to make her own laws'

... I must further say that we have proposed this measure because Ireland wants to make her own laws. It is not enough to say that you are prepared to make good laws. You were prepared to make good laws for the colonies. You did make good laws for the colonies according to the best of your light. The colonists were totally dissatisfied with them. You accepted their claim to make their own laws. Ireland, in our opinion, has a claim not less urgent.

Now, sir, what is before us? What is before us in the event of the rejection of this bill? What alternatives have been proposed? Here I must for a moment comment on the fertile imagination of my right honourable friend the Member for West Birmingham⁕. He has proposed alternatives, and plenty of them. My right honourable friend says that a dissolution [of Parliament] has no terrors for him. I do not wonder at it. I do not see how a dissolution can have any terrors for him. He has trimmed his vessel and he has touched his rudder in such a masterly way that in whichever direction the winds of Heaven may blow they must fill his sails. Let me illustrate my meaning. I will suppose different cases. Supposing at the election – I mean that an election is a thing like Christmas, it is always coming – supposing that at an election public opinion should be very strong in favour of the bill. My right honourable friend would then be perfectly prepared to meet that public opinion, and tell it – 'I declared strongly that I adopted the principle of the bill.' On the other hand, if public opinion was very adverse to the bill, my right honourable friend, again, is in complete armour, because he says – 'Yes, I voted against the bill.' Supposing, again, public opinion is in favour of a very large plan for Ireland. My right honourable friend is perfectly provided for that case also. The government plan was not large enough for him, and he proposed in his speech on the introduction of the bill that we should have a measure on the basis of federation, which goes beyond this bill. Lastly – and now I have very nearly boxed the compass – supposing that public opinion should take quite a different turn, and instead of wanting very large measures for Ireland should demand very small measures for Ireland, still the resources of my right honourable friend are not exhausted, because then he is able to point out that the last of his plans was four provincial councils controlled from London. Under other circumstances I should, perhaps, have been tempted to ask the secret of my right honourable friend's recipe; as it is, I am afraid I am too old to learn it. But I do not wonder that a dissolution has no terrors for him, because he is prepared in such a way and with such a series of expedients to meet all the possible contingencies of the case. Well, sir, when I come to look at these practical alternatives and provisions, I find that they are visibly creations of the vivid imagination born of the hour and perishing with the hour, totally and absolutely unavailable for the solution of a great and difficult problem, the weight of which, and the urgency of which, my right honourable friend himself in other days has seemed to feel.

'The loudest manifestations of displeasure'

But I should not say now that our plan has possession of the field without a rival. Lord Salisbury* has given us a rival plan. My first remark is that Lord Salisbury's policy has not been disavowed. It is, therefore, adopted. What is it? (*A laugh*) Another laugh? It has been disavowed; what is it? Great complaints are made because it has been called a policy of coercion; and Lord Salisbury is stated to have explained in 'another place' that he is not favourable to coercion, but only to legislative provisions for preventing interference by one man with the liberty of another, and for insuring the regular execution of the law. And that, you say, is not coercion? Was that your view six months ago? ... these proposals which we were about to make were defined as coercion by the Tories at the election, and Lord Salisbury now denies them to be coercion; and it is resented with the loudest manifestations of displeasure when anyone on this side of the House states that Lord Salisbury has recommended 20 years of coercion. Lord Salisbury recommended, as he says himself, 20 years of those measures which last year were denounced by the Tories. But what did Lord Salisbury call them himself? What were his own words? His words were – 'My alternative policy is that Parliament should enable the government of England to govern Ireland.'

What is the meaning of those words? Their meaning, in the first instance, is this – the Government does not want the aid of Parliament to exercise their executive power; it wants the aid of Parliament for fresh legislation. The demand that the Parliament should enable the government of England to govern Ireland is a demand for fresh legislative power. This fresh legislative power, how are they to use?

'Apply that recipe honestly, consistently, and resolutely for 20 years, and at the end of that time you will find Ireland will be fit to accept any gift in the way of local government or repeal of coercion laws that you may wish to give.'

'The cup was at her lips, and she was ready to drink it'

And yet objections and complaints of misrepresentation teem from that side of the House when anyone on this side says that Lord Salisbury recommended coercion, when he himself applies that same term in his own words. A question was put to me by my honourable friend the Member for Bermondsey [Thorold Rogers], in the course of his most instructive speech. My honourable friend had a serious misgiving as to the point of time. Were we right in introducing this measure now? He did not object to the principle; he intimated a doubt as to the moment. I may ask my honourable friend to consider what would have happened had we hesitated as to the duty before us, had we used the constant efforts that would have been necessary to keep the late government in office, and allowed them to persevere in their intentions. On the 26th of January they proposed what we termed a measure of coercion, and I think we were justified in so terming it, because anything attempting to put down a political association can hardly have another name. Can it be denied that that legislation must have been accompanied by legislation against the press, legislation against public meetings, and other legislation without which it would have been totally ineffective? Would it have been better if a great controversy cannot (*sic*) be avoided – and I am sensible of the evil of this great controversy – I say it is better that Parties should be matched in conflict upon a question of giving a great boon to Ireland, rather than – as we should have been if the policy of January 26 had proceeded – that we should have been matched and brought into conflict, and the whole country torn with dispute and discussion upon the policy of a great measure of coercion. That is my first reason.

My second reason is this. Let my honourable friend recollect that this is the earliest moment in our parliamentary history when we have the voice of Ireland authentically expressed in our hearing. Majorities of Home Rulers there may have been upon other occasions; a practical majority of Irish Members never has been brought together for such a purpose. Now, first, we can understand her; now, first, we are able to deal with her; we are able to learn authentically what she wants and wishes, what she offers and will do; and as we ourselves enter into the strongest moral and honourable obligations by the steps which we take in this House, so we have before us practically an Ireland under the representative system able to give us equally authentic information, able morally to convey to us an assurance the breach and rupture of which would cover Ireland with disgrace.

… In 1795 … it is historically clear that the Parliament of Grattan [the last independent Dublin Parliament before Union] was on the point of solving the Irish problem. The two great knots of that problem were – in the first place, Roman Catholic Emancipation; and, in the second place, the reform of Parliament. The cup was at her lips, and she was ready to drink it, when the hand of England rudely and ruthlessly dashed it to the ground in obedience to the wild and dangerous intimations of an Irish faction. '*Ex illo fluere ac retro sublapsa referri, Spes Danaum.*'*

'We have given Ireland a voice: we must all listen for a moment to what she says'

There has been no great day of hope for Ireland, no day when you might hope completely and definitely to end the controversy till now – more than 90 years. The long periodic time has at last run out, and the star has again mounted into the heavens. What Ireland was doing for herself in 1795 we at length have done. The Roman Catholics have been emancipated – emancipated after a woeful disregard of solemn promises through 29 years, emancipated slowly, sullenly, not from goodwill, but from abject terror, with all the fruits and consequences which will always follow that method of legislation. The second problem has been also solved, and the representation of Ireland has been thoroughly reformed; and I am thankful to say that the franchise was given to Ireland on the re-adjustment of last year with a free heart, with an open hand, and the gift of that franchise was the last act required to make the success of Ireland in her final effort absolutely sure. We have given Ireland a voice: we must all listen for a moment to what she says. We must all listen – both sides, both Parties, I mean as they are, divided on this question – divided, I am afraid, by an almost immeasurable gap. We do not undervalue or despise the forces opposed to us. I have described them as the forces of class and its dependents; and that as a general description – as a slight and rude outline of a description – is, I believe, perfectly true. I do not deny that many are against us whom we should have expected to be for us. I do not deny that some whom we see against us have caused us by their conscientious action the bitterest disappointment. You have power, you have wealth, you have rank, you have station, you have organization. What have we? We think that we have the people's heart; we believe and we know we have the promise of the harvest of the future. As to the people's heart, you may dispute it, and dispute it with perfect sincerity. Let that matter make its own proof. As to the harvest of the future, I doubt if you have so much confidence, and I believe that there is in the breast of many a man who means to vote against us to-night a profound misgiving, approaching even to a deep conviction, that the end will be as we foresee, and not as you do – that the ebbing tide is with you and the flowing tide is with us. Ireland stands at your bar expectant, hopeful, almost suppliant. Her words are the words of truth and soberness. She asks a blessed oblivion of the past and in that oblivion our interest is deeper than even hers.

'A sad exception to the glory of our country'

My right honourable friend the Member for East Edinburgh** asks us to-night to abide by the traditions of which we are the heirs. What traditions? By the Irish traditions? Go into the length and breadth of the world, ransack the literature of all countries, find, if you can, a single voice, a single book, find, I would almost say, as much as a single newspaper article, unless the product of the day, in which the conduct of England towards Ireland is anywhere treated except with profound and bitter condemnation. Are these the traditions by which we are exhorted to stand? No; they are a sad exception to the glory of our country. They are a broad and black blot upon the pages of its history; and what we want to do is to stand by the traditions of which we are the heirs in all matters except our relations with Ireland, and to make our relations with Ireland to conform to the other traditions of our country. So we treat our traditions – so we hail the demand of Ireland for what I call a blessed oblivion of the past. She asks also a boon for the future; and that boon for the future, unless we are much mistaken, will be a boon to us in respect of honour, no less than a boon to her in respect of happiness, prosperity, and peace. Such, Sir, is her prayer. Think, I beseech you, think well, think wisely, think, not for the moment, but for the years that are to come, before you reject this bill.

♥ Daniel O'Connell (1775–1847), Irish politician and modern father of Irish nationalism.
♦ Joseph Chamberlain (1836–1914), one of those Liberals who led the break with Gladstone over Home Rule, and who had recently resigned from Gladstone's administration on the question.
♣ Robert Gascoyne Cecil, 3rd Marquess of Salisbury (1830–1903), leader of the Conservative Party, prime minister 1885–January 1886, July 1886–1892, 1895–1902.
♠ 'From then onwards the tide of fortune left the shores of Troy and ebbed faster than it flowed earlier' (Virgil, *Aeneid*, Book II).
♥♥ George Goschen, 1st Viscount Goschen (1831–1907), one of the founders of the Liberal Unionist Party, who lost his seat in the ensuing election, defeated by a Home Rule candidate. He was appointed chancellor of the exchequer in Salisbury's administration on Lord Randolph Churchill's resignation in December 1886.

'Methods of barbarism'

National Reform Union, London, 14 June 1901

Sir Henry Campbell-Bannerman

on the treatment of the Boers

Henry Campbell-Bannerman (1836–1908) was born into a prosperous Glasgow wholesaler's family. He worked in the firm after university until 1868, when he was elected as a Liberal MP for the seat of Stirling Burghs, which he represented until his death. He was a committed Gladstonian, and in 1871 he was given his first office by his patron, becoming financial secretary to the war office. During W.E. Gladstone's second administration he served at the Admiralty and as chief secretary for Ireland. In 1886, in the brief third administration, he entered the Cabinet as secretary of state for war. He served in this post again when Gladstone returned to office in 1892, and under Gladstone's successor, Lord Rosebery.

In 1899 Campbell-Bannerman was elected leader of the Liberal Party in the Commons, and would become prime minister on the resignation of the Conservative government in December 1905. When the second Anglo-Boer War broke out in October 1899, Campbell-Bannerman made it clear that he felt it was unjustified, and that Britain had provoked it following the Jameson raid (1895–6), in which a force under Dr L.S. Jameson, sponsored by Cecil Rhodes (prime minister of the Cape Colony), invaded the Boer Transvaal Republic to support non-Dutch European ('Uitlander') rebels. When war broke out in 1899 Campbell-Bannerman argued that Britain was unjustifiably belligerent and should restore self-government to the Boer territories. Edward VII, who ascended the throne in January 1901, became so angry at Campbell-Bannerman's consistent attacks on the government's prosecution of the war that he privately urged Rosebery to resume his leadership of the Liberal Party; nothing came of this.

Meanwhile, Campbell-Bannerman was deeply affected by an account given to him by a young woman, Emily Hobhouse, who had visited concentration camps containing 60,000 Boer women and children, and who had seen the aftermath of the burning of villages and other settlements by the British Army. He let his anger boil over in public at an after-dinner speech, in which he railed against the 'methods of barbarism' being used against the Boers. A journalist present wrote of the 'strong suppressed emotion' from which Campbell-Bannerman was evidently 'suffering', and said that he spoke – unusually for him – without notes. Once the speech was reported, Campbell-Bannerman was denounced as having betrayed the Army, his treachery the worse as he was a former war secretary – this despite the fact that he took care, as politicans have subsequently done when criticising unpopular wars, to commend the heroism and sacrifice of the armed forces.

Campbell-Bannerman remained resolute in the aftermath, emphasising that he had been attacking the policies of the government, not the Army that had obeyed the orders to implement them. Although he had to endure a great deal of abuse from his opponents, the speech largely united his Party behind him – with the exception of a few Liberal imperialists around Rosebery – and brought a fierce spotlight, internationally as well as nationally, on the philosophical question of the conduct of war.

'We cannot disguise from ourselves that at every gathering there is present the spectre of this terrible war. (*'Hear, hear'*) What would not all of our countrymen give, whatever party they belong to, if we could be free from the fear and misgivings and the horrors associated with this war? I have been taken to task, and some writers in the Unionist press have used great acerbity of language, because the other day I said that there could only be an insignificant fraction of the Liberal Party who approved the policy – as I said, the unwise and unworthy policy (*Cheers*) – of pressing unconditional surrender on those who are opposing us in this war. I have been called upon to produce a single Liberal anywhere who has approved that policy. What is that policy? That now that we have got the men we have been fighting against down, we should punish them as severely as possible, devastate their country, burn their homes, break up their very instruments of agriculture, and destroy the machinery by which food is produced. (*Cries of 'shame'*) It is that we should sweep – as the Spaniards did in Cuba; and how we denounced the Spaniards – the women and children into camps in which they are destitute of all the decencies and comforts, and many of the necessities of life, and in some of which the death-rate rose so high as 430 in the 1000. (*'Shame'*) I do not say for a moment, because I do not think for a moment, that this is an intentional policy of His Majesty's government, but it is the policy of the writers in the press who support them; and, at all events, it is the thing which is being done at this moment in the name and by the authority of this most humane and Christian nation. (*'Shame'*) Yesterday I asked the Leader of the House of Commons when the information would be afforded, of which we are so sadly in want. My request was refused. Mr Balfour treated us with a short disquisition on the nature of the war. (*Laughter*) A phrase often used was that 'war is war', but when one comes to ask about it, one is told that no war is going on – that it is not war. (*Laughter*) When is a war not a war? When it is carried on by methods of barbarism in South Africa. (*Cheers*) ...

'A conspiracy conducted with every circumstance of falsehood'

Do you think that we can be intimidated today by being taunted as Little Englanders and pro-Boers? ... Let us disregard all this nonsense. Little Englanders! Well, Sir, I was born a good many years ago. I was born a citizen of a great England – an England that has grown greater

THE 2ND ANGLO-BOER WAR

1898

The Cape Colony governor Alfred Milner meets colonial secretary Joseph Chamberlain to explain tensions over the rights and taxation of British 'Uitlanders' (many of them gold prospectors) in the Boer Transvaal Republic.

1899

Over 20,000 British Uitlanders petition Queen Victoria (April); a conference at Bloemfontein fails to solve the issues (May–June); rejecting British terms, the leaders of the Transvaal Republic, including Paul Kruger and Jan Smuts, declare war (Oct.), to be supported still. It has grown in a century of almost unbroken peace. It has grown mainly under the principles and under the conduct of the Liberal Party. (*Cheers*) It has grown, and I hope it will grow greater still if the Liberal Party never desert their name and never abandon their faith. (*Cheers*) ...

With reference to this war, I regard it as the greatest disaster which in modern times has befallen the British nation, both in its conduct and in what I fear must be its consequences. I am not going tonight elaborately into the causes of the war. But this must be said with confidence, that the war has arisen from the alienation of two races. Up to a few years ago, a very few years ago, the reconciliation of the British and the Dutch races had made great and satisfactory progress. The two peoples were living in absolute cordiality and friendship. There had been no doubt in the Transvaal friction in minor matters, but nothing that would have led to any collision. (*Cheers*) Suddenly there was perpetrated the crime that has been the root of the whole mischief, a subsidised insurrection. (*Cheers*) And an armed invasion of the South African Republic organised by the prime minister of the Cape Colony, a privy counsellor of the queen, with his confederates the gold gamblers of the Rand. (*Cheers*) A conspiracy conducted with every circumstance of falsehood. It was the manner – I say it with shame and regret – in which that infamous transaction was regarded and treated by the people here and in South Africa – they were made the heroes of the British party as it was called – which shook to its foundation the confidence of the Dutch people in the good faith of this country. That is the origin of the war. (*Cheers*) Now, gentlemen, in my opinion, you have no right to forget or disregard that circumstance when you are dealing with the question of the hostility of the Boers ... I do not propose to enter either tonight upon the question of the conduct of the war. The valour of our soldiers and the fortitude of our people we all recognise. ('*Hear, Hear*') They have saved us; they have repaired the blunders, and have enabled us to face the disasters of this war.

1900

by Boers in the Orange Free State (Oct.); superior Boer forces inflict defeats at Stormberg (10 Dec.) and Magersfontein (11 Dec.); Boer sieges of Colonel Baden-Powell in Mafeking (Oct.) and a British column in Ladysmith (Dec.) begin.

Lord Roberts, assisted by Kitchener, becomes commander-in-chief of British forces in South Africa; the British suffer large losses at Battle of Spion Kop (24/5 Jan.), but finally relieve Ladysmith (Feb.) and Mafeking (May), and capture Bloemfontein (March); forces

under Roberts occupy Johannesburg and Pretoria (May–June); with the end of Boer resistance, the Orange Free State is renamed the Orange River Colony (May), while the Transvaal is formally annexed (Oct.).

'Their day of reckoning is at hand'

Limehouse, London, 30 July 1909

David Lloyd George
attacks the vested interests of landowners and landlords

David Lloyd George (1863–1945), prime minister from 1916 to 1922 and later 1st Earl Lloyd George of Dwyfor, was elected to the Commons in 1890 and appointed president of the board of trade by Campbell-Bannerman in December 1905. On the succession to the premiership of H.H. Asquith in 1908 Lloyd George was appointed chancellor of the exchequer, a post he held until becoming minister of munitions in 1915. As chancellor he sought to impose a redistributive programme that would provide a basic social security system for the poor – starting with old age pensions, the legislation for which he introduced the month after his appointment.

The main framework for his reforms was signalled in his first budget – known as the People's Budget – that he introduced on 29 April 1909. To finance both pensions and new Dreadnought battleships for the Navy, the budget proposed increased death duties and income taxes, brought in a super-tax on incomes over £5,000, and introduced new land taxes. Seen as a naked assault on the landed interest, it was subsequently thrown out by the Conservative-dominated House of Lords, by 350 votes to 75. The budget was eventually passed in April 1910 after a general election, but the Liberals then introduced a bill to curb the power of the House of Lords. This led to a protracted and dramatic constitutional clash between the two Houses, which was not resolved until August 1911, when the Tories backed down in the face of the threat by Asquith to force the king to create up to 500 Liberal peers and thereby neuter the Tory majority in the Upper House.

This speech, made in London's East End at the height of the attacks on Lloyd George by the landed interest, shows both his rhetorical skill and his great pugnacity. This outburst of naked socialism horrified Edward VII so much that he sent for Asquith two days later and told him that such incitements to class warfare as this had to stop. 'I have never known him more agitated, or difficult to appease', Asquith told his chancellor.

'A few months ago a meeting was held not far from this hall in the heart of the City of London, demanding that the government should launch into enormous expenditure on the Navy. That meeting ended up with a resolution promising that those who passed the resolution would give financial support to the government in their undertaking. There have been two or three meetings held in the City of London since, attended by the same class of people but not ending up with a resolution promising to pay. On the contrary, we are spending the money, but they won't pay. What has happened since to alter their tone? Simply that we have sent in the bill. We started our four Dreadnoughts. They cost eight millions of money. We promised them four more. They cost another eight millions.

Somebody has got to pay; and then these gentlemen say: 'Perfectly true; somebody has got to pay but we would rather that somebody were somebody else.' We started building; we wanted money to pay for the building; so we sent the hat round. We sent it round amongst the

THE ROAD TO THE PARLIAMENT ACT OF 1911

1909

Lloyd George introduces the so-called People's Budget (29 April): it is rejected by the House of Lords (30 Nov.); Prime Minister Asquith dissolves Parliament to enable a general election that highlights the constitutional issue of the Lords' actions.

1910

The Liberals win the election (15 Jan.); the Parliament Bill, limiting the House of Lords' right of veto, gets its first reading in the Commons; Edward VII dies (6 May); negotiations attempt to solve the constitutional crisis, but without result (June–Dec.); George V confirms to Asquith that, should the Liberals win a new election fought on the issue of parliamentary reform and the House of Lords still obstruct legislation, he would be prepared to create sufficient new peers to pass the Parliament Bill; the Liberals are returned in a minority government (19 Dec.).

1911

A new Parliament Bill is introduced by Asquith (21 Feb.), passing the House of Lords (10 Aug.) to become law: the Lords can no longer veto a bill, only delay it by two years, and the maximum life of a Parliament is reduced from seven years to five.

workmen and winders of Derbyshire and Yorkshire, the weavers of High Peak and the Scotsmen of Dumfries who, like all their countrymen, know the value of money. They all dropped in their coppers. We went round Belgravia; and there has been such a howl ever since that it has completely deafened us.

But they say 'It is not so much the Dreadnoughts we object to; it is pensions.' If they objected to pensions, why did they promise them? They won elections on the strength of their promises. It is true they never carried them out. Deception is always a pretty contemptible vice, but to deceive the poor is the meanest of all. But they say, 'When we promised pensions, we meant pensions at the expense of people for whom they were provided. We simply meant to bring in a bill to compel workmen to contribute to their own pensions.' If that is what they meant why did they not say so? The budget, as your Chairman has already so well reminded you, is introduced not merely for the purpose of raising barren taxes, but taxes that are fertile, taxes that will bring forth fruit – the security of the country which is paramount in the minds of all. The provision for the aged and deserving poor – it was time it was done. It is rather a shame for a rich country like ours – probably the richest in the world, if not the richest the world has ever seen, that it should allow those who have toiled all their days to end in penury and possibly starvation. It is rather hard that an old workman should have to find his way to the gates of the tomb, bleeding and footsore, through the brambles and thorns of poverty. We cut a new path for him, an easier one, a pleasanter one, through fields of waving corn. We are raising money to pay for the new road, aye, and to widen it, so that 200,000 paupers shall be able to join in the march. There are so many in the country blessed by Providence with great wealth, and if there are amongst them men who grudge out of their riches a fair contribution towards the less fortunate of their fellow-countrymen they are very shabby rich men. We propose to do more by means of the budget. We are raising money to provide against the evils and the sufferings that follow from unemployment. We are raising money for the purpose of assisting our great friendly societies to provide for the sick and the widows and orphans. We are providing money to enable us to develop the resources of our own land. I do not believe any fair-minded man would challenge the justice and the fairness of the objects which we have in view in raising this money.

But there are some of them who say, 'The taxes themselves are unjust, unfair, unequal, oppressive – notably so the land taxes.' They are engaged, not merely in the House of Commons, but outside the House of Commons, in assailing these taxes with a concentrated and sustained ferocity which will not allow even a comma to escape with its life. Now, are these taxes really so wicked? Let us examine them; because it is perfectly clear that the one part of the budget that attracts all the hostility and animosity is that part which deals with the taxation of land. Well, now let us examine it. I do not want you to consider merely abstract principles. I want to invite your attention to a number of concrete cases; fair samples to show you how in these concrete illustrations our budget proposals work. Now let us take them. Let us take first of all the tax on undeveloped land and on increment.

'The fraud of the few'

Not far from here, not so many years ago, between the Lea and the Thames you had hundreds of acres of land which was not very useful even for agricultural purposes. In the main it was a sodden marsh. The commerce and the trade of London increased under free trade, the tonnage of your shipping went up by hundreds of thousands of tons and by millions; labour was attracted from all parts of the country to cope with all this trade and business which was done here. What happened? There was no housing accommodation. This Port of London became overcrowded, and the population overflowed. That was the opportunity of the owners of the marsh. All that land became valuable building land, and land which used to be rented at £2 or £3 an acre has been selling within the last few years at £2,000 an acre, £3,000 an acre, £6,000 an acre, £8,000 an acre. Who created that increment? Who made that golden swamp? Was it the landlord? Was it his energy? Was it his brains – a very bad look out for the place if it were – his forethought? It was purely the combined efforts of all the people engaged in the trade and commerce of the Port of London – trader, merchant, shipowner, dock labourer, workman, everybody except the landlord. Now, you follow that transaction. Land worth £2 or £3 an acre running up to thousands.

'Only a halfpenny! And that is what all the howling is about'

During the time it was ripening the landlord was paying his rates and taxes, not on £2 or £3 an acre. It was agricultural land, and because it was agricultural land a munificent Tory government voted a sum of two millions to pay half the rates of those poor distressed landlords, and you and I had to pay taxes in order to enable those landlords to pay half their rates on agricultural land, while it was going up every year by hundreds of pounds through your efforts and the efforts of your neighbours. Well, now, that is coming to an end. On the walls of Mr Balfour's meeting last Friday were the words: 'We protect against fraud and folly.' So do I. These things I am going to tell you of have only been possible up to the present through the fraud of the few and the folly of the many.

Now, what is going to happen in the future? In future those landlords will have to contribute to the taxation of the country on the basis of the real value – only one halfpenny in the pound! Only a halfpenny! And that is what all the howling is about. But there is another little tax called the increment tax. For the future what will happen? We mean to value all the land in the kingdom. And here you can draw no distinction between agricultural land and other land, for the simple reason that East and West Ham was agricultural land a few years ago! And if land goes up in the future by hundreds and thousands an acre through the efforts of the community, the community will get 20 per cent. of that increment. Ah! What a misfortune it is that there was not a chancellor of the exchequer who did this thirty years ago. Only thirty years ago, and we should now be enjoying an abundant revenue from this source.

... Who is the landlord? The landlord is a gentleman – I have not a word to say about him in his personal capacity – the landlord is a gentleman who does not earn his wealth. He does not even take the trouble to receive his wealth. He has a host of agents and clerks to receive it for him. He does not even take the trouble to spend his wealth. He has a host of people around him to do the actual spending for him. He never sees it until he comes to enjoy it. His sole function, his chief pride, is stately consumption of wealth produced by others. What about the doctor's income? How does the doctor earn his income? The doctor is a man who visits our homes when they are darkened with the shadow of death: who, by his skill, his trained courage, his genius, wrings hope out of the grip of despair, wins life out of the fangs of the Great Destroyer. All blessings upon him and his divine art of healing that mends bruised bodies and anxious hearts. To compare the reward which he gets for that labour with the wealth which pours into the pockets of the landlord purely owing to the possession of his monopoly is a piece – if they will forgive me for saying so – of insolence which no intelligent man would tolerate. Now that is the halfpenny tax on unearned increment.

... The landlord has threatened us that if we proceed with the budget he will take his sack clean away from the hopper, and the grain which we are all grinding our best to fill his sack will go into our own. Oh, I cannot believe it.

There is a limit even to the wrath of outraged landlords. We must really appease them; we must offer up some sacrifice to them. Suppose we offer the House of Lords to them? Well, you seem rather to agree with that. I will make the suggestion to them.

'What did the landlord put in?'

Now, unless I am wearying you, I have just one other land tax, and that is a tax on royalties. The landlords are receiving eight millions a year by way of royalties.

What for? They never deposited the coal there. It was not they who planted these great granite rocks in Wales, who laid the foundations of the mountains.

Was it the landlord? And yet he, by some divine right, demands as his toll – for merely the right for men to risk their lives in hewing these rocks – eight millions a year. Take any coalfield. I went down to a coalfield the other day, and they pointed out to me many collieries there. They said: 'You see that colliery there. The first man who went there spent a quarter of a million in sinking shafts, in driving mains and levels. He never got coal, and he lost his quarter of a million. The second man who came spent £100,000 – and he failed. The third man came along, and he got the coal.' What was the landlord doing in the meantime? The first man failed; but the landlord got his royalty, the landlord got his dead-rent – and a very good name for it. The second man failed, but the landlord got his royalty.

These capitalists put their money in, and I said: 'When the cash failed what did the landlord put in?' He simply put in the bailiffs. The capitalist risks, at any rate, the whole of his money; the engineer puts his brains in; the miner risks his life.

I was telling you I went down a coalmine the other day. We sank into a pit half a mile deep. We then walked underneath the mountain, and we did about three-quarters of a mile with rock and shale above us. The earth seemed to be straining – around us and above us – to crush us in.

'They are broken, they can earn no more'

You could see the pit-props bent and twisted and sundered until you saw their fibres split in resisting the pressure. Sometimes they give way, and then there is mutilation and death. Often a spark ignites, the whole pit is deluged in fire, and the breath of life is scorched out of hundreds of breasts by the consuming flame. In the very next colliery to the one I descended just a few years ago three hundred people lost their lives in that way. And yet when the Prime Minister and I knock at the door of these great landlords, and say to them: 'Here, you know these poor fellows who have been digging up royalties at the risk of their lives, some of them are old, they have survived the perils of their trade, they are broken, they can earn no more. Won't you give them something towards keeping them out of the workhouse?' they scowl at us, and we say: 'Only a ha'penny, just a copper.' They say: 'You thieves!' and they turn their dogs on to us, and you can hear their bark every morning. If this is an indication of the view taken by these great landlords of their responsibility to the people who at the risk of life create their wealth, then I say their day of reckoning is at hand.

The other day at the great Tory meeting held at the Cannon Street Hotel they had blazoned on the walls, 'We protest against the budget in the name of democracy, liberty and justice.' Where does the democracy come in in this landed system? Where is the liberty in our leasehold system? Where is the seat of justice in all these transactions?

I claim that the tax we impose on land is fair, is just and is moderate. They go on threatening that if we proceed, they will cut down their benefactions and discharge labour. What kind of labour? What is the labour they are going to choose for dismissal? Are they going to threaten to devastate rural England by feeding and dressing themselves? Are they going to reduce their gamekeepers? Ah, that would be sad! The agricultural labourer and the farmer might then have some part of the game which they fatten with their labour. But what would happen to you in the season? No weekend shooting with the Duke of Norfolk or anyone.

But that is not the kind of labour they are going to cut down. They are going to cut down productive labour – their builders and their gardeners – and they are going to ruin their property so that it shall not be taxed.

All I can say is this – the ownership of land is not merely an enjoyment, it is a stewardship. It has been reckoned as such in the past; and if they cease to discharge their functions, the security and defence of the country, looking after the broken in their villages and in their neighbourhoods – then these functions which are part of the traditional duties attached to the ownership of land, and which have given to it its title – if they cease to discharge those functions, the time will come to reconsider the conditions under which the land is held in this country.

'It is one of the prime duties of statesmanship to investigate those conditions'

No country, however rich, can permanently afford to have quartered upon its revenue a class which declines to do the duty which it was called upon to perform since the beginning. And, therefore, it is one of the prime duties of statesmanship to investigate those conditions. But I do not believe it. They have threatened and menaced like that before. They have seen it is not to their interest to carry out these futile menaces. They are not protesting against paying their fair share of taxation of the land, and they are doing so by saying: 'You are burdening industry; you are putting burdens upon the people which they cannot bear.' Ah! They are not thinking of themselves. Noble souls! It is not the great dukes they are feeling for, it is the market gardener, it is the builder; and it was, until recently, the smallholder. In every debate in the House of Commons they said: 'We are not worrying for ourselves. We can afford it without broad acres; but just think of the little man who has only got a few acres.' And we were so very impressed with this tearful appeal that at last we said: 'We will leave him out.' And I almost expected to see Mr Pretyman♥ jump over the table when I said it, fall on my neck and embrace me. Instead of that he stiffened up, his face wreathed with anger, and he said: 'The budget is more unjust than ever.'

'No cupboard should be barer'

We are placing burdens on the broadest shoulders. Why should I put burdens on the people? I am one of the children of the people. I was brought up amongst them. I know their trials; and God forbid that I should add one grain of trouble to the anxieties which they bear with such patience and fortitude. When the prime minister did me the honour of inviting me to take charge of the national exchequer at a time of great difficulty, I made up my mind, in framing the budget which was in front of me, that at any rate no cupboard should be barer, no lot would be harder. By that test I challenge them to judge the budget.

♥ Captain Ernest Pretyman (1860–1931), Unionist MP for Chelmsford.

'A *fit country*
for heroes to live in'

Wolverhampton, 23 November 1918

David Lloyd George
on Britain's prospects following
the Great War

This speech, made 12 days after the Armistice was signed in 'the war to end all wars', contains Lloyd George's vision for a country that had lost one-sixth of its fighting men in the conflict, and whose economy was now going to have to shift from war production to peace. There is much talk in it of providing for all classes, notably in ensuring that all ex-combatants should have some land to call their own and that new areas of Britain should be developed economically. The most famous line in the speech – often misquoted as a pledge to build 'homes fit for heroes' – was to be a severe hostage to fortune. It played well during an election campaign – for Lloyd George had, as he intimates in this extract, decided to call an election immediately on victory being secured in order to have a mandate to carry forward a new programme. The *Dictionary of National Biography* recorded that Lloyd George's 'demagogic conduct of the election did his reputation permanent harm'. He and the Unionist Party leader, Andrew Bonar Law (1858–1923), agreed to fight the election as a coalition, maintaining political unity the better to rebuild the country.

The coalition won an overwhelming victory in December 1918 – 526 of the 707 seats in the House of Commons – but its promise was short-lived. Lloyd George's own Liberal followers were in a minority, with only 133 of the seats – and a faction of Liberals under the last prime minister, H.H. Asquith, had split away before the election. Lloyd George's idea that the land would give a living to millions more able-bodied men, until such time as there was an industrial revival, was pie in the sky. By the early 1920s Britain was in severe econonomic depression, with many ex-servicemen unemployed, and the prime minister's great hopes of 1918 were largely unfulfilled. Indeed, most of the period until war broke out again in 1939 was to be marked by poverty, depression and slump. The coalition fell in 1922. Lloyd George, who died in 1945 shortly after being created an earl, never held office again, and neither did the Liberal Party.

'What is our task? To make Britain a fit country for heroes to live in. I am not using the word 'heroes' in any spirit of boastfulness, but in the spirit of humble recognition of the fact. I cannot think what these men have gone through. I have been there at the door of the furnace and witnessed it, but that is not being in it, and I saw them march into the furnace. There are millions of men who will come back. Let us make this a land fit for such men to live in. There is no time to lose. I want us to take advantage of this new spirit. Don't let us waste this victory merely in ringing joybells. Let us make victory the motive power to link the old land up in such measure that it will be nearer the sunshine than ever before, and that at any rate it will lift those who have been living in the dark places to a plateau where they will get the rays of the sun. We cannot undertake that without a new Parliament. Those of you who have been at the front have seen the star shells, how they light up the darkness and illuminate all the obscure places. The Great War has been like a gigantic star shell, flashing all over the land, illuminating the country and showing up the deep, dark places. We have seen places that we have never noticed before, and we mean to put these things right.

What is the first thing the Great War has shown us? The appalling waste of human material in the country. There is hardly any material placed by Providence in this country which is so much wasted as human life and human strength and human intellect – the most precious and irreplaceable material of all. I have previously said something about the figures of recruiting officers. Those who were in charge of recruiting came to the conclusion that if the people of this country had lived under proper conditions, were properly fed and housed, and lived under healthy conditions – had lived their lives in their full vigour – you could have had a milion more men available and fit to put into the Army. It is not merely that. When life has not been lost, its vitality has been depressed. There are millions who are below par. You cannot keep even animals in their full vigour unless you give them good conditions. You cannot do it with men and women, and you cannot bring up children under bad conditions.

'Slums are not fit homes for the men who have won this war'

There are millions of men's lives which have been lost as a result of the war, but there are millions more of maimed lives in the sense of undermined constitutions through atrocious social conditions in consequence of the terrors of this Great War. You must put that right. Put it at its lowest – trade, commerce and industry all suffer through it. A vigorous community of strong, healthy men and women is more valuable even from the commercial and industrial point of view than a community which is below par in consequence of bad conditions. Treat it if you like not as a human proposition, but as a business proposition. It is a good business, to see that the men, the women and the children of this country are brought up and sustained under conditions that will give strength and vigour to their frames, more penetration and endurance to their intelligence, and more spirit and heart than ever to face the problems of life which will always be problems that will require fighting right from the cradle to the tomb. That is the first problem.

THE END OF WAR

1918
Armistice with Germany comes into force (11 Nov.); the Westminster coalition government is returned in an election in which many women vote for the first time (14 Dec.).

1919
The Paris Peace Conference opens (18 Jan.); the murder of two policemen sparks the Anglo-Irish War (or Irish War of Independence, 21 Jan.); Germany and the Allies sign Treaty of Versailles (28 June); Britain celebrates Peace Day (19 July); the Treaty of St Germain is signed with Austria; a two-minute silence remembers the war dead (11 Nov.); Lady Astor becomes the first woman MP (29 Nov.).

1920
The council of the new League of Nations meets (Feb.); military conscription in Britain is abolished (30 April); peace treaties are signed with Hungary (June) and Turkey (Aug.); the British Communist Party is founded (July); a Remembrance parade at the newly built Cenotaph is held in Whitehall, and the Unknown Soldier is buried in Westminster Abbey (11 Nov.); the Government of Ireland Act offers Home Rule to Ireland.

One of the ways of dealing with that is, of course, to deal with housing conditions. Slums are not fit homes for the men who have won this war or for their children. They are not fit nurseries for the children who are to make an imperial race, and there must be no patching up. This problem has got to be undertaken in a way never undertaken before, as a great national charge and duty. The housing of the people must be a national concern.

'Bring people back to the land'

What is the next revelation of the Great War? The enormous waste of the resources of our land. What do I mean? I mean on the surface and under the surface. Britain is a rich country so far as its soil is concerned. We import hundreds of millions of our supplies from abroad. I do not mean to say that we can grow them all, but we can grow a very much larger proportion of our supplies than we have done in past years. Take food. You can grow vast quantities of food in this country for which you have been dependent on foreign imports, but you want a much more intelligent policy than that. The land must be cultivated to its full capacity. That ought to be an essential feature in the new Britain … a great agricultural policy is a great industrial policy. It relieves the labour market, and when you have got periods of depression there is always the land. You don't have the same competition which throws men out of employment. On the other hand, you have got a nursery to train vigorous men who will sustain other industries, and unless you have agriculture to do that, believe me you cannot keep alive an industrial system in this country. An intelligent agricultural policy is the basis of a great industrial policy, and a systematic effort must be made to bring people back to the land. (*Cheers*) That is the place to grow strong men. The touch of the soil reinvigorates and reinforces. When there are any signs of exhaustion bring them back to the mother land, and the old life that is in the veins of Britain flows through them, and you find them reinvigorated and strong.

'*Glittering prizes*'

Glasgow, 7 November 1923

Lord Birkenhead
on the need to counter 'Idealism' in
foreign affairs

Frederick Edwin Smith (1872–1930) was the son of a Birkenhead estate agent who rose, by the age of 46, to be lord chancellor, and who had a reputation as one of the most flamboyant and provocative politicians of his era. Smith's father had died when he was only 15, but his resolute and resourceful mother ensured he completed his education, and he won a scholarship to Oxford in 1891. After taking a first class degree in jurisprudence he became a law don, and then as a practising barrister soon made a substantial fortune and a great career.

Smith's father had been active in Liverpool politics and his son followed him in this pursuit, soon becoming one of the leading figures in the city's public life. In January 1906 he had been elected Unionist MP for Liverpool Walton, joining the Commons when his Party had suffered a landslide defeat at the hands of Sir Henry Campbell-Bannerman's Liberals. He had used the full force of his intelligence, wit and personality to make an unconventionally biting and memorable maiden speech.

His subsequent political career showed a meteoric rise. In 1919 he had become, at the age of 46, lord chancellor in the Lloyd George coalition government. Two days after the fall of that coalition three years later, he had been elected lord rector of Glasgow University, beating the Liberal Sir John Simon and the novelist and socialist H.G. Wells by an absolute majority. Birkenhead (as he had become on taking his peerage) chose for his rectorial address the theme of 'Idealism in International Politics'. Had any in his audience expected a pious exposition of this subject, they would have been disappointed.

Using all the rhetorical and intellectual gifts at his disposal – not to mention his profound desire to shock and provoke – Birkenhead embarked on an interesting definition of idealism, using Jesus Christ as his example. He proceeded to argue that war was not necessarily a bad thing, since no people should be given a freehold on a nation, and that international boundaries would in the end be determined on the basis of force: something akin to Thomas Carlyle's 'might is right' principle. It was this description not of idealism, but of the lack of idealism as a reality, that caused an explosion in response to his words. Birkenhead had made it clear he was not advocating war, just observing that it would happen – 'we diagnose certain diseases'. However, in the anti-war climate of the time, only five years after the end of the Great War, the speech immediately acquired notoriety. He certainly went against the prevailing orthodoxy, and as such his reputation was damaged. Dying as he did in 1930, worn out by drink and women, he did not live long enough to see his pessimism proved right.

From the very dawn of the world man has been a combative animal. To begin with, he fought violently for his own elemental needs; later, perhaps in tribal or communal quarrel; later still, with the growth of greater communities, upon a larger and more sophisticated scale. And it is to be specially noted that there have nevertheless almost always existed men who sincerely but very foolishly believed; firstly, that no war would arise in their own day; and, secondly (when that war did arise), that for some reason or other it would be the last. At this point the idealist degenerates into the pacifist; and it is at this point consequently that he becomes a danger to the community of which he is citizen. Athens, in her decline, had no lack of such advisers; and, unhappily for the City of the Violet Crown, she preferred their sloppy folly to the ardent eloquence of Demosthenes. In the days of Napoleon (who had a very just contempt for these 'ideologues') Charles Fox harnessed his eloquence to the chariot of sentimentalism. But he switched rather abruptly as soon as he became prime minister. And in our own day we have been afforded convincing evidence of the real peril to national security which arises when idealists grow too strong in the conduct of public affairs. Perhaps this happened in 1906. Every sensible person now realises that even in that year the German scheme was being nebulously conceived; and its deadly menace increased with every year which passed. I myself, in a book called *Unionist Policy*, published in 1910, devoted a long article, of which I shall presume to say that it was closely and clearly reasoned, to demonstrating the soundness of Lord Roberts's warnings. But the immense increase in the German Army, the construction of strategic railways upon the Belgian boundary; the creation of a mighty fleet, which had no enemy but ours, left our idealist unconvinced.

'Idealism became rampant with those in power ... And all the time the armies grew'

And accordingly, every year the annual meetings of a great federation, with pathetic faith and sincerity, passed resolutions in favour of reducing our military and naval expenditure; and a Member of Parliament, in private life

THE LEAGUE OF NATIONS

1919
The proposal to create the League of Nations, following US President Wilson's 'Fourteen Points for Peace', is accepted at the Paris Peace Conference (25 Jan.); the League's Covenant is incorporated into the Treaty of Versailles (28 June); there are 42 founding members, excluding the USA, which never joins.

1920
The first meeting is held in London to ratify the Treaty of Versailles, officially ending World War I (10 Jan.); the League moves to Geneva (1 Nov.), where the first general assembly is held (15 Nov.).

1926
Germany joins the League of Nations (but leaves in 1933, together with Japan).

1930s
Some of the main powers leave the League, further reducing its global influence.

1946
After World War II, all assets of the League are transferred to its successor organisation, the United Nations (18 April).

an admirable citizen and a sagacious chemist, produced the immortal saying that he would rather trust to the doctrines of international law than to the protection of the British Fleet[v]. Even the robust patriotism of my friend Mr Winston Churchill succumbed for a fugitive moment to the miasma; though the lapse in his case was to be nobly retrieved by the demoniac energy elicited by actual contact with the Admiralty. It was, indeed, in these years that Idealism became rampant with those in power. Notorious and almost vital facts were everywhere ignored. German editors were entertained by English editors in London; and dilated with fluent eloquence upon the pacific intentions of the fatherland. English editors in their turn visited Berlin to enjoy, in that martial capital, the same agreeable reassurances. And all the time the armies grew. All the time a mighty instrument was being fashioned in the German fleet. All the time Heligoland frowned more impregnably upon the North Sea. All the time those great military railways, unneeded for peacetime traffic, were debouching upon the defenceless Belgian frontier. In the welter of sentimentality, amid which Great Britain might easily have mouldered into ruin, my valued colleague, Lord Haldane, presented a figure alike interesting, individual, and arresting. In speech fluent and even infinite, he yielded to no living idealist in the easy coinage of sentimental phraseology. Here, indeed, he was a match for those who distributed the chloroform of Berlin. Do we not remember, for instance, that Germany was his spiritual home? But he none the less prepared himself, and the empire, to talk when the time came with his spiritual friends in language not in the least spiritual. He devised the Territorial Army, which was capable of becoming the easy nucleus of national conscription; and which unquestionably ought to have been used for that purpose at the outbreak of war. He created the Imperial General Staff. He founded the Officers' Training Corps.

And two other names require special and honourable mention in an age of incredible self-deceit. Lord Roberts devoted the evening of an illustrious life to warnings of marvellous prescience which passed almost unheeded. General Baden-Powell used the laurels which he had gained at Mafeking to inspire and sustain the noblest and most promising movement which has taken place in our lifetime. The foundation of the Boy Scouts established for this gifted and imaginative soldier a monument more lasting than bronze.

It has been thought worthwhile to retrace the events of these fateful years with some particularity in order to show that Idealism in national affairs is not merely impracticable, but that it may easily degenerate into a deadly source of national peril.

'The signing of the Armistice immediately released all the sentimentalists'

Still a further illustration may be drawn from recent events. The signing of the Armistice immediately released all the sentimentalists. Not only was the Great War ended, but there was never to be another. The League of Nations was to be equipped with functions and resources which would in effect enthrone it in super-sovereignty over the contributory nations. But herein the statesman who of all others should most completely have understood the American people demonstrated that in fact he understood them least of all. That people is the most generous people in the world in the field of international charity. The United States have lavished countless millions of dollars upon the starving population of Russia. They were first in the field with bountiful relief to stricken Japan. But they draw – and rightly draw – a sharp and logical distinction between idealism in their capacity as private citizens for private charities; and idealism in their corporate or national character. And accordingly they exercised their undoubted right in repudiating at the first opportunity an idealist conception which they believed to be at once impracticable, strange to their traditions, and incompatible with their interests.

A broader consideration must now in its turn be examined. We are told that the object aimed at is the abolition of war. Everybody recognises that war is both cruel and hateful. But is it even conceivable that it can ever be abolished? Is the ownership of the world to be stereotyped by perpetual tenure in the hands of those who possess its different territories today? If it is, very strange and undesirable consequences will one day follow. For nations wax and wane, so that a power competent in one age to govern an empire, perhaps remote, in the general interest of the world, will in another abuse a dominion for which it no longer possesses the necessary degree of vigour. The history of Spain supplies a familiar illustration.

Her chivalry was second to none in Europe. Her high standard of gallant conduct was disfigured only by the cruelties of the Inquisition. Her stately galleons brought a quiver of apprehension even to the stout bosom of Queen Elizabeth; and were never discredited until the rout of the superb Armada. And in exuberant colonial enterprise she was the mistress and pioneer of Europe. In the last-named enterprise, indeed, she flung her civilisation and her language into the remote parts of the world, deriving incredible titles from successive papal bulls. And coincidentally, or almost so, with her immense maritime enterprise, she flung the martial Moor in root from Spain. But her decline was as rapid as her ascension. She proved no adequate custodian of her overseas possessions. Had a League of Nations existed when she began to lose them, would it have sustained Spain, or the insurgents of Spain, or in another case, the despoilers of Spain?

'The emergence of new and martial nations has been gradually marked by violent readjustments'

And the general extrusion of savage races from regions, for instance, the Americas continent, and certain of the South Sea islands, to which they had some considerable legal right, shows that, rightly or wrongly, nations of stronger fibre, confronted by indigenous weaklings, have always asserted the right of forcible expropriation. No one (to make the argument short) who has studied the history of the world has ever defended the view that the supreme interest of evolutionary humanity can support a definitive delimination for all time of the surface of the world.

But if such a final distribution is impracticable and even undesirable, by what agency are modifications to be made? Voluntary cessations of territory have not been frequent in the past; and there seems little reason to suppose that they will become more fashionable in the future. For many thousands of years the emergence of new and martial nations has been gradually marked by violent readjustments of national boundaries. It may, of course, be the case that human nature has so completely altered that some new method is discoverable. I confess, however, that none has up to the present occurred to my own mind.

It may, perhaps, be charged against those who sincerely hold the views which I have attempted to make plain, that we carry in our veins the virus which coloured the sombre and unmoral genius of Treitschke♦, and which found popular expression in the mosquito propaganda of von Bernhardi♣. But such a charge, if made, would be patently unjust. We neither hold nor have we preached these doctrines. We diagnose certain diseases. We did not create them. A distinction must surely be drawn between him who calls attention to the risk of conflagration and that other who puts his torch to inflammable material.

'Glittering prizes to those who have stout hearts'

The purpose and moral of these general observations may be summarised in a few concluding observations. For as long a time as the records of history have been preserved human societies passed through a ceaseless process of evolution and adjustment. This process has been sometimes pacific; but more often it has resulted from warlike disturbance. The strength of different nations, measured in terms of arms, varies from century to century. The world continues to offer glittering prizes to those who have stout hearts and sharp swords; it is therefore extremely improbable that the experience of future ages will differ in any material respect from that which has happened since the twilight of the human race. It is for us, therefore, who in our history have proved ourselves a martial, rather than a military, people to abstain, as has been our habit, from provocation; but to maintain in our own hand the adequate means for our own protection; and, so equipped, to march with heads erect and bright eyes along the road of our imperial destiny.

♥ Sir John Tomlinson Brunner, MP and industrialist (1842–1919).
♦ Heinrich von Treitschke (1834–96), German historian, anti-Semite and anti-Briton.
♣ Friedrich von Bernhardi (1849–1930), German writer on military subjects, famous for his advocacy of German aggression before the Great War.

'The king has made his decision'

House of Commons, 10 December 1936

Stanley Baldwin
on events surrounding the abdication of
Edward VIII

In the autumn of 1936 Edward VIII began to make it clear to his prime minister, Stanley Baldwin (1867–1947), that he proposed to marry Mrs Simpson. Baldwin – a Worcestershire businessman who entered Parliament in middle age – had been prime minister twice already (1923–4 and 1924–9), had served in the National Coalition government from 1931, and had been prime minister since the previous year. Supported by the Cabinet, much of the Commons and most of the royal family, he advised the king that his marriage to a divorcee was not constitutionally possible given the king's role as supreme governor of the Church of England, and that it would not be accepted by the British people. The British people, however, seemed largely to disagree with this contention, though thanks to a remarkable press blackout they were largely unaware of the crisis until shortly before its denouement.

On 10 December, adamantly resolved to put his private happiness before his duty as sovereign, the king abdicated, and his brother succeeded him as George VI. It fell to Baldwin, as the sovereign's principal adviser, to explain the outcome to the House of Commons and the nation, which he did that afternoon. His speech is a masterpiece not only of oratory, but also in conveying the full solemnity of the occasion and revealing the enormous stress the episode had placed on both Baldwin and the British constitution.

Queen Mary, the mother of the abdicating king, felt Baldwin had spoken in 'a wonderfully dignified manner'. The MP Harold Nicolson, who heard the speech, recorded in his diary after what had been regarded as a stunning triumph for Baldwin that 'I suppose that in after-centuries men will read the words of that speech and exclaim, "what an opportunity wasted!". They will never know the tragic force of its simplicity.' The unity for which Baldwin called in support of the new king would indeed become essential in the years ahead. Baldwin retired at the coronation in May 1937 and was created Earl Baldwin of Bewdley.

'No more grave message has ever been received by Parliament and no more difficult, I may almost say repugnant, task has ever been imposed upon a prime minister. I would ask the House, which I know will not be without sympathy for me in my position today, to remember that in this last week I have had but little time in which to compose a speech for delivery today, as I must tell what I have to tell truthfully, sincerely and plainly, with no attempt to dress up or to adorn. I shall have little or nothing to say in the way of comment or criticism, or of praise or of blame. I think my best course today, and the one that the House would desire, is to tell them, as far as I can, what has passed between His Majesty and myself and what has led up to the present situation.

I should like to say at the start that His Majesty as Prince of Wales has honoured me for many years with a friendship which I value, and I know that he would agree with me in saying to you that it was not only a friendship, but, between man and man, a friendship of affection. I would like to tell the House that when we said 'Good-bye' on Tuesday night at

Fort Belvedere we both knew and felt and said to each other that that friendship, so far from being impaired by the discussions of this last week, bound us more closely together than ever and would last for life.

Now, sir, the House will want to know how it was that I had my first interview with His Majesty. I may say that His Majesty has been most generous in allowing me to tell the House the pertinent parts of the discussions which took place between us. As the House is aware, I had been ordered in August and September a complete rest which, owing to the kindness of my staff and the consideration of all my colleagues, I was able to enjoy to the full, and when October came, although I had been ordered to take a rest in that month, I felt that I could not in fairness to my work take a further holiday, and I came, as it were, on half-time before the middle of October, and, for the first time since the beginning of August, was in a position to look into things.

'All expressing perturbation and uneasiness'

There were two things that disquieted me at that moment. There was coming to my office a vast volume of correspondence, mainly at that time from British subjects and American citizens of British origin in the United States of America, from some of the Dominions and from this country, all expressing perturbation and uneasiness at what was then appearing in the American press. I was aware also that there was in the near future a divorce case coming on, as a result of which, I realised that possibly a difficult situation might arise later, and I felt that it was essential that someone should see His Majesty and warn him of the difficult situation that might arise later if occasion was given for a continuation of this kind of gossip and of criticism, and the danger that might come if that gossip and that criticism spread from the other side of the Atlantic to this country. I felt that in the circumstances there was only one man who could speak to him and talk the matter over with him, and that man was the prime minister. I felt doubly bound to do it by my duty, as I conceived it, to the country and my duty to him not only as a counsellor, but as a friend. I consulted, I am ashamed to say – and they have forgiven me – some of my colleagues.

I happened to be staying in the neighbourhood of Fort Belvedere about the middle of October, and I ascertained that His Majesty was leaving his house on Sunday, 18th October, to entertain a small shooting party at Sandringham, and that he was leaving on the Sunday afternoon. I telephoned from my friend's house on the Sunday morning and found that he had left earlier than was expected. In those circumstances, I communicated with him through his secretary and stated that I desired to see him – this is the first and only occasion on which I was the one who asked for an interview – that I desired to see him, that the matter was urgent. I told him what it was. I expressed my willingness to come to Sandringham on Tuesday, the 20th, but I said that I thought it wiser, if His Majesty thought fit, to see me at Fort Belvedere, for I was anxious that no one at that time should know of my visit, and that at any rate our first talk should be in complete privacy. The reply came from His Majesty that he would motor back on the Monday, 19th October, to Fort Belvedere, and he would see me on the Tuesday morning. And on the Tuesday morning I saw him.

Sir, I may say, before I proceed to the details of the conversation, that an adviser to the crown can be of no possible service to his master unless he tells him at all times the truth as he sees it, whether that truth be welcome or not. And let me say here, as I may say several times before I finish, that during those talks, when I look back, there is nothing I have not told His Majesty of which I felt he ought to be aware – nothing. His Majesty's attitude all through has been – let me put it in this way: Never has he shown any sign of offence, of being hurt at anything I have said to him. The whole of our discussions have been carried out, as I have said, with an increase, if possible, of that mutual respect and regard in which we stood. I told His Majesty that I had two great anxieties – one the effect of a continuance of the kind of criticism that at that time was proceeding in the American press, the effect it would have in the Dominions and particularly in Canada, where it was widespread, the effect it would have in this country.

'The British monarchy is a unique institution'

That was the first anxiety. And then I reminded him of what I had often told him and his brothers in years past. The British monarchy is a unique institution. The crown in this country through the centuries has been deprived of many of its prerogatives, but today, while that is true, it stands for far more than it ever has done in its history. The importance of its integrity is, beyond all question, far greater than it has ever been, being as it is not only the last link of the empire that is left, but the guarantee in this country, so long as it exists in that integrity, against many evils that have affected and afflicted other countries. There is no man in this country, to whatever party he may belong, who would not subscribe to that. But while this feeling largely depends on the respect that has grown up in the last three generations for the monarchy, it might not take so long, in face of the kind of criticism to which it was being exposed, to lose that power far more rapidly than it was built up, and once lost I doubt if anything could restore it.

That was the basis of my talk on that aspect, and I expressed my anxiety and desire, that such criticism should not have cause to go on. I said that in my view no popularity in the long run would weigh against the effect of such criticism. I told His Majesty that I for one had looked forward to his reign being a great reign in a new age – he has so many of the qualities necessary – and that I hoped we should be able to see our hopes realised. I told him I had come – naturally, I was his prime minister – but I wanted to talk it over with him as a friend to see if I could help him in this matter. Perhaps I was saying what I should not say here; I

EUROPE IN 1936

20 JANUARY
George V dies and is succeeded by his son Edward VIII.

7 MARCH
The German Army reoccupies the Rhineland, in contravention of the Treaty of Versailles.

17 JULY
The Spanish Civil War starts (ending in 1939).

AUGUST
In the Soviet Union the first show trials of Stalin's Great Purge are held: 8–10 million will die in the

following two years; the 11th Olympic Games are held in Berlin, and the African-American sprinter Jesse Owens wins four gold medals, which Hitler refuses to present to him.

have not asked him whether I might say this, but I will say it because I do not think he would mind, and I think it illustrates the basis on which our talks proceeded. He said to me, not once, but many times during those many, many hours we have had together and especially towards the end, 'You and I must settle this matter together; I will not have anyone interfering.'

I then pointed out the danger of the divorce proceedings, that if a verdict was given in that case that left the matter in suspense for some time, that period of suspense might be dangerous, because then everyone would be talking, and when once the press began, as it must begin some time in this country, a most difficult situation would arise for me, for him, and there might well be a danger which both he and I had seen all through this – I shall come to that later – and it was one of the reasons why he wanted to take this action quickly – that is, that there might be sides taken and factions grow up in this country in a matter where no faction ought ever to exist.

It was on that aspect of the question that we talked for an hour, and I went away glad that the ice had been broken, because I knew that it had to be broken. For some little time we had no further meetings. I begged His Majesty to consider all that I had said. I said that I pressed him for no kind of answer, but would he consider everything I had said? The next time I saw him it was on Monday 16th November. That was at Buckingham Palace. By that date the decree nisi had been pronounced in the divorce case. His Majesty had sent for me on that occasion. I had meant to see him later in the week, but he had sent for me first. I felt it my duty to begin the conversation, and I spoke to him for a quarter of an hour or 20 minutes on the question of marriage.

Again, we must remember that the Cabinet had not been in this at all – I had reported to about four of my senior colleagues the conversation at Fort Belvedere. I saw the king on Monday, 16th November, and I began by giving him my view of a possible marriage. I told him that I did not think that a particular marriage was one that would receive the approbation of the country. That marriage would have involved the lady becoming queen. I did tell His Majesty once that I might be a remnant of the old Victorians, but that my worst enemy would not say of me that I did not know what the reaction of the English people would be to any particular course of action, and I told him that so far as they went I was certain that that would be impracticable. I cannot go further into the details, but that was the substance. I pointed out to him that the position of the king's wife was different from the position of the wife of any other citizen in the country; it was part of the price which the king

6 OCTOBER
Germany and Italy form a coalition.

11 OCTOBER
Members of Oswald Mosley's British Union of Fascists march into a volatile area of East London, provoking the so-

called 'Battle of Cable Street'.

2 NOVEMBER
The BBC television service begins broadcasting from Alexandra Palace, North London.

10 NOVEMBER
A Public Order Bill prohibits private armed groups and imposes controls on marches.

25 NOVEMBER
Germany and Japan sign an Anti-Comintern Pact against the Soviet Union.

10 DECEMBER
Edward VIII finally abdicates to marry US divorcee Wallis Simpson: he is created Duke of Windsor, and his younger brother, the Duke of York, succeeds him as George VI.

has to pay. His wife becomes queen; the queen becomes the queen of the country; and, therefore, in the choice of a queen the voice of the people must be heard. It is the truth expressed in those lines that may come to your minds:

> His will is not his own;
> For he himself is subject to his birth,
> He may not, as unvalued persons do,
> Carve for himself; for on his choice depends
> The safety and the health of the whole State.

'I am going to marry Mrs Simpson, and I am prepared to go'

Then His Majesty said to me – I have his permission to state this – that he wanted to tell me something that he had long wanted to tell me. He said, 'I am going to marry Mrs Simpson, and I am prepared to go.' I said, 'Sir, that is most grievous news and it is impossible for me to make any comment on it today.' He told the queen that night; he told the Duke of York and the Duke of Gloucester the next day, and the Duke of Kent, who was out of London, either on the Wednesday or the Thursday; and for the rest of the week, so far as I know, he was considering that point.

He sent for me again on Wednesday, 25th November. In the meantime a suggestion had been made to me that a possible compromise might be arranged to avoid those two possibilities that had been seen, first in the distance and then approaching nearer and nearer. The compromise was that the king should marry, that Parliament should pass an act enabling the lady to be the king's wife without the position of queen; and when I saw His Majesty on 25th November he asked me whether that proposition had been put to me, and I said yes. He asked me what I thought of it. I told him that I had not considered it. I said, 'I can give you no considered opinion.' If he asked me my first reaction informally, my first reaction was that Parliament would never pass such a bill. But I said that if he desired it I would examine it formally. He said he did so desire. Then I said, 'It will mean my putting that formally before the whole Cabinet and communicating with the prime ministers of all the Dominions, and was that his wish?' He told me that it was. I said that I would do it.

On 2nd December the king asked me to go and see him. Again I had intended asking for an audience later that week, because such inquiries as I thought proper to make I had not completed. The inquiries had gone far enough to show that neither in the Dominions nor here would there be any prospect of such legislation being accepted. His Majesty asked me if I could answer his question. I gave him the reply that I was afraid it was impracticable for those reasons. I do want the House to realise this: His Majesty said that he was not surprised at that answer. He took my answer with no question and he never returned to it again. I want the House to realise – because if you can put yourself in His Majesty's place and you know what His Majesty's feelings are, and you know how glad you would have been had this been possible – that he behaved there as a great gentleman; he said no more about it. The matter was closed. I never heard another word about it from him. That decision was, of course, a formal decision, and that was the only formal decision of any kind taken by the Cabinet until I come to the history of yesterday. When we had finished that conversation, I pointed out that the possible alternatives had been narrowed, and that it really had brought him into the position that he would be placed in a grievous situation between two conflicting loyalties in his own heart – either complete abandonment of the project on which his heart was set, and remaining as king, or doing as he intimated to me that he was prepared to do, in the talk which I have reported, going, and later on contracting that marriage, if it were possible. During the last days, from that day until now, that has been the struggle in which His Majesty has been engaged. We had many talks, and always on the various aspects of this limited problem.

'If he went he would go with dignity'

The House must remember – it is difficult to realise – that His Majesty is not a boy, although he looks so young. We have all thought of him as our prince, but he is a mature man, with wide and great experience of life and the world, and he always had before him three, nay, four, things, which in these conversations at all hours, he repeated again and again – that if he went he would go with dignity. He would not allow a situation to arise in which he could not do that. He wanted to go with as little disturbance of his ministers and his people as possible. He wished to go in circumstances that would make the succession of his brother as little difficult for his brother as possible; and I may say that any idea to him of what might be called a king's party, was abhorrent. He stayed down at Fort Belvedere because he said that he was not coming to London while these things were in dispute, because of the cheering crowds. I honour and respect him for the way in which he behaved at that time.

I have something here which, I think, will touch the House. It is a pencilled note, sent to me by His Majesty this morning, and I have his authority for reading it. It is just scribbled in pencil:

'Duke of York. He and the king have always been on the best of terms as brothers, and the king is confident that the duke deserves and will receive the support of the whole empire.'

I would say a word or two on the king's position. The king cannot speak for himself. The king has told us that he cannot carry, and does not see his way to carry, these almost intolerable burdens of kingship without a woman at his side, and we know that. This crisis, if I may use the word, has arisen now rather than later from that very frankness of His Majesty's character which is one of his many attractions. It would have been perfectly possible for His Majesty not to have told me of this at the date when he did, and not to have told me for some months to come. But he realised the damage that might be done in the interval by gossip, rumours and talk, and he made that declaration to me when he did, on purpose to avoid what he felt might be dangerous, not only here but throughout the empire, to the moral force of the crown which we are all determined to sustain.

He told me his intentions, and he has never wavered from them. I want the House to understand that. He felt it his duty to take into his anxious consideration all the representations that his advisers might give him and not until he had fully considered them did he make public his decision. There has been no kind of conflict in this matter. My efforts during these last days have been directed, as have the efforts of those most closely round him, in trying to help him to make the choice which he has not made, and we have failed. The king has made his decision to take this moment to send this gracious message because of his confident hope that by that he will preserve the unity of this country and of the whole empire, and avoid those factious differences which might so easily have arisen.

'There is not a soul here today that wants to judge'

It is impossible, unfortunately, to avoid talking to some extent today about one's-self. These last days have been days of great strain, but it was a great comfort to me, and I hope it will be to the House, when I was assured before I left him on Tuesday night, by that intimate circle that was with him at the Fort that evening, that I had left nothing undone that I could have done to move him from the decision at which he had arrived, and which he has communicated to us. While there is not a soul among us who will not regret this from the bottom of his heart, there is not a soul here today that wants to judge. We are not judges. He has announced his decision. He has told us what he wants us to do, and I think we must close our ranks, and do it ...

... My last words on that subject are that I am convinced that where I have failed no one could have succeeded. His mind was made up, and those who know His Majesty best will know what that means.

This House today is a theatre which is being watched by the whole world. Let us conduct ourselves with that dignity which His Majesty is showing in this hour of his trial. Whatever our regret at the contents of the Message, let us fulfil his wish, do what he asks, and do it with speed. Let no word be spoken today that the utterer of that word may regret in days to come, let no word be spoken that causes pain to any soul, and let us not forget today the revered and beloved figure of Queen Mary, what all this time has meant to her, and think of her when we have to speak, if speak we must, during this debate. We have, after all, as the guardians of democracy in this little island to see that we do our work to maintain the integrity of that democracy and of the monarchy, which, as I said at the beginning of my speech, is now the sole link of our whole empire and the guardian of our freedom. Let us look forward and remember our country and the trust reposed by our country in this, the House of Commons, and let us rally behind the new king (*'Hear, hear'*), stand behind him, and help him; and let us hope that, whatever the country may have suffered by what we are passing through, it may soon be repaired and that we may take what steps we can in trying to make this country a better country for all the people in it.

'The woman I love'

Radio broadcast, London, 10 December 1936

Edward VIII
on his decision to abdicate

Edward VIII (1872–1972) had succeeded his father, George V, as king on 20 January 1936. The new king had had difficult relations with his father and objected fundamentally to the hidebound, Victorian conventionality that the late king had imposed on the monarchy and his family. George's prediction that, when he was gone, his son would come into trouble within a year proved spot-on.

Like many of his generation who had experienced the horror and the immediate consequences of the Great War, the new king had taken his pleasures whenever he could. Aside from the relatively harmless activities of foxhunting four or five days a week, and actively socialising with the *beau monde*, he was also a keen pursuer of married women. One of these was the already once-divorced American Wallis Simpson (1896–1986); he was deeply involved with her when he came to the throne. In the autumn of 1936 she divorced her second husband, Ernest Simpson, and the way was clear for the king to become her third husband. Once this proved constitutionally impossible (see Baldwin's speech previously in this volume) the king chose instead to abdicate.

Angered that Baldwin had not, in his speech to the Commons, stressed that Mrs Simpson had done everything in her power to talk the king out of abdicating, he demanded the right to address the nation on the occasion of his going. This he did from Windsor Castle, that evening, introduced as 'Prince Edward' by Sir John Reith, the Director-General of the BBC. The speech he gave had been written with the help of his legal adviser, Walter Monckton, and some final rhetorical flourishes were added by Edward's friend and close partisan Winston Churchill. Monckton noted that the prince began nervously but, growing in confidence, ended almost at a shout. The diarist and Conservative MP Chips Channon described it as 'a manly, sincere farewell'.

Edward was then created Duke of Windsor, married Mrs Simpson the following year in France, and spent the rest of his life in exile, mostly in Paris. It was a signal of his disaffection from the royal family that while he retained the style of 'His Royal Highness', the duchess, as she became after their marriage, was refused the same style for herself.

At long last I am able to say a few words of my own. I have never wanted to withhold anything, but until now it has not been constitutionally possible for me to speak.

'I have found it impossible to carry the heavy burden'

A few hours ago I discharged my last duty as king and emperor, and now that I have been succeeded by my brother, the Duke of York, my first words must be to declare my allegiance to him. This I do with all my heart.

ROYAL BROADCASTS

1932
The first Christmas broadcast is made by George V, speaking live on the wireless from Sandringham, the idea suggested by Sir John Reith (later Lord Reith) to inaugurate the Empire Service (now the BBC World Service); the time chosen is 3pm, the best time for reaching most of the empire, and the text is provided by Rudyard Kipling.

1936
Edward VIII takes to the airwaves to justify his abdication.

1939
The outbreak of war establishes royal broadcasts as annual events (there had been none in 1936 or 1938).

1945
George VI's speech celebrates the end of World War II.

1952
Elizabeth II, 26 years old, gives her first speech as queen.

1957
The first televised Christmas broadcast is made.

1966
Elizabeth II speaks in a broadcast about the important role of women in society.

1969
This is the only year since 1939 when no broadcast is made; a repeat of a documentary of the royal family is shown instead.

1992
The Queen refers in her Christmas broadcast to her 'annus horribilis', which saw her children's marriages fail and a serious fire at Windsor Castle.

1997
The Queen accedes to public opinion and makes a special television broadcast (5 Sept.) following the death of Princess Diana on 31 August.

You all know the reasons which have impelled me to renounce the throne. But I want you to understand that in making up my mind I did not forget the country or the empire which as Prince of Wales, and lately as king, I have for twenty-five years tried to serve. But you must believe me when I tell you that I have found it impossible to carry the heavy burden of responsibility and to discharge my duties as king as I would wish to do without the help and support of the woman I love.

'The decision I have made has been mine and mine alone'

And I want you to know that the decision I have made has been mine and mine alone. This was a thing I had to judge entirely for myself. The other person most nearly concerned has tried up to the last to persuade me to take a different course. I have made this, the most serious decision of my life, only upon the single thought of what would in the end be best for all.

This decision has been made less difficult to me by the sure knowledge that my brother, with his long training in the public affairs of this country and with his fine qualities, will be able to take my place forthwith, without interruption or injury to the life and progress of the empire. And he has one matchless blessing, enjoyed by so many of you and not bestowed on me – a happy home with his wife and children.

During these hard days I have been comforted by Her Majesty my mother and by my family. The ministers of the crown, and in particular Mr Baldwin, the prime minister, have always treated me with full consideration. There has never been any constitutional difference between me and them and between me and Parliament. Bred in the constitutional tradition by my father, I should never have allowed any such issue to arise.

Ever since I was Prince of Wales, and later on when I occupied the throne, I have been treated with the greatest kindness by all classes of the people, wherever I have lived or journeyed throughout the empire. For that I am very grateful.

'I lay down my burden'

I now quit altogether public affairs, and I lay down my burden. It may be some time before I return to my native land, but I shall always follow the fortunes of the British race and empire with profound interest, and if at any time in the future I can be found of service to His Majesty in a private station I shall not fail.

And now we all have a new king. I wish him, and you, his people, happiness and prosperity with all my heart. God bless you all. God save the king.

'The suppression of all
that we hold dear'

Radio broadcast, 25 December 1939

George VI
at the first Christmas of the war

Following the abdication of his elder brother Edward VIII, Prince Albert, Duke of York (1895–1952), became King George VI. He had not been schooled for the role of monarch, though it had widely been considered even before Edward VIII's abdication that the duke's daughter, Princess Elizabeth, would probably one day succeed her childless uncle to the throne – as, in 1952, she did.

As a younger man Bertie, as he was known in his family, had been in the shadow of his glamorous and far more self-confident elder brother, and had been overpowered by the forceful personality of their father, King George V. He had had such a terrible stammer that speaking in public had been a terrible ordeal for him, and sometimes one fraught with embarrassment. However, with commendable resolution and with the firm support of his redoubtable wife Queen Elizabeth (1900–2003), he had sought to overcome these handicaps and to devote himself completely to the service of his people when fate intervened in December 1936.

With his happy and settled family life the king embodied the Christian domesticity and values of decency that would come to represent much of what Britain was fighting for against the Nazis once war broke out in September 1939. A leader who would be a constant support to his prime ministers – first Neville Chamberlain, then Winston Churchill – rather than a charismatic inspiration, he allied himself directly with the hopes and fears of his people as his country entered into perhaps the darkest passage in its history.

This speech – his Christmas message of 1939, the first Christmas of the war – was heard by tens of millions of Britons on their wirelesses, and relayed to hundreds of millions more around the British empire and the globe. It sums up both the king's simplicity and his absolute recognition that he, and his people, were all in it together.

The festival which we know as Christmas is above all the festival of peace and of the home. Among all free peoples the love of peace is profound, for this alone gives security to the home.

But true peace is in the hearts of men, and it is the tragedy of this time that there are powerful countries whose whole direction and policy are based on aggression and the suppression of all that we hold dear for mankind.

'We are fighting against wickedness'

It is this that has stirred our peoples and given them a unity unknown in any previous war. We feel in our hearts that we are fighting against wickedness, and this conviction will give us strength from day to day to persevere until victory is assured.

At home we are, as it were, taking the strain for what may lie ahead of us, resolved and confident. We look with pride and thankfulness on the never-failing courage and devotion of the Royal Navy upon which, throughout the last four months, has burst the storm of ruthless and unceasing war.

And when I speak of our Navy today, I mean all the men of our empire who go down to the sea in ships, the Mercantile Marine, the mine sweepers, the trawlers and drifters, from the senior officers to the last boy who has joined up. To every one in this great fleet I send a message of gratitude and greeting, from myself as from all my peoples.

The same message I send to the gallant Air Force, which, in co-operation with the Navy, is our sure shield of defence. They are daily adding laurels to those that their fathers won.

'I would send a special word of greeting to the armies of the empire'

I would send a special word of greeting to the armies of the empire, to those who have come from afar, and in particular to the British Expeditionary Force. Their task is hard. They are waiting, and waiting is a trial of nerve and discipline. But I know that when the moment comes for action they will prove themselves worthy of the highest traditions of their great Service.

And to all who are preparing themselves to serve their country, on sea or land or in the air, I send my greeting at this time. The men and women of our far-flung empire, working in their several vocations, with the one same purpose, all are members of the great family of nations which is prepared to sacrifice everything that freedom of spirit may be saved to the world.

Such is the spirit of empire; of the great Dominions; of India; of every colony, large or small. From all alike have come offers for (sic) help, for which the mother country can never be sufficiently grateful. Such unity in aim and in effort has never been seen in the world before.

I believe from my heart that the cause which binds together my peoples and our gallant and faithful Allies is

---

THE OUTBREAK OF WAR
1939

29 APRIL
Conscription is re-introduced in Britain

31 AUGUST
Children begin to be evacuated from London.

1 SEPTEMBER
German forces invade Poland from the west.

3 SEPTEMBER
The British and French governments, having guaranteed the independence of Poland, declare war on Nazi Germany.

9 SEPTEMBER
British Expeditionary Force begins crossing the Channel.

10 SEPTEMBER
Canada declares war on Germany; the Battle of the Atlantic begins.

17 SEPTEMBER
Soviet troops invade Poland from the east, claiming to be saving the country from German occupation.

27 SEPTEMBER
Warsaw surrenders and Poland is partitioned between Germany and the Soviet Union (28 Sept.).

14 OCTOBER
The British battleship HMS *Royal Oak* is sunk by a German U-boat in Scapa Flow, off the north coast of Scotland.

the cause of Christian civilisation. On no other basis can a true civilisation be built.

Let us remember this through the dark times ahead of us and when we are making that peace for which all men pray.

> *'A new year is at hand. We cannot tell what it will bring.'*

A new year is at hand. We cannot tell what it will bring. If it brings peace, how thankful we shall all be. If it brings us continued struggle we shall remain undaunted.

In the meantime, I feel that we may all find a message of encouragement in the lines which, in my closing words, I would like to say to you:

> I said to the man who stood at the gate of the year, 'Give me a light that I may tread safely into the unknown.' And he replied, 'Go out into the darkness, and put your hand into the hand of God. That shall be to you better than light, and safer than a known way.

May that Almighty hand guide and uphold us all.

'Blood, toil, tears and sweat'

House of Commons, London, 13 May 1940

Winston Churchill
on becoming prime minister and the
challenges of war

Winston Churchill (1874–1965) had perhaps the most remarkable career of any statesman in British history. The son of Lord Randolph Churchill (1849–95), who had served as Lord Salisbury's chancellor before petulantly resigning in 1886, Winston Churchill was from his earliest years determined to live up to the reputation of his father. An unimpressive schoolboy, he joined the Army, was captured during the second Anglo-Boer War, and became a Conservative MP in 1900. He crossed the floor in 1903 on the issue of free trade, and became home secretary and First Lord of the Admiralty. His responsibility in the latter job for the disaster of Gallipoli saw him out of office and serving in the trenches; but he was soon back in office in the Lloyd George administration of 1916–22.

With the collapse of the Liberal Party after 1922 he returned to Parliament first as a Constitutional candidate, then rejoining the Conservative Party. From 1924 to 1929 he was chancellor of the exchequer, but spent the 1930s as an increasingly frustrated and embittered backbencher, championing unpopular causes such as the maintenance of the Indian empire and the rights of Edward VIII. He was, however, a consistent critic of disarmament and appeasement, and this earned him an immediate recall to the Admiralty in September 1939 when the Second World War broke out. When Neville Chamberlain was defeated in the Norway debate in the spring of 1940, many Conservatives hoped Lord Halifax would succeed him as prime minister: but others recognised that Churchill was the only man with the gumption and resolve to see Britain through the terrible crisis that followed the fall of France, with the threat of invasion increasing daily.

Churchill's reputation as a great war leader is firmly rooted in this and the two succeeding speeches, in which he displays his mastery of oratory and his sheer pugnacity. They are three of the most important speeches ever made in Britain, for their effect in galvanising support for the war effort and for the resistance against a potentially mortal threat from Hitler. When Churchill met his Cabinet on 13 May 1940, he told them he had nothing to offer except 'blood, toil, tears and sweat', a phrase he repeated when he spoke for the government in a vote of confidence in the Commons later that day. Ironically, his warmest support that day came from the Labour benches, the Conservatives for the most part still hankering after Chamberlain and worried by Churchill's record of failure, lack of judgment, and caprice during earlier spells in office.

'On Friday evening last I received His Majesty's commission to form a new administration. It is the evident wish and will of Parliament and the nation that this should be conceived on the broadest possible basis and that it should include all parties, both those who supported the late government and also the parties of the Opposition. I have completed the most important part of this task. A War Cabinet has been formed of five members, representing, with the opposition Liberals, the unity of the nation. The three Party leaders have agreed to serve, either in the War Cabinet or in high

THE END OF THE PHONEY WAR

MAY 1940

10 MAY
German armies invade Belgium and the Netherlands.

12 MAY
The German Army, having bypassed the defensive Maginot Line by advancing through the forested and mountainous Ardennes region, crosses the Meuse at Sedan, northern France; French forces crumble.

13 MAY
The French government evacuates from Paris.

14 MAY
Rotterdam is destroyed by bombers.

15 MAY
The Netherlands surrenders.

17 MAY
A French armoured counter-attack under Charles de Gaulle fails to stem the German advance.

21 MAY
Amiens and Arras in northern France fall to the Germans, and by mid-June France is defeated.

26 MAY
British and French troops begin their evacuation across the Channel from Dunkirk.

28 MAY
Belgium surrenders to Germany.

executive office. The three fighting services have been filled. It was necessary that this should be done in one single day, on account of the extreme urgency and rigour of events. A number of other positions, key positions, were filled yesterday, and I am submitting a further list to His Majesty tonight. I hope to complete the appointment of the principal ministers during to-morrow. The appointment of the other ministers usually takes a little longer, but I trust that, when Parliament meets again, this part of my task will be completed, and that the administration will be complete in all respects.

'To form an administration of this scale and complexity is a serious undertaking'

I considered it in the public interest to suggest that the House should be summoned to meet today. Mr Speaker agreed, and took the necessary steps, in accordance with the powers conferred upon him by the Resolution of the House. At the end of the proceedings today, the adjournment of the House will be proposed until Tuesday, 21st May, with, of course, provision for earlier meeting, if need be. The business to be considered during that week will be notified to members at the earliest opportunity. I now invite the House, by the motion which stands in my name, to record its approval of the steps taken and to declare its confidence in the new government.

To form an administration of this scale and complexity is a serious undertaking in itself, but it must be remembered that we are in the preliminary stage of one of the greatest battles in history, that we are in action at many other points in Norway and in Holland, that we have to be prepared in the Mediterranean, that the air battle is continuous and that many preparations, such as have been indicated by my hon. Friend below the gangway, have to be made here at home. In this crisis I hope I may be pardoned if I do not address the House at any length today. I hope that any of my friends and colleagues, or former colleagues, who are affected by the political reconstruction, will make allowance, all allowance, for any lack of ceremony with which it has been necessary to act. I would say to the House, as I said to those who have joined this government: 'I have nothing to offer but blood, toil, tears and sweat.'

'I have nothing to offer but blood, toil, tears and sweat'

We have before us an ordeal of the most grievous kind. We have before us many, many long months of struggle and of suffering. You ask, what is our policy? I can say: It is to wage war, by sea, land and air, with all our might and with all the strength that God can give us; to wage war against a monstrous tyranny, never surpassed in the dark, lamentable catalogue of human crime. That is our policy. You ask, what is our aim? I can answer in one word: It is victory, victory at all costs, victory in spite of all terror, victory, however long and hard the road may be; for without victory, there is no survival. Let that be realised; no survival for the British empire, no survival for all that the British empire has stood for, no survival for the urge and impulse of the ages, that mankind will move forward towards its goal. But I take up my task with buoyancy and hope. I feel sure that our cause will not be suffered to fail among men. At this time I feel entitled to claim the aid of all, and I say, 'Come then, let us go forward together with our united strength.'

'We shall fight on the beaches'

House of Commons, London, 4 June 1940

Winston Churchill
on the evacuation from Dunkirk and the spirit of resistance

In the weeks after Churchill became prime minister the French forces crumpled in the face of the German onslaught, and the British, heavily outnumbered, had no choice but to look for a route to the sea. In one of the most remarkable operations ever carried out, 335,000 men of the British Expeditionary Force and Allied troops were evacuated by a flotilla of 'little ships' from the beaches of Dunkirk on the Channel coast of France at the end of May and beginning of June 1940. A carefully managed retreat, a series of mistakes by the Germans, calm seas and a fine fight by the RAF to deny the *Luftwaffe* air superiority had conspired to bring this miracle about. Yet it was a defeat for the British Expeditionary Force nonetheless, and Churchill came to the Commons to explain the nature of the operation, to warn against complacency, and to make one of many appeals to the United States for support in Britain's fight against Germany. At 4am the next morning, the Germans, massed on the Somme, began their advance on Paris.

'When, a week ago today, I asked the House to fix this afternoon as the occasion for a statement, I feared it would be my hard lot to announce the greatest military disaster in our long history. I thought – and some good judges agreed with me – that perhaps 20,000 or 30,000 men might be re-embarked. But it certainly seemed that the whole of the French First Army and the whole of the British Expeditionary Force north of the Amiens-Abbeville gap would be broken up in the open field or else would have to capitulate for lack of food and ammunition. These were the hard and heavy tidings for which I called upon the House and the nation to prepare themselves a week ago. The whole root and core and brain of the British Army, on which and around which we were to build, and are to build, the great British armies in the later years of the war, seemed about to perish upon the field or to be led into an ignominious and starving captivity.

... I asked the House a week ago to suspend its judgment because the facts were not clear, but I do not feel that any reason now exists why we should not form our own opinions upon this pitiful episode. The surrender of the Belgian Army compelled the British at the shortest notice to cover a flank to the sea more than 30 miles in length. Otherwise all would have been cut off, and all would have shared the fate to which King Leopold [of Belgium] had condemned the finest army his country had ever formed. So in doing this and in exposing this flank, as anyone who followed the operations on the map will see, contact was lost between the British and two out of the three corps forming the First French Army, who were still farther from the coast than we were, and it seemed impossible that any large number of Allied troops could reach the coast.

'The enemy attacked on all sides with great strength and fierceness'

The enemy attacked on all sides with great strength and fierceness, and their main power, the power of their far more numerous Air Force, was thrown into the battle or else concentrated upon Dunkirk and the beaches. Pressing in upon the narrow exit, both from the east and from the west, the enemy began to fire with cannon upon the beaches by which alone the shipping could approach or depart. They sowed magnetic mines in the channels and seas; they sent repeated waves of hostile aircraft, sometimes more than a hundred strong in one formation, to cast their bombs upon the single pier that remained, and upon the sand dunes upon which the troops had their eyes for shelter. Their U-boats, one of which was sunk, and their motor launches took their toll of the vast traffic which now began. For four or five days an intense struggle reigned. All their armoured divisions – or what was left of them – together with great masses of infantry and artillery, hurled themselves in vain upon the ever-narrowing, ever-contracting appendix within which the British and French Armies fought.

Meanwhile, the Royal Navy, with the willing help of countless merchant seamen, strained every nerve to embark the British and Allied troops; 220 light warships and 650 other vessels were engaged. They had to operate upon the difficult coast, often in adverse weather, under an almost ceaseless hail of bombs and an increasing concentration of artillery fire. Nor were the seas, as I have said, themselves free from mines and torpedoes. It was in conditions such as these that our men carried on, with little or no rest, for days and nights on end, making trip after trip across the dangerous waters, bringing with them always men whom they had rescued. The numbers they have brought back are the measure of their devotion and their courage. The hospital ships, which brought off many thousands of British and French wounded, being so plainly marked were a special target for Nazi bombs; but the men and women on board them never faltered in their duty.

'Out of the jaws of death and shame'

Meanwhile, the Royal Air Force, which had already been intervening in the battle, so far as its range would allow, from home bases, now used part of its main metropolitan fighter strength, and struck at the German bombers and at the fighters which in large numbers protected them. This struggle was protracted and fierce. Suddenly the scene has cleared, the crash and thunder has for the moment – but only for the moment – died away. A miracle of

---

THE BRITISH EXPEDITIONARY FORCE (BEF) 1908–40

1908
The BEF is created by Secretary of War Richard Burdon (later Viscount Haldane), in case Britain ever needs to deploy quickly overseas.

1914
With the outbreak of the Great War, the BEF is sent to France and Belgium under the command of General Sir John French; heavy casualties are suffered at Mons (Aug.); its nickname, the 'Old Contemptibles', supposedly originates from an 'Order of the Day' for 19 August from the Kaiser, though it is now thought the order emerged from the British War Office for propaganda purposes; the BEF helps to halt the German advance at the Marne (6–12 Sept.).

1939
The BEF is sent to France at the outbreak of World War II under the command of General Lord Gort.

1940
Over 300,000 of the BEF are evacuated from Dunkirk, as France falls to the German onslaught (30 May–4 June).

deliverance, achieved by valour, by perseverance, by perfect discipline, by faultless service, by resource, by skill, by unconquerable fidelity, is manifest to us all. The enemy was hurled back by the retreating British and French troops. He was so roughly handled that he did not hurry their departure seriously. The Royal Air Force engaged the main strength of the German Air Force, and inflicted upon them losses of at least four to one; and the Navy, using nearly 1,000 ships of all kinds, carried over 335,000 men, French and British, out of the jaws of death and shame, to their native land and to the tasks which lie immediately ahead. We must be very careful not to assign to this deliverance the attributes of a victory. Wars are not won by evacuations. But there was a victory inside this deliverance, which should be noted. It was gained by the Air Force. Many of our soldiers coming back have not seen the Air Force at work; they saw only the bombers which escaped its protective attack. They underrate its achievements. I have heard much talk of this; that is why I go out of my way to say this. I will tell you about it.

This was a great trial of strength between the British and German Air Forces. Can you conceive a greater objective for the Germans in the air than to make evacuation from these beaches impossible, and to sink all these ships which were displayed, almost to the extent of thousands? Could there have been an objective of greater military importance and significance for the whole purpose of the war than this? They tried hard, and they were beaten back; they were frustrated in their task. We got the Army away; and they have paid fourfold for any losses which they have inflicted. Very large formations of German aeroplanes – and we know that they are a very brave race – have turned on several occasions from the attack of one-quarter of their number of the Royal Air Force, and have dispersed in different directions. Twelve aeroplanes have been hunted by two. One aeroplane was driven into the water and cast away by the mere charge of a British aeroplane, which had no more ammunition. All of our types – the Hurricane, the Spitfire and the new Defiant – and all our pilots have been vindicated as superior to what they have at present to face.

'I will pay my tribute to these young airmen'

When we consider how much greater would be our advantage in defending the air above this island against an overseas attack, I must say that I find in these facts a sure basis upon which practical and reassuring thoughts may rest. I will pay my tribute to these young airmen. The great French Army was very largely, for the time being, cast back and disturbed by the onrush of a few thousands of armoured vehicles. May it not also be that the cause of civilisation itself will be defended by the skill and devotion of a few thousand airmen? There never has been, I suppose, in all the world, in all the history of war, such an opportunity for youth. The Knights of the Round Table, the Crusaders, all fall back into the past – not only distant but prosaic; these young men, going forth every morn to guard their native land and all that we stand for, holding in their hands these instruments of colossal and shattering power, of whom it may be said that:

> Every morn brought forth a noble chance
> And every chance brought forth a noble knight,

deserve our gratitude, as do all the brave men who, in so many ways and on so many occasions, are ready, and continue to be ready to give life and all for their native land.

I return to the Army. In the long series of very fierce battles, now on this front, now on that, fighting on three fronts at once, battles fought by two or three divisions against an equal or somewhat larger number of the enemy, and fought fiercely on some of the old grounds that so many of us knew so well – in these battles our losses in men have exceeded 30,000 killed, wounded and missing. I take occasion to express the sympathy of the House to all who have suffered bereavement or who are still anxious. The president of the board of trade* is not here today. His son has been killed, and many in the House have felt the pangs of affliction in the sharpest form. But I will say this about the missing: we have had a large number of wounded come home safely to this country, but I would say about the missing that there may be very many reported missing who will come back home, some day, in one way or another. In the confusion of this fight it is inevitable that many have been left in positions where honour required no further resistance from them.

Against this loss of over 30,000 men, we can set a far heavier loss certainly inflicted upon the enemy. But our losses in material are enormous. We have perhaps lost one-third of the men we lost in the opening days of the battle of 21st March, 1918, but we have lost nearly as many guns – nearly one thousand – and all our transport, all the armoured vehicles that were with the Army in the north. This loss will impose a further delay on the expansion of our military strength. That expansion had not been proceeding as far as we had hoped. The best of all we had to give had gone to the British Expeditionary Force, and although they had not the numbers of tanks and some articles of equipment which were desirable, they were a very well and finely equipped Army. They had the first-fruits of all that our industry had to give, and that is gone. And now here is this further delay. How long it will be, how long it will last, depends upon the exertions which we make in this island. An effort the like of which has never been seen in our records is now being made. Work is proceeding everywhere, night and day, Sundays and week days. Capital and labour have cast aside their interests, rights, and customs and put them into the common stock. Already the flow of munitions has leaped forward. There is no reason why we should not in a few months overtake the sudden and serious loss that has come upon us, without retarding the development of our general programme.

'What has happened in France and Belgium is a colossal military disaster'

Nevertheless, our thankfulness at the escape of our Army and so many men, whose loved ones have passed through an agonising week, must not blind us to the fact that what has happened in France and Belgium is a colossal military disaster. The French Army has been weakened, the Belgian Army has been lost, a large part of those fortified lines upon which so much faith had been reposed is gone, many valuable mining districts and factories have passed into the enemy's possession, the whole of the Channel ports are in his hands, with all the tragic consequences that follow from that, and we must expect another blow to be struck almost immediately at us or at France. We are told that Herr Hitler has a plan for invading the British Isles. This has often been thought of before. When Napoleon lay at Boulogne for a year with his flat-bottomed boats and his Grand Army, he was told by someone, 'There are bitter weeds in England.' There are certainly a great many more of them since the British Expeditionary Force returned.

The whole question of home defence against invasion is, of course, powerfully affected by the fact that we have for the time being in this island incomparably more powerful military forces than we have ever had at any moment in this war or the last. But this will not continue. We shall not be content with a defensive war. We have our duty to our ally. We have to reconstitute and build up the British Expeditionary Force once again, under its gallant commander-in-chief, Lord Gort. All this is in train; but in the interval we must put our defences in this island into such a high state of organisation that the fewest possible numbers will be required to give effective security and that the largest possible potential of offensive effort may be realised. On this we are now engaged.

'We have found it necessary to take measures of increasing stringency'

... We have found it necessary to take measures of increasing stringency, not only against enemy aliens and suspicious characters of other nationalities, but also against British subjects who may become a danger or a nuisance should the war be transported to the United Kingdom. I know there are a great many people affected by the orders which we have made who are the passionate enemies of Nazi Germany. I am very sorry for them, but we cannot, at the present time and under the present stress, draw all the distinctions which we should like to do. If parachute landings were attempted and fierce fighting attendant upon them followed, these unfortunate people would be far better out of the way, for their own sakes as well as for ours. There is, however, another class, for which I feel not the slightest sympathy. Parliament has given us the powers to put down fifth column activities with a strong hand, and we shall use those powers subject to the supervision and correction of the House, without the slightest hesitation until we are satisfied, and more than satisfied, that this malignancy in our midst has been effectively stamped out.

Turning once again, and this time more generally, to the question of invasion, I would observe that there has never been a period in all these long centuries of which we boast when an absolute guarantee against invasion, still less against serious raids, could have been given to our people. In the days of Napoleon the same wind which would have carried his transports across the Channel might have driven away the blockading fleet. There was always the chance, and it is that chance which has excited and befooled the imaginations of many continental tyrants. Many are the tales that are told. We are assured that novel methods will be adopted, and when we see the originality of malice, the ingenuity of aggression, which our enemy displays, we may certainly prepare ourselves for every kind of novel stratagem and every kind of brutal and treacherous manoeuvre. I think that no idea is so outlandish that it should not be considered and viewed with a searching, but at the same time, I hope, with a steady eye. We must never forget the solid assurances of sea power and those which belong to air power if it can be locally exercised.

'We shall never surrender'

I have, myself, full confidence that if all do their duty, if nothing is neglected, and if the best arrangements are made, as they are being made, we shall prove ourselves once again able to defend our island home, to ride out the storm of war, and to outlive the menace of tyranny, if necessary for years, if necessary alone. At any rate, that is what we are going to try to do. That is the resolve of His Majesty's government – every man of them. That is the will of Parliament and the nation. The British empire and the French Republic, linked together in their cause and in their need, will defend to the death their native soil, aiding each other like good comrades to the utmost of their strength. Even though large tracts of Europe and many old and famous states have fallen or may fall into the grip of the Gestapo and all the odious apparatus of Nazi rule, we shall not flag or fail. We shall go on to the end, we shall fight in France, we shall fight on the seas and oceans, we shall fight with growing confidence and growing strength in the air, we shall defend our island, whatever the cost may be, we shall fight on the beaches, we shall fight on the landing grounds, we shall fight in the fields and in the streets, we shall fight in the hills; we shall never surrender, and even if, which I do not for a moment believe, this island or a large part of it were subjugated and starving, then our empire beyond the seas, armed and guarded by the British fleet, would carry on the struggle, until, in God's good time, the New World, with all its power and might, steps forth to the rescue and the liberation of the old.

♥ Sir Andrew Duncan (1884–1952), MP for the City of London.

'*This was their finest hour*'

House of Commons, London, 18 June 1940

Winston Churchill
on the British determination to resist
German invasion

By the sixth week of Churchill's premiership the tale of disaster facing Britain had become even worse. France had fallen, and the miracle of Dunkirk – with its 335,000 men evacuated from northern France – could not conceal the fact that Britain was very nearly broken as well as now standing alone against Nazi Germany. There seemed little doubt that a German invasion would come.

In this speech, Churchill set out to convince Parliament and the people that such an invasion could, and would, be resisted. His peroration, in which he coined the phrase 'the Battle of Britain' but spoke inspirationally of 'broad, sunlit uplands', is especially magnificent. That evening he broadcast the same speech on the wireless to the nation.

The air battle that ultimately saved Britain from invasion took place in August and September, and the Blitz began after it. Nonetheless, the fact that Britain warded off an invasion was to be crucial to the outcome of the war, though victory would still be almost five years away.

'The disastrous military events which have happened during the past fortnight have not come to me with any sense of surprise. Indeed, I indicated a fortnight ago as clearly as I could to the House that the worst possibilities were open; and I made it perfectly clear then that whatever happened in France would make no difference to the resolve of Britain and the British empire to fight on, 'if necessary for years, if necessary alone'. During the last few days we have successfully brought off the great majority of the troops we had on the line of communication in France; and seven-eighths of the troops we have sent to France since the beginning of the war – that is to say, about 350,000 out of 400,000 men – are safely back in this country. Others are still fighting with the French, and fighting with considerable success in their local encounters against the enemy. We have also brought back a great mass of stores, rifles and munitions of all kinds which had been accumulated in France during the last nine months.

We have, therefore, in this island today a very large and powerful military force. This force comprises all our best-trained and our finest troops, including scores of thousands of those who have already measured their quality against the Germans and found themselves at no disadvantage. We have under arms at the present time in this island over a million and a quarter men. Behind these we have the Local Defence Volunteers [Home Guard], numbering half a million, only a portion of whom, however, are yet armed with rifles or other firearms. We have incorporated into our defence forces every man for whom we have a weapon. We expect very large additions to our weapons in the near future, and in preparation for this we intend forthwith to call up, drill and train further large numbers. Those who are not called up, or else are employed during the vast business of munitions production in all its branches – and their ramifications are innumerable – will serve their country best by remaining at their ordinary work until they receive their summons. We have also over here Dominions armies. The Canadians had actually landed in France, but have now been safely withdrawn, much disappointed, but in perfect order, with all their artillery and equipment. And these very high-class forces from the Dominions will now take part in the defence of the mother country.

Lest the account which I have given of these large forces should raise the question: why did they not take part in the great battle in France? I must make it clear that, apart from the divisions training and organising at home, only 12 divisions were equipped to fight upon a scale which justified their being sent abroad. And this was fully up to the number which the French had been led to expect would be available in France at the ninth month of the war. The rest of our forces at home have a fighting value for home defence which will, of course, steadily increase every week that passes. Thus, the invasion of Great Britain would at this time require the transportation across the sea of hostile armies on a very large scale, and after they had been so transported they would have to be continually maintained with all the masses of munitions and supplies which are required for continuous battle – as continuous battle it will surely be.

'Some people seem to forget that we have a Navy'

Here is where we come to the Navy – and after all, we have a Navy. Some people seem to forget that we have a Navy. We must remind them. For the last thirty years I have been concerned in discussions about the possibilities of overseas invasion, and I took the responsibility on behalf of the Admiralty, at the beginning of the last war, of allowing all regular troops to be sent out of the country. That was a very serious step to take, because our Territorials had only just been called up and were quite untrained. Therefore, this island was for several months particularly denuded of fighting troops. The Admiralty had confidence at that time in their ability to prevent a mass invasion even though at that time the Germans had a magnificent battle fleet in the proportion of 10 to 16, even though they were capable of fighting a general engagement every day and any day, whereas now they have only a couple of heavy ships worth speaking of – the *Scharnhorst* and the *Gneisenau*. We are also told that the Italian Navy is to come out and gain sea superiority in these waters. If they seriously intend it, I shall only say that we shall be delighted to offer Signor Mussolini a free and safeguarded passage through the Strait of Gibraltar in order that he may play the part to which he aspires. There is a general curiosity in the British Fleet to find out whether the Italians are up to the level they were at in the last war or whether they have fallen off at all.

Therefore, it seems to me that as far as sea-borne invasion on a great scale is concerned, we are far more capable of meeting it today than we were at many periods in the last war and

THE HOME GUARD

1940
The Local Defence Volunteers (LDV) are founded by Gen. Kirke, as a means of defending Dover (Feb.), and they are officially recognised in a radio appeal by Anthony Eden, the secretary of war, who asks for more volunteers (14 May): in the following 24 hours, 250,000 men register at local police stations, rising to 1.5 million by the end of June: only 200,000 volunteers were anticipated, and there are subsequent delays in supplying uniforms

during the early months of this war, before our other troops were trained, and while the BEF [British Expeditionary Force] had proceeded abroad. Now, the Navy have never pretended to be able to prevent raids by bodies of 5,000 or 10,000 men flung suddenly across and thrown ashore at several points on the coast some dark night or foggy morning. The efficacy of sea power, especially under modern conditions, depends upon the invading force being of large size; it has to be of large size, in view of our military strength, to be of any use. If it is of large size, then the Navy have something they can find and meet and, as it were, bite on. Now, we must remember that even five divisions, however lightly equipped, would require 200 to 250 ships, and with modern air reconnaissance and photography it would not be easy to collect such an armada, marshal it, and conduct it across the sea without any powerful naval forces to escort it; and there would be very great possibilities, to put it mildly, that this armada would be intercepted long before it reached the coast, and all the men drowned in the sea or at the worst blown to pieces with their equipment while they were trying to land. We also have a great system of minefields, recently strongly reinforced, through which we alone know the channels. If the enemy tries to sweep passages through these minefields, it will be the task of the Navy to destroy the mine-sweepers and any other forces employed to protect them. There should be no difficulty in this, owing to our great superiority at sea.

'The enemy is crafty and there is no dirty trick he will not do'

Those are the regular, well-tested, well-proved arguments on which we have relied during many years in peace and war. But the question is whether there are any new methods by which those solid assurances can be circumvented. Odd as it may seem, some attention has been given to this by the Admiralty, whose prime duty and responsibility is to destroy any large sea-borne expedition before it reaches, or at the moment when it reaches, these shores. It would not be a good thing for me to go into details of this. It might suggest ideas to other people which they have not thought of, and they would not be likely to give us any of their ideas in exchange. All I will say is that untiring vigilance and mind-searching must be devoted to the subject, because the enemy is crafty and cunning and full of novel treacheries and stratagems. The House may be assured that the utmost ingenuity is being displayed and imagination is being evoked from large numbers of competent officers, well-trained in tactics and thoroughly up to date, to measure and counterwork novel possibilities. Untiring vigilance

and weapons; the LDV is renamed the Home Guard, a name suggested by Churchill (23 July); units are affiliated to county army regiments (Aug.), and the Home Guard is a key contributor to civil defence (Sept.).

1941
Conscription is extended to include service in the Home Guard (Dec.).

1943
Numbers reach a peak of 1.8 million, organised into 1,100 battalions (March); 'nominated women' join the Home Guard from 20 April.

1945
With the end of war, the Home Guard is disbanded (31 Dec.).

and untiring searching of the mind is being, and must be, devoted to the subject, because, remember, the enemy is crafty and there is no dirty trick he will not do.

... This brings me, naturally, to the great question of invasion from the air, and of the impending struggle between the British and German Air Forces. It seems quite clear that no invasion on a scale beyond the capacity of our land forces to crush speedily is likely to take place from the air until our Air Force has been definitely overpowered. In the meantime, there may be raids by parachute troops and attempted descents of airborne soldiers. We should be able to give those gentry a warm reception both in the air and on the ground, if they reach it in any condition to continue the dispute. But the great question is: can we break Hitler's air weapon? Now, of course, it is a very great pity that we have not got an Air Force at least equal to that of the most powerful enemy within striking distance of these shores. But we have a very powerful Air Force which has proved itself far superior in quality, both in men and in many types of machine, to what we have met so far in the numerous and fierce air battles which have been fought with the Germans. In France, where we were at a considerable disadvantage and lost many machines on the ground when they were standing round the aerodromes, we were accustomed to inflict in the air losses of as much as two and two-and-a-half to one. In the fighting over Dunkirk, which was a sort of no-man's-land, we undoubtedly beat the German Air Force, and gained the mastery of the local air, inflicting here a loss of three or four to one day after day. Anyone who looks at the photographs which were published a week or so ago of the re-embarkation, showing the masses of troops assembled on the beach and forming an ideal target for hours at a time, must realise that this re-embarkation would not have been possible unless the enemy had resigned all hope of recovering air superiority at that time and at that place.

In the defence of this island the advantages to the defenders will be much greater than they were in the fighting around Dunkirk. We hope to improve on the rate of three or four to one which was realised at Dunkirk; and in addition all our injured machines and their crews which get down safely – and, surprisingly, a very great many injured machines and men do get down safely in modern air fighting – all of these will fall, in an attack upon these islands, on friendly soil and live to fight another day; whereas all the injured enemy machines and their complements will be total losses as far as the war is concerned.

'Our fighter pilots – these splendid men, this brilliant youth'

During the great battle in France, we gave very powerful and continuous aid to the French Army, both by fighters and bombers; but in spite of every kind of pressure we never would allow the entire metropolitan fighter strength of the Air Force to be consumed. This decision was painful, but it was also right, because the fortunes of the battle in France could not have been decisively affected even if we had thrown in our entire fighter force. That battle was lost by the unfortunate strategical opening, by the extraordinary and unforeseen power of the armoured columns, and by the great preponderance of the German Army in numbers. Our fighter Air Force might easily have been exhausted as a mere accident in that great struggle, and then we should have found ourselves at the present time in a very serious plight. But as it is, I am happy to inform the House that our fighter strength is stronger at the present time relatively to the Germans, who have suffered terrible losses, than it has ever been; and consequently we believe ourselves possessed of the capacity to continue the war in the air under better conditions than we have ever experienced before. I look forward confidently to the exploits of our fighter pilots – these splendid men, this brilliant youth – who will have the glory of saving their native land, their island home, and all they love, from the most deadly of all attacks.

There remains, of course, the danger of bombing attacks, which will certainly be made very soon upon us by the bomber forces of the enemy. It is true that the German bomber force is superior in numbers to ours; but we have a very large bomber force also, which we shall use to strike at military targets in Germany without intermission. I do not at all underrate the severity of the ordeal which lies before us; but I believe our countrymen will show themselves capable of standing up to it, like the brave men of Barcelona, and will be able to stand up to it, and carry on in spite of it, at least as well as any other people in the world. Much will depend upon this; every man and every woman will have the chance to show the finest qualities of their race, and render the highest service to their cause. For all of us, at this time, whatever our sphere, our station, our occupation or our duties, it will be a help to remember the famous lines:

> He nothing common did or mean,
> Upon that memorable scene.

'Absolutely devoted to the ancient motherland'

I have thought it right upon this occasion to give the House and the country some indication of the solid, practical grounds upon which we base our inflexible resolve to continue the war. There are a good many people who say, 'Never mind. Win or lose, sink or swim, better die than submit to tyranny – and such a tyranny.' And I do not dissociate myself from them. But I can assure them that our professional advisers of the three Services unitedly advise that we should carry on the war, and that there are good and reasonable hopes of final victory. We have fully informed and consulted all the self-governing Dominions, these great communities far beyond the oceans who have been built up on our laws and on our civilisation, and who are absolutely free to choose their course, but are absolutely devoted to the ancient motherland, and who feel themselves inspired by the same emotions which lead me to stake our all upon duty and honour. We have fully consulted them, and I have received from their Prime Ministers, Mr Mackenzie King of Canada, Mr Menzies of Australia, Mr Fraser of New Zealand, and General Smuts of South Africa – that wonderful man, with his immense profound mind, and his eye watching from a distance the whole panorama of European affairs – I have received from all these eminent men, who all have governments behind them elected on wide franchises, who are all there because they represent the will of their people, messages couched in the most moving terms in which they endorse our decision to fight on, and declare themselves ready to share our fortunes and to persevere to the end. That is what we are going to do.

We may now ask ourselves: in what way has our position worsened since the beginning of the war? It has worsened by the fact that the Germans have conquered a large part of the coast line of Western Europe, and many small countries have been overrun by them. This aggravates the possibilities of air attack and adds to our naval preoccupations. It in no way diminishes, but on the contrary definitely increases, the power of our long-distance blockade.

Similarly, the entrance of Italy into the war increases the power of our long-distance blockade. We have stopped the worst leak by that. We do not know whether military resistance will come to an end in France or not, but should it do so, then of course the Germans will be able to concentrate their forces, both military and industrial, upon us. But for the reasons I have given to the House these will not be found so easy to apply. If invasion has become more imminent, as no doubt it has, we, being relieved from the task of maintaining a large army in France, have far larger and more efficient forces to meet it.

'I see great reason for intense vigilance and exertion'

If Hitler can bring under his despotic control the industries of the countries he has conquered, this will add greatly to his already vast armament output. On the other hand, this will not happen immediately, and we are now assured of immense, continuous and increasing support in supplies and munitions of all kinds from the United States; and especially of aeroplanes and pilots from the Dominions and across the oceans coming from regions which are beyond the reach of enemy bombers.

I do not see how any of these factors can operate to our detriment on balance before the winter comes; and the winter will impose a strain upon the Nazi regime, with almost all Europe writhing and starving under its cruel heel, which, for all their ruthlessness, will run them very hard. We must not forget that from the moment when we declared war on the 3rd September it was always possible for Germany to turn all her Air Force upon this country, together with any other devices of invasion she might conceive, and that France could have done little or nothing to prevent her doing so. We have, therefore, lived under this danger, in principle and in a slightly modified form, during all these months. In the meanwhile, however, we have enormously improved our methods of defence, and we have learned what we had no right to assume at the beginning, namely, that the individual aircraft and the individual British pilot have a sure and definite superiority. Therefore, in casting up this dread balance sheet and contemplating our dangers with a disillusioned eye, I see great reason for intense vigilance and exertion, but none whatever for panic or despair.

'During the first four years of the last war the Allies experienced nothing but disaster'

During the first four years of the last war the Allies experienced nothing but disaster and disappointment. That was our constant fear: one blow after another, terrible losses, frightful dangers. Everything miscarried. And yet at the end of those four years the morale of the Allies was higher than that of the Germans, who had moved from one aggressive triumph to another, and who stood everywhere triumphant invaders of the lands into which they had broken. During that war we repeatedly asked ourselves the question: how are we going to win? and no one was able ever to answer it with much precision, until at the end, quite suddenly, quite unexpectedly, our terrible foe collapsed before us, and we were so glutted with victory that in our folly we threw it away.

We do not yet know what will happen in France or whether the French resistance will be prolonged, both in France and in the French empire overseas. The French government will be throwing away great opportunities and casting adrift their future if they do not continue the war in accordance with their treaty obligations, from which we have not felt able to release them. The House will have read the historic declaration in which, at the desire of many Frenchmen – and of our own hearts – we have proclaimed our willingness at the darkest hour in French history to conclude a union of common citizenship in this struggle. However matters may go in France or with the French government, or other French governments, we in this island and in the British empire will never lose our sense of comradeship with the French people. If we are now called upon to endure what they have been suffering, we shall emulate their courage, and if final victory rewards our toils they shall share the gains, aye, and freedom shall be restored to all. We abate nothing of our just demands; not one jot or tittle do we recede. Czechs, Poles, Norwegians, Dutch, Belgians have joined their causes to our own. All these shall be restored.

'Upon this battle depends the survival of Christian civilisation'

What General Weygand called the Battle of France is over. I expect that the Battle of Britain is about to begin. Upon this battle depends the survival of Christian civilisation. Upon it depends our own British life, and the long continuity of our institutions and our empire. The whole fury and might of the enemy must very soon be turned on us. Hitler knows that he will have to break us in this island or lose the war. If we can stand up to him, all Europe may be free and the life of the world may move forward into broad, sunlit uplands. But if we fail, then the whole world, including the United States, including all that we have known and cared for, will sink into the abyss of a new Dark Age made more sinister, and perhaps more protracted, by the lights of perverted science. Let us therefore brace ourselves to our duties, and so bear ourselves that, if the British empire and its Commonwealth last for a thousand years, men will still say, 'This was their finest hour.'

'Never in the field of
human conflict'

House of Commons, London, 20 August 1940

Winston Churchill
on the Battle of Britain and the current
state of the war

By late August 1940, the air battle over South-East England had raged for six weeks and, in the view of most of the British public, was the prelude to an invasion. German troops could not hope to cross the English Channel until the *Luftwaffe* had gained air superiority; and to achieve that it had to defeat the fighter pilots of the Royal Air Force. Winston Churchill made this speech during a brief lull in the Battle of Britain, coining one of the many phrases by which he would be immortalised – 'the Few'. With those two words he immortalised in turn the heroic pilots of Fighter Command who would, within a month, cause Hitler to abandon his invasion plans. A failed, final surge by the *Luftwaffe* on 15 September – thereafter Battle of Britain Day – was the last straw for the Nazis. Knowing he could not invade, Hitler instead changed his tactics to cause maximum damage and demoralisation to the British people and their property, in a *Blitzkrieg* ('lightning war') – the Blitz – that lasted throughout the winter of 1940–1.

'Almost a year has passed since the war began, and it is natural for us, I think, to pause on our journey at this milestone and survey the dark, wide field. It is also useful to compare the first year of this second war against German aggression with its forerunner a quarter of a century ago. Although this war is in fact only a continuation of the last, very great differences in its character are apparent. In the last war millions of men fought by hurling enormous masses of steel at one another. 'Men and shells' was the cry, and prodigious slaughter was the consequence.

In this war nothing of this kind has yet appeared. It is a conflict of strategy, of organisation, of technical apparatus, of science, mechanics, and morale. The British casualties in the first 12 months of the Great War amounted to 365,000. In this war, I am thankful to say, British killed, wounded, prisoners, and missing, including civilians, do not exceed 92,000, and of these a large proportion are alive as prisoners of war. Looking more widely around, one may say that throughout all Europe for one man killed or wounded in the first year perhaps five were killed or wounded in 1914–15.

The slaughter is only a small fraction, but the consequences to the belligerents have been even more deadly. We have seen great countries with powerful armies dashed out of coherent existence in a few weeks. We have seen the French Republic and the renowned French Army beaten into complete and total submission with less than the casualties which they suffered in any one of half a dozen of the battles of 1914–18.

'Dashed out of coherent existence in a few weeks'

The entire body – it might almost seem at times the soul – of France has succumbed to physical effects incomparably less terrible than those which were sustained with fortitude and undaunted will power 25 years ago. Although up to the present the loss of life has been mercifully diminished, the decisions reached in the course of the struggle are even more profound upon the fate of nations than anything that has ever happened since barbaric times. Moves are made upon the scientific and strategic boards, advantages are gained by mechanical means, as a result of which scores of millions of men become incapable of further resistance, or judge themselves incapable of further resistance, and a fearful game of chess proceeds from check to mate by which the unhappy players seem to be inexorably bound.

There is another more obvious difference from 1914. The whole of the warring nations are engaged, not only soldiers, but the entire population, men, women, and children. The fronts are everywhere. The trenches are dug in the towns and streets. Every village is fortified. Every road is barred. The front line runs through the factories. The workmen are soldiers with different weapons but the same courage. These are great and distinctive changes from what many of us saw in the struggle of a quarter of a century ago.

There seems to be every reason to believe that this new kind of war is well suited to the genius and the resources of the British nation and the British empire and that, once we get properly equipped and properly started, a war of this kind will be more favourable to us than the sombre mass slaughters of the Somme and Passchendaele. If it is a case of the whole nation fighting and suffering together, that ought to suit us, because we are the most united of all the nations, because we entered the war upon the national will and with our eyes open, and because we have been nurtured in freedom and individual responsibility and are the products, not of totalitarian uniformity but of tolerance and variety.

'The sole champion of the liberties of all Europe'

If all these qualities are turned, as they are being turned, to the arts of war, we may be able to show the enemy quite a lot of things that they have not thought of yet. Since the Germans drove the Jews out and lowered their technical standards, our science is definitely ahead of theirs. Our geographical position, the command of the sea, and the friendship of the United States enable us to draw resources from the whole world and to manufacture weapons of war of every kind, but especially of the superfine kinds, on a scale hitherto practised only by Nazi Germany.

THE BATTLE OF BRITAIN 1940

10 JULY
The battle begins with a month of attacks by the *Luftwaffe* on freight convoys crossing the English Channel.

12 AUGUST
The *Luftwaffe* attacks four radar stations, with three of them briefly taken off the air; attacks begin on coastal airfields, with further attacks inland in the following days.

15 AUGUST
The *Luftwaffe* makes the largest number of sorties of the campaign.

18 AUGUST
The day sees the greatest number of casualties on both

Hitler is now sprawled over Europe. Our offensive springs are being slowly compressed, and we must resolutely and methodically prepare ourselves for the campaigns of 1941 and 1942. Two or three years are not a long time, even in our short, precarious lives. They are nothing in the history of the nation, and when we are doing the finest thing in the world, and have the honour to be the sole champion of the liberties of all Europe, we must not grudge these years or weary as we toil and struggle through them. It does not follow that our energies in future years will be exclusively confined to defending ourselves and our possessions. Many opportunities may lie open to amphibious power, and we must be ready to take advantage of them.

'The road to victory may not be so long as we expect. But we have no right to count upon this'

One of the ways to bring this war to a speedy end is to convince the enemy, not by words, but by deeds, that we have both the will and the means, not only to go on indefinitely but to strike heavy and unexpected blows. The road to victory may not be so long as we expect. But we have no right to count upon this. Be it long or short, rough or smooth, we mean to reach our journey's end.

It is our intention to maintain and enforce a strict blockade not only of Germany but of Italy, France, and all the other countries that have fallen into the German power. I read in the papers that Herr Hitler has also proclaimed a strict blockade of the British Islands. No one can complain of that. I remember the Kaiser doing it in the last war. What indeed would be a matter of general complaint would be if we were to prolong the agony of all Europe by allowing food to come in to nourish the Nazis and aid their war effort, or to allow food to go in to the subjugated peoples, which certainly would be pillaged off them by their Nazi conquerors.

There have been many proposals, founded on the highest motives, that food should be allowed to pass the blockade for the relief of these populations. I regret that we must refuse these requests. The Nazis declare that they have created a new unified economy in Europe.

sides, but then exhaustion and weather halt the battle for nearly a week.

7 SEPTEMBER
The Blitz starts with 57 consecutive nights of bombing on London, following RAF raids on Berlin on the night of 25/6 Aug.; the *Luftwaffe* has already bombed a number of British cities during the months of July and Aug.

15 SEPTEMBER
The RAF repulses two waves of German attacks.

17 SEPTEMBER
Hitler finally orders postponement of his invasion of Britain.

31 OCTOBER
The Battle of Britain ends, but German air attacks continue into 1941 (Coventry is devastated, 14 Nov.).

They have repeatedly stated that they possess ample reserves of food and that they can feed their captive peoples …

… The only agencies which can create famine in any part of Europe now and during the coming winter, will be German exactions or German failure to distribute the supplies which they command.

There is another aspect. Many of the most valuable foods are essential to the manufacture of vital war material. Fats are used to make explosives. Potatoes make the alcohol for motor spirit. The plastic materials now so largely used in the construction of aircraft are made of milk. If the Germans use these commodities to help them to bomb our women and children, rather than to feed the populations who produce them, we may be sure that imported foods would go the same way, directly or indirectly, or be employed to relieve the enemy of the responsibilities he has so wantonly assumed.

Let Hitler bear his responsibilities to the full and let the peoples of Europe who groan beneath his yoke aid in every way the coming of the day when that yoke will be broken. Meanwhile, we can and we will arrange in advance for the speedy entry of food into any part of the enslaved area, when this part has been wholly cleared of German forces, and has genuinely regained its freedom. We shall do our best to encourage the building up of reserves of food all over the world, so that there will always be held up before the eyes of the peoples of Europe, including – I say deliberately – the German and Austrian peoples, the certainty that the shattering of the Nazi power will bring to them all immediate food, freedom and peace.

'What a cataract of disaster has poured out upon us'

Rather more than a quarter of a year has passed since the new government came into power in this country. What a cataract of disaster has poured out upon us since then. The trustful Dutch overwhelmed; their beloved and respected Sovereign driven into exile; the peaceful city of Rotterdam, the scene of a massacre as hideous and brutal as anything in the Thirty Years War. Belgium invaded and beaten down; our own fine Expeditionary Force, which King Leopold [of Belgium] called to his rescue, cut off and almost captured, escaping as it seemed only by a miracle and with the loss of all its equipment; our ally, France, out; Italy in against us; all France in the power of the enemy, all its arsenals and vast masses of military material converted or convertible to the enemy's use; a puppet government set up at Vichy which may at any moment be forced to become our foe; the whole Western seaboard of Europe from the North Cape to the Spanish frontier in German hands; all the ports, all the air-fields on this immense front, employed against us as potential springboards of invasion. Moreover, the German air power, numerically so far outstripping ours, has been brought so close to our island that what we used to dread greatly has come to pass and the hostile bombers not only reach our shores in a few minutes and from many directions, but can be escorted by their fighting aircraft.

Why, sir, if we had been confronted at the beginning of May with such a prospect, it would have seemed incredible that at the end of a period of horror and disaster, or at this point in a period of horror and disaster, we should stand erect, sure of ourselves, masters of our fate and with the conviction of final victory burning unquenchable in our hearts. Few would have believed we could survive; none would have believed that we should today not only feel stronger but should actually be stronger than we have ever been before.

Let us see what has happened on the other side of the scales. The British nation and the British empire finding themselves alone, stood undismayed against disaster. No one flinched or wavered; nay, some who formerly thought of peace, now think only of war. Our people are united and resolved, as they have never been before. Death and ruin have become small things compared with the shame of defeat or failure in duty.

'We have not only fortified our hearts but our island'

We cannot tell what lies ahead. It may be that even greater ordeals lie before us. We shall face whatever is coming to us. We are sure of ourselves and of our cause and that is the supreme fact which has emerged in these months of trial.

Meanwhile, we have not only fortified our hearts but our island. We have rearmed and rebuilt our armies in a degree which would have been deemed impossible a few months ago. We have ferried across the Atlantic, in the month of July, thanks to our friends over there, an immense mass of munitions of all kinds, cannon, rifles, machine-guns, cartridges, and shell, all safely landed without the loss of a gun or a round. The output of our own factories, working as they have never worked before, has poured forth to the troops. The whole British Army is at home. More than 2,000,000 determined men have rifles and bayonets in their hands tonight and three-quarters of them are in regular military formations. We have never had armies like this in our island in time of war. The whole island bristles against invaders, from the sea or from the air …

Our Navy is far stronger than it was at the beginning of the war. The great flow of new construction set on foot at the outbreak is now beginning to come in. We hope our friends across the ocean will send us a timely reinforcement to bridge the gap between the peace flotillas of 1939 and the war flotillas of 1941. There is no difficulty in sending such aid. The seas and oceans are open. The U-boats are contained. The magnetic mine is, up to the present time, effectively mastered. The merchant tonnage under the British flag, after a year of unlimited U-boat war, after eight months of intensive mining attack, is larger than when we began. We have, in addition, under our control at least 4,000,000 tons of shipping from the captive countries which has taken refuge here or in the harbours of the empire. Our stocks of food of all kinds are far more abundant than in the days of peace and a large and growing programme of food production is on foot.

'There will presently come cleansing and devouring flame'

Why do I say all this? Not assuredly to boast; not assuredly to give the slightest countenance to complacency. The dangers we face are still enormous, but so are our advantages and resources.

I recount them because the people have a right to know that there are solid grounds for the confidence which we feel, and that we have good reason to believe ourselves capable, as I said in a very dark hour two months ago, of continuing the war 'if necessary alone, if necessary for years'. I say it also because the fact that the British empire stands invincible, and that Nazidom is still being resisted, will kindle again the spark of hope in the breasts of hundreds of millions of downtrodden or despairing men and women throughout Europe, and far beyond its bounds, and that from these sparks there will presently come cleansing and devouring flame.

The great air battle which has been in progress over this island for the last few weeks has recently attained a high intensity. It is too soon to attempt to assign limits either to its scale or to its duration. We must certainly expect that greater efforts will be made by the enemy than any he has so far put forth. Hostile air fields are still being developed in France and the Low Countries, and the movement of squadrons and material for attacking us is still proceeding.

It is quite plain that Herr Hitler could not admit defeat in his air attack on Great Britain without sustaining most serious injury. If, after all his boastings and blood-curdling threats and lurid accounts trumpeted round the world of the damage he has inflicted, of the vast numbers of our Air Force he has shot down, so he says, with so little loss to himself; if after tales of the panic-stricken British crushed in their holes cursing the plutocratic Parliament which has led them to such a plight; if after all this his whole air onslaught were forced after a while tamely to peter out, the Fuehrer's reputation for veracity of statement might be seriously impugned. We may be sure, therefore, that he will continue as long as he has the strength to do so, and as long as any preoccupations he may have in respect of the Russian Air Force allow him to do so.

'Never ... was so much owed by so many to so few'

On the other hand, the conditions and course of the fighting have so far been favourable to us. I told the House two months ago that whereas in France our fighter aircraft were wont to inflict a loss of two or three to one upon the Germans, and in the fighting at Dunkirk, which was a kind of no-man's-land, a loss of about three or four to one, we expected that in an attack on this island we should achieve a larger ratio. This has certainly come true. It must also be remembered that all the enemy machines and pilots which are shot down over our island, or over the seas which surround it, are either destroyed or captured; whereas a considerable proportion of our machines, and also of our pilots, are saved, and soon again in many cases come into action …

The enemy is, of course, far more numerous than we are. But our new production already, as I am advised, largely exceeds his, and the American production is only just beginning to flow in. It is a fact, as I see from my daily returns, that our bomber and fighter strength now, after all this fighting, are larger than they have ever been. We believe that we shall be able to continue the air struggle indefinitely and as long as the enemy pleases, and the longer it continues the more rapid will be our approach, first towards that parity, and then into that superiority in the air, upon which in a large measure the decision of the war depends.

The gratitude of every home in our island, in our empire, and indeed throughout the world, except in the abodes of the guilty, goes out to the British airmen who, undaunted by odds, unwearied in their constant challenge and mortal danger, are turning the tide of the world war by their prowess and by their devotion. Never in the field of human conflict was so much owed by so many to so few.

All hearts go out to the fighter pilots, whose brilliant actions we see with our own eyes day after day; but we must never forget that all the time, night after night, month after month, our bomber squadrons travel far into Germany, find their targets in the darkness by the highest navigational skill, aim their attacks, often under the heaviest fire, often with serious loss, with deliberate careful discrimination, and inflict shattering blows upon the whole of the technical and war-making structure of the Nazi power. On no part of the Royal Air Force does the weight of the war fall more heavily than on the daylight bombers who will play an invaluable part in the case of invasion and whose unflinching zeal it has been necessary in the meanwhile on numerous occasions to restrain.

We are able to verify the results of bombing military targets in Germany, not only by reports which reach us through many sources, but also, of course, by photography. I have no hesitation in saying that this process of bombing the military industries and communications of Germany and the air bases and storage depots from which we are attacked, which process will continue upon an ever-increasing scale until the end of the war, and may in another year attain dimensions hitherto undreamed of, affords one at least of the most certain, if not the shortest of all the roads to victory. Even if the Nazi legions stood triumphant on the Black Sea, or indeed upon the Caspian, even if Hitler was at the gates of India, it would profit him nothing if at the same time the entire economic and scientific apparatus of German war power lay shattered and pulverised at home.

'The defection of France has, of course, been deeply damaging to our position'

The fact that the invasion of this island upon a large scale has become a far more difficult operation with every week that has passed since we saved our Army at Dunkirk, and our very great preponderance of sea-power enable us to turn our eyes and to turn our strength increasingly towards the Mediterranean and against that other enemy [Italy] who, without the slightest provocation, coldly and deliberately, for greed and gain, stabbed France in the back in the moment of her agony, and is now marching against us in Africa.

The defection of France has, of course, been deeply damaging to our position in what is called, somewhat oddly, the Middle East. In the defence of Somaliland, for instance, we had counted upon strong French forces attacking the Italians from Jibuti. We had counted also upon the use of the French naval and air bases in the Mediterranean, and particularly upon the North African shore. We had counted upon the French Fleet. Even though metropolitan France was temporarily overrun, there was no reason why the French Navy, substantial parts of the French Army, the French Air Force and the French empire overseas should not have continued the struggle at our side.

Shielded by overwhelming sea-power, possessed of invaluable strategic bases and of ample funds, France might have remained one of the great combatants in the struggle. By so doing, France would have preserved the continuity of her life, and the French empire might have advanced with the British empire to the rescue of the independence and integrity of the French motherland.

In our own case, if we had been put in the terrible position of France, a contingency now happily impossible, although, of course, it would have been the duty of all war leaders to fight on here to the end, it would also have been their duty, as I indicated in my speech of 4th June, to provide as far as possible for the Naval security of Canada and our Dominions and to make sure they had the means to carry the struggle from beyond the oceans. Most of the other countries that have been overrun by Germany for the time being have persevered valiantly and faithfully. The Czechs, the Poles, the Norwegians, the Dutch, the Belgians are still in the field, sword in hand, recognised by Great Britain and the United States as the sole representative authorities and lawful governments of their respective states.

'Our old comradeship with France is not dead'

That France alone should lie prostrate at this moment is the crime, not of a great and noble nation, but of what are called 'the men of Vichy'. We have profound sympathy with the French people. Our old comradeship with France is not dead. In General de Gaulle and his gallant band, that comradeship takes an effective form. These free Frenchmen have been condemned to death by Vichy, but the day will come, as surely as the sun will rise tomorrow, when their names will be held in honour, and their names will be graven in stone in the streets and villages of a France restored in a liberated Europe to its full freedom and its ancient fame …

A good many people have written to me to ask me to make on this occasion a fuller statement of our war aims, and of the kind of peace we wish to make after the war, than is contained in the very considerable declaration which was made early in the autumn. Since then we have made common cause with Norway, Holland, and Belgium. We have recognised the Czech government of Dr Beneš, and we have told General de Gaulle that our success will carry with it the restoration of France.

I do not think it would be wise at this moment, while the battle rages and the war is still perhaps only in its earlier stage, to embark upon elaborate speculations about the future shape which should be given to Europe or the new securities which must be arranged to spare mankind the miseries of a third World War. The ground is not new, it has been frequently traversed and explored, and many ideas are held about it in common by all good men, and all free men. But before we can undertake the task of rebuilding we have not only to be convinced ourselves, but we have to convince all other countries that the Nazi tyranny is going to be finally broken.

The right to guide the course of world history is the noblest prize of victory. We are still toiling up the hill; we have not yet reached the crest-line of it; we cannot survey the landscape or even imagine what its condition will be when that longed-for morning comes. The task which lies before us immediately is at once more practical, more simple and more stern. I hope – indeed I pray – that we shall not be found unworthy of our victory if after toil and tribulation it is granted to us. For the rest, we have to gain the victory. That is our task.

There is, however, one direction in which we can see a little more clearly ahead. We have to think not only for ourselves but for the lasting security of the cause and principles for which we are fighting and of the long future of the British Commonwealth of Nations.

Some months ago we came to the conclusion that the interests of the United States and of the British empire both required that the United States should have facilities for the naval and air defence of the Western hemisphere against the attack of a Nazi power which might have acquired temporary but lengthy control of a large part of Western Europe and its formidable resources.

We had therefore decided spontaneously, and without being asked or offered any inducement, to inform the government of the United States that we would be glad to place such defence facilities at their disposal by leasing suitable sites in our Transatlantic possessions for their greater security against the unmeasured dangers of the future.

The principle of association of interests for common purposes between Great Britain and the United States had developed even before the war. Various agreements had been reached about certain small islands in the Pacific Ocean which had become important as air fuelling points. In all this line of thought we found ourselves in very close harmony with the government of Canada.

'Let it roll on full flood, inexorable'

Presently we learned that anxiety was also felt in the United States about the air and naval defence of their Atlantic seaboard, and President Roosevelt has recently made it clear that he would like to discuss with us, and with the Dominion of Canada and with Newfoundland, the development of American naval and air facilities in Newfoundland and in the West Indies. There is, of course, no question of any transference of sovereignty – that has never been suggested – or of any action being taken, without the consent or against the wishes of the various colonies concerned, but for our part, His Majesty's government are entirely willing to accord defence facilities to the United States on a 99 years' leasehold basis, and we feel sure that our interests no less than theirs, and the interests of the colonies themselves and of Canada and Newfoundland will be served thereby.

These are important steps. Undoubtedly this process means that these two great organisations of the English-speaking democracies, the British empire and the United States, will have to be somewhat mixed up together in some of their affairs for mutual and general advantage.

For my own part, looking out upon the future, I do not view the process with any misgivings. I could not stop it if I wished; no one can stop it. Like the Mississippi, it just keeps rolling along. Let it roll. Let it roll on full flood, inexorable, irresistible, benignant, to broader lands and better days.

'An iron curtain'

Westminster College, Fulton, Missouri, United States, 5 March 1946

Winston Churchill
on the post-war world and the
division of Europe

Although Churchill had been hailed as a hero by his countrymen for his role in leading Britain to victory in the war against Hitler, they had not seen fit to return the Conservative Party to power in the general election of 1945. Therefore, his visit to Fulton, in the presence of US President Harry S Truman, was as leader of the Opposition. He used the trip to make the most important speech by any politician in the immediate post-war period, a speech from which many historians date the beginning of the Cold War. Britain and the United States were in the process of changing enemies: from the Germans, defeated and de-Nazified, to the Soviet Union, the recent ally whose ruthless occupation of Eastern Europe had, in the eyes of Churchill and many others, replaced one brutal tyranny with another.

The speech is another masterpiece of Churchillian rhetoric, displaying yet again the power of his phrase-making – the 'iron curtain' and 'the special relationship' having both entered the language. Ironically, much of enslaved Eastern Europe was in that position because of the careless concession of lands and spheres of influence to Stalin during the wartime 'big three' conferences, in which Churchill was one of the main players.

The 'iron curtain' would not finally be lifted until the early 1990s, as the Eastern European countries under Soviet sway followed the lead of East Germany in the autumn of 1989, and demanded freedom.

‘ I am glad to come to Westminster College this afternoon, and am complimented that you should give me a degree. The name 'Westminster' is somehow familiar to me.

I seem to have heard of it before. Indeed, it was at Westminster that I received a very large part of my education in politics, dialectic, rhetoric, and one or two other things. In fact we have both been educated at the same, or similar, or, at any rate, kindred establishments.

It is also an honour, perhaps almost unique, for a private visitor to be introduced to an academic audience by the president of the United States. Amid his heavy burdens, duties, and responsibilities – unsought but not recoiled from – the president has travelled a thousand miles to dignify and magnify our meeting here today and to give me an opportunity of addressing this kindred nation, as well as my own countrymen across the ocean, and perhaps some other countries too. The president has told you that it is his wish, as I am sure it is yours, that I should have full liberty to give my true and faithful counsel in these anxious and baffling times. I shall certainly avail myself of this freedom, and feel the more right to do so because any private ambitions I may have cherished in my younger days have been satisfied beyond my wildest dreams. Let me, however, make it clear that I have no official mission or status of any kind, and that I speak only for myself. There is nothing here but what you see.

I can therefore allow my mind, with the experience of a lifetime, to play over the problems which beset us on the morrow of our absolute victory in arms, and to try to make sure with what strength I have that what has been gained with so much sacrifice and suffering shall be preserved for the future glory and safety of mankind.

'The United States stands at … the pinnacle of world power'

The United States stands at this time at the pinnacle of world power. It is a solemn moment for the American democracy. For with primacy in power is also joined an awe inspiring accountability to the future. If you look around you, you must feel not only the sense of duty done but also you must feel anxiety lest you fall below the level of achievement. Opportunity is here now, clear and shining for both our countries. To reject it or ignore it or fritter it away will bring upon us all the long reproaches of the after-time. It is necessary that constancy of mind, persistency of purpose, and the grand simplicity of decision shall guide and rule the conduct of the English-speaking peoples in peace as they did in war. We must, and I believe we shall, prove ourselves equal to this severe requirement.

When American military men approach some serious situation they are wont to write at the head of their directive the words 'over-all strategic concept'. There is wisdom in this, as it leads to clarity of thought. What then is the over-all strategic concept which we should inscribe today? It is nothing less than the safety and welfare, the freedom and progress, of all the homes and families of all the men and women in all the lands. And here I speak partic-ularly of the myriad cottage or apartment homes where the wage-earner strives amid the accidents and difficulties of life to guard his wife and children from privation and bring the family up in the fear of the Lord, or upon ethical conceptions which often play their potent part.

To give security to these countless homes, they must be shielded from the two giant marauders, war and tyranny. We all know the frightful disturbances in which the ordinary family is plunged when the curse of war swoops down upon the breadwinner and those for whom he works and contrives. The awful ruin of Europe, with all its vanished glories, and of large parts of Asia glares us in the eyes. When the designs of wicked men or the aggressive urge of mighty states dissolve over large areas the frame of civilised society, humble folk are confronted with difficulties with which they cannot cope. For them all is distorted, all is broken, even ground to pulp.

When I stand here this quiet afternoon I shudder to visualise what is actually happening to millions now and what is going to happen in this period when famine stalks the earth. None can compute what has been called 'the unestimated sum of human pain'. Our supreme task and duty is to guard the homes of the common people from the horrors and miseries of another war. We are all agreed on that.

'Not merely a cockpit in a Tower of Babel'

Our American military colleagues, after having proclaimed their 'over-all strategic concept' and computed available resources, always proceed to the next step–namely, the method. Here again there is widespread agreement. A world organisation has already been erected for the prime purpose of preventing war, UNO [United Nations Organisation], the successor of the League of Nations, with the decisive addition of the United States and all that that means, is already at work. We must make sure that its work is fruitful, that it is a reality and not a sham, that it is a force for action, and not merely a frothing of words, that it is a true temple of peace in which the shields of many nations can some day be hung up, and not merely a cockpit in a Tower of Babel. Before we cast away the solid assurances of national armaments for self-preservation we must be certain that our temple is built, not upon shifting sands or quagmires, but upon the rock. Anyone can see with his eyes open that our path will be difficult and also long, but if we persevere together as we did in the two world wars – though not, alas, in the interval between them – I cannot doubt that we shall achieve our common purpose in the end.

I have, however, a definite and practical proposal to make for action. Courts and magistrates may be set up but they cannot function without sheriffs and constables. The United Nations Organisation must immediately begin to be equipped with an international armed force. In such a matter we can only go step by step, but we must begin now. I propose that each of the Powers and States should be invited to delegate a certain number of air squadrons to the service of the world organisation. These squadrons would be trained and prepared in their own countries, but would move around in rotation from one country to another. They would wear the uniform of their own countries but with different badges. They would not be required to act against their own nation, but in other respects they would be directed by the world organisation. This might be started on a modest scale and would grow as confidence grew. I wished to see this done after the First World War, and I devoutly trust it may be done forthwith.

'The secret knowledge or experience of the atomic bomb'

It would nevertheless be wrong and imprudent to entrust the secret knowledge or experience of the atomic bomb, which the United States, Great Britain, and Canada now share, to the world organisation, while it is still in its infancy. It would be criminal madness to cast it adrift in this still agitated and un-united world. No one in any country has slept less well in their beds because this knowledge, and the method and the raw materials to apply it, are at present largely retained in American hands. I do not believe we should all have slept so soundly had the positions been reversed and if some Communist or

THE UNITED NATIONS

1942
The first formal use of the term 'United Nations' (1 Jan.): the Declaration by the United Nations is signed by 26 countries (plus 21 more before the end of World War II), committing the Allies to the principles of the Atlantic Charter; the term becomes synonymous during the war with the Allies.

1944
Representatives of France, the Republic of China (Taiwan), UK, USA and the Soviet Union (subsequently the five permanent members of the Security Council) meet in Washington, D.C., to discuss the setting up of the organisation (Aug.–Oct.).

1945
The UN Conference on International Organisations begins in San Francisco (25 April); 50 nations that were at the conference, plus Poland, sign the UN Charter (25 June); the UN comes into existence (24 Oct.).

1971
The seat for the Republic of China (Taiwan) is transferred to the People's Republic of China.

2006
Newly independent Montenegro joins the UN, taking its membership to 192 countries.

neo-Fascist state monopolised for the time being these dread agencies. The fear of them alone might easily have been used to enforce totalitarian systems upon the free democratic world, with consequences appalling to human imagination. God has willed that this shall not be and we have at least a breathing space to set our house in order before this peril has to be encountered: and even then, if no effort is spared, we should still possess so formidable a superiority as to impose effective deterrents upon its employment, or threat of employment, by others. Ultimately, when the essential brotherhood of man is truly embodied and expressed in a world organisation with all the necessary practical safeguards to make it effective, these powers would naturally be confided to that world organisation.

'The great principles of freedom'

Now I come to the second danger of these two marauders which threatens the cottage, the home, and the ordinary people – namely, tyranny. We cannot be blind to the fact that the liberties enjoyed by individual citizens throughout the British Empire are not valid in a considerable number of countries, some of which are very powerful. In these states control is enforced upon the common people by various kinds of all-embracing police governments. The power of the state is exercised without restraint, either by dictators or by compact oligarchies operating through a privileged party and a political police. It is not our duty at this time when difficulties are so numerous to interfere forcibly in the internal affairs of countries which we have not conquered in war. But we must never cease to proclaim in fearless tones the great principles of freedom and the rights of man which are the joint inheritance of the English-speaking world and which through Magna Carta, the Bill of Rights, the Habeas Corpus, trial by jury, and the English common law find their most famous expression in the American Declaration of Independence.

All this means that the people of any country have the right, and should have the power by constitutional action, by free unfettered elections, with secret ballot, to choose or change the character or form of government under which they dwell; that freedom of speech and thought should reign; that courts of justice, independent of the executive, unbiased by any party, should administer laws which have received the broad assent of large majorities or are consecrated by time and custom. Here are the title deeds of freedom which should lie in every cottage home. Here is the message of the British and American peoples to mankind. Let us preach what we practise – let us practise what we preach.

I have now stated the two great dangers which menace the homes of the people: war and tyranny. I have not yet spoken of poverty and privation which are in many cases the prevailing anxiety. But if the dangers of war and tyranny are removed, there is no doubt that science and co-operation can bring in the next few years to the world, certainly in the next few decades newly taught in the sharpening school of war, an expansion of material well-being beyond anything that has yet occurred in human experience. Now, at this sad and breathless moment, we are plunged in the hunger and distress which are the aftermath of our stupendous struggle; but this will pass and may pass quickly, and there is no reason except human folly or sub-human crime which should deny to all the nations the inauguration and enjoyment of an age of plenty. I have often used words which I learned fifty years ago from a great Irish-American orator, a friend of mine, Mr Bourke Cockran. 'There is enough for all. The earth is a generous mother; she will provide in plentiful abundance food for all her children if they will but cultivate her soil in justice and in peace.' So far I feel that we are in full agreement.

'This means a special relationship'

Now, while still pursuing the method of realising our overall strategic concept, I come to the crux of what I have travelled here to say. Neither the sure prevention of war, nor the continuous rise of world organisation will be gained without what I have called the fraternal association of the English-speaking peoples. This means a special relationship between the British Commonwealth and empire and the United States. This is no time for generalities, and I will venture to be precise. Fraternal association requires not only the growing friendship and mutual understanding between our two vast but kindred systems of society, but the continuance of the intimate relationship between our military advisers, leading to common study of potential dangers, the similarity of weapons and manuals of instructions, and to the interchange of officers and cadets at technical colleges. It should carry with it the continuance of the present facilities for mutual security by the joint use of all Naval and Air Force bases in the possession of either country all over the world. This would perhaps double the mobility of the American Navy and Air Force. It would greatly expand that of the British Empire Forces and it might well lead, if and as the world calms down, to important financial savings. Already we use together a large number of islands; more may well be entrusted to our joint care in the near future.

... There is however an important question we must ask ourselves. Would a special relationship between the United States and the British Commonwealth be inconsistent with our over-riding loyalties to the World Organisation? I reply that, on the contrary, it is probably the only means by which that organisation will achieve its full stature and strength. There are already the special United States relations with Canada which I have just mentioned, and there are the special relations between the United States and the South American republics. We British have our twenty years Treaty of Collaboration and Mutual Assistance with Soviet Russia. I agree with Mr Bevin, the foreign secretary of Great Britain, that it might well be a fifty years treaty so far as we are concerned. We aim at nothing but mutual assistance and collaboration. The British have an alliance with Portugal unbroken since 1384, and which produced fruitful results at critical moments in the late war. None of these clash with the general interest of a world agreement, or a world organisation; on the contrary they help it. 'In my father's house are many mansions.' Special associations between members of the United Nations which have no aggressive point against any other country, which harbour no design incompatible with the Charter of the United Nations, far from being harmful, are beneficial and, as I believe, indispensable.

'The dark ages may return'

I spoke earlier of the Temple of Peace. Workmen from all countries must build that temple. If two of the workmen know each other particularly well and are old friends, if their families are inter-mingled, and if they have 'faith in each other's purpose, hope in each other's future and charity towards each other's shortcomings' – to quote some good words I read here the other day – why cannot they work together at the common task as friends and partners? Why cannot they share their tools and thus increase each other's working powers? Indeed they must do so or else the temple may not be built, or, being built, it may collapse, and we shall all be proved again unteachable and have to go and try to learn again for a third time in a school of war, incomparably more rigorous than that from which we have just been released.

The dark ages may return, the Stone Age may return on the gleaming wings of science, and what might now shower immeasurable material blessings upon mankind, may even bring about its total destruction. Beware, I say; time may be short. Do not let us take the course of allowing events to drift along until it is too late. If there is to be a fraternal association of the kind I have described, with all the extra strength and security which both our countries can derive from it, let us make sure that that great fact is known to the world, and that it plays its part in steadying and stabilising the foundations of peace. There is the path of wisdom. Prevention is better than cure.

A shadow has fallen upon the scenes so lately lighted by the Allied victory. Nobody knows what Soviet Russia and its Communist international organisation intends to do in the immediate future, or what are the limits, if any, to their expansive and proselytising tendencies. I have a strong admiration and regard for the valiant Russian people and for my wartime comrade, Marshal Stalin. There is deep sympathy and goodwill in Britain – and I doubt not here also – towards the peoples of all the Russias and a resolve to persevere through many differences and rebuffs in establishing lasting friendships. We understand the Russian need to be secure on her western frontiers by the removal of all possibility of German aggression. We welcome Russia to her rightful place among the leading nations of the world. We welcome her flag upon the seas. Above all, we welcome constant, frequent and growing contacts between the Russian people and our own people on both sides of the Atlantic. It is my duty however, for I am sure you would wish me to state the facts as I see them to you, to place before you certain facts about the present position in Europe.

'An iron curtain has descended across the Continent'

From Stettin in the Baltic to Trieste in the Adriatic, an iron curtain has descended across the Continent. Behind that line lie all the capitals of the ancient states of Central and Eastern Europe. Warsaw, Berlin, Prague, Vienna, Budapest, Belgrade, Bucharest and Sofia, all these famous cities and the populations around them lie in what I must call the Soviet sphere, and all are subject in one form or another, not only to Soviet influence but to a very high and, in many cases, increasing measure of control from Moscow. Athens alone – Greece with its immortal glories – is free to decide its future at an election under British, American and French observation. The Russian-dominated Polish government has been encouraged to make enormous and wrongful inroads upon Germany, and mass expulsions of millions of Germans on a scale grievous and undreamed of are now taking place. The Communist Parties, which were very small in all these eastern states of Europe, have been raised to pre-eminence and power far beyond their numbers and are seeking everywhere to obtain totalitarian control. Police governments are prevailing in nearly every case, and so far, except in Czechoslovakia, there is no true democracy.

Turkey and Persia are both profoundly alarmed and disturbed at the claims which are being made upon them and at the pressure being exerted by the Moscow government. An attempt is being made by the Russians in Berlin to build up a quasi-Communist Party in their zone of occupied Germany by showing special favours to groups of left-wing German leaders. At the end of the fighting last June, the American and British Armies withdrew westwards, in accordance with an earlier agreement, to a depth at some points of 150 miles upon a front of nearly four hundred miles, in order to allow our Russian allies to occupy this vast expanse of territory which the Western democracies had conquered.

If now the Soviet government tries, by separate action, to build up a pro-Communist Germany in their areas, this will cause new serious difficulties in the British and American zones, and will give the defeated Germans the power of putting themselves up to auction between the Soviets and the Western democracies. Whatever conclusions may be drawn from these facts – and facts they are – this is certainly not the liberated Europe we fought to build up. Nor is it one which contains the essentials of permanent peace.

'Walk forward in sedate and sober strength'

The safety of the world requires a new unity in Europe, from which no nation should be permanently outcast. It is from the quarrels of the strong parent races in Europe that the world wars we have witnessed, or which occurred in former times, have sprung. Twice in our own lifetime we have seen the United States, against their wishes and their traditions, against arguments, the force of which it is impossible not to comprehend, drawn by irresistible forces, into these wars in time to secure the victory of the good cause, but only after frightful slaughter and devastation had occurred. Twice the United States has had to send several millions of its young men across the Atlantic to find the war; but now war can find any nation, wherever it may dwell between dusk and dawn. Surely we should work with conscious purpose for a grand pacification of Europe, within the structure of the United Nations and in accordance with its Charter. That I feel is an open cause of policy of very great importance.

'Let no man underrate the abiding power of the British empire and Commonwealth'

In front of the iron curtain which lies across Europe are other causes for anxiety. In Italy the Communist Party is seriously hampered by having to support the Communist-trained Marshal Tito's claims to former Italian territory at the head of the Adriatic. Nevertheless the future of Italy hangs in the balance. Again one cannot imagine a regenerated Europe without a strong France. All my public life I have worked for a strong France and I never lost faith in her destiny, even in the darkest hours. I will not lose faith now. However, in a great number of countries, far from the Russian frontiers and throughout the world, Communist fifth columns are established and work in complete unity and absolute obedience to the directions they receive from the Communist centre. Except in the British Commonwealth and in the United States where Communism is in its infancy, the Communist Parties or fifth columns constitute a growing challenge and peril to Christian civilisation. These are sombre facts for anyone to have to recite on the morrow of a victory gained by so much splendid comradeship in arms and in the cause of freedom and democracy; but we should be most unwise not to face them squarely while time remains.

... Let no man underrate the abiding power of the British empire and Commonwealth. Because you see the 46 millions in our island harassed about their food supply, of which they only grow one half, even in war-time, or because we have difficulty in restarting our industries and export trade after six years of passionate war effort, do not suppose that we shall not come through these dark years of privation as we have come through the glorious years of agony, or that half a century from now, you will not see 70 or 80 millions of Britons spread about the world and united in defence of our traditions, our way of life, and of the world causes which you and we espouse. If the population of the English-speaking Commonwealths be added to that of the United States with all that such co-operation implies in the air, on the sea, all over the globe and in science and in industry, and in moral force, there will be no quivering, precarious balance of power to offer its temptation to ambition or adventure. On the contrary, there will be an overwhelming assurance of security. If we adhere faithfully to the Charter of the United Nations and walk forward in sedate and sober strength seeking no one's land or treasure, seeking to lay no arbitrary control upon the thoughts of men; if all British moral and material forces and convictions are joined with your own in fraternal association, the high-roads of the future will be clear, not only for us but for all, not only for our time, but for a century to come.

'Never had
it so good'

Bedford, 20 July 1957

Harold Macmillan

on the dangers of
overheating in the
economy

Harold Macmillan, later 1st Earl of Stockton (1894–1986), made much of being a crofter's grandson. He was, however, a scion of the notable London publishing house that bore his family name, and after an Eton schooling and Oxford University education married a daughter of the Duke of Devonshire – who spent much of their married life cuckolding him with a fellow MP, Robert Boothby. Macmillan first sat in the Commons for Stockton-on-Tees in industrial northeast England, and his experience of the poverty of his constituents sent him so far to the left of the Conservative Party that he was rumoured during the 1930s to be contemplating joining the Labour Party.

After a good World War II – he became minister resident in North Africa, and was admired by Churchill – he found himself at the top table of the post-war Conservative Party. Once the Party returned to power in 1951, he held a succession of Cabinet posts, including minister of housing (in which he made, and kept, a pledge to build 300,000 council houses), foreign secretary and chancellor of the exchequer. Always an ambitious man, he changed tack halfway through the Suez debacle in the autumn of 1956 and set himself up as one of the main rivals to succeed Sir Anthony Eden. When Eden resigned in January 1957, Macmillan duly 'emerged' ahead of his main challenger, R.A. Butler, as the new leader and prime minister.

The country was shell-shocked after the ill-thought actions and humiliating retreat of the Suez crisis, and its economy seriously damaged. A run on sterling had put the currency at risk of devaluation, the gold reserves were plummeting and the deficit rising. Macmillan was warned by his chancellor, Peter Thorneycroft, that Britain was living way beyond its means, and that inflation was a serious threat to prosperity.

All that is the background to this much-misunderstood speech, which Macmillan made in July 1957, six months after taking office. Far from being a smug and complacent reflection on a country clearly – it seemed – far wealthier than ever before, Macmillan was asking whether the rise in the standard of living could continue at this rate, and subtly trying to warn the country that belts might have to be tightened. Within two months the bank rate had risen from 5 to 7 per cent, and the following January Thorneycroft and his two junior ministers at the treasury all resigned over Macmillan's refusal to demand further spending cuts from the Cabinet. Macmillan famously dismissed that crisis as a 'little local difficulty'.

'We want to re-equip our own factories and farms with the most up-to-date plant and machinery. We want to maintain, and, if we can, improve, our social services. And we must of course play our proper part in defence.

All these things together make up a heavy task, which we have succeeded in meeting over the last six years. We have fulfilled our widespread defence obligations. We have made a great drive for capital investment; at first the emphasis was on house building, because we were so short of accommodation, and then in recent years the surge has been in industrial building. Last year we devoted £3,000 million to fixed capital investment – one-sixth of our national income. We have improved social services. Real expenditure on them, that is the value allowing for the rise in prices, is 10% higher than it was six years ago. We are building hospitals. We are opening new schools. (I remember they used to blame me for keeping back the schools to make way for the houses. It wasn't true even then; and it certainly isn't true now. On average every week in this country ten new schools are opened.) Our technical and technological work is going ahead fast. A £100 million programme it is, over five years, and we need it. Without the expert men and women we cannot handle the new inventions and techniques.

Our general economic prospects are good. The balance of payments prospects are favourable – we look like earning a really worthwhile surplus this year. That is because our exports are holding up well in world markets. In the first half of this year they were 6% higher by value – 7 higher to North America – than a year before. Our invisible earnings too – from shipping, and oil particularly – are doing well. The gold and dollar reserves rose £88 million in the first half of this year. So we have not had to use either the loan we negotiated with the Export/Import Bank or the stand-by credit with the International Monetary Fund, which are both being held in reserve. These increased earnings come from the increasing production of most of our main industries – steel, coal, motor cars – a large part of the increase in output is going to exports or to investment. That is all to the good.

A RECOVERING ECONOMY IN THE 1950s

1950
Wartime petrol rationing ends.

1951
The largest oil refinery in Europe opens at Fawley; prescription charges for dentures and spectacles are introduced to help fund the defence budget (April); the Festival of Britain is opened by George VI (May); the steel industry is nationalised.

1952
Rab Butler introduces an 'austerity' budget (Jan.); the De Havilland Comet – the first jet airliner – makes its maiden flight, from London to Johannesburg (2 May), but two later crash in mid-air (Oct.); Britain tests an atom bomb (Oct.).

1953
The steel industry is denationalised by the Conservative government (July); sugar and sweet rationing ends.

1954
London's gold market reopens after 15 years (March); 14 years of food rationing ends (July).

1955
A motorway construction plan is announced (Jan.), with the first section of the M1 opening in 1959; strikes hit docks, railways and printing presses (May); the Independent Television Authority begins to broadcast.

1956
Petrol rationing is reintroduced (Nov.) as a result of the Suez Crisis (ends May 1957).

1958
The chancellor of the exchequer and two treasury ministers resign, having been prevented by Macmillan from implementing spending cuts (Jan.); the Clean Air Act is introduced (June); the Rent Act frees up rent charges (June).

1959
Britain and seven other countries form the European Free Trade Association (EFTA).

Indeed, let's be frank about it; most of our people have never had it so good. Go around the country, go to the industrial towns, go to the farms, and you will see a state of prosperity such as we have never had in my life time – nor indeed ever in the history of this country.

'Is it too good to last?'

What is beginning to worry some of us is 'Is it too good to be true?', or perhaps I should say 'Is it too good to last?' For, amidst all this prosperity, there is one problem that has troubled us – in one way or another – ever since the war. It's the problem of rising prices. Our constant concern today is – can prices be steadied while at the same time we maintain full employment in an expanding economy? Can we control inflation? This is the problem of our time. It is true that prices have risen less since we took office. It is true that wages, and, in the main, salaries, have more than held their own in the race. Taking the nation as a whole, compared with six years ago, personal incomes are 40% up, and though prices have risen they have only risen by 20%.

I read in the *Daily Mirror* this week a statement which said that the people were worried at 'too small wages chasing too big bills'. Whatever else is true, this isn't true. Wages have risen far beyond prices.

But we must not, and we do not intend to allow these facts to blind us to the dangers. The great mass of the country has for the time being, at any rate, been able to contract out of the effects of rising prices. But they will not be able to contract out for ever, if inflation prices us out of world markets. For, if that happens, we will be back in the old nightmare of unemployment. The older ones among you will know what this meant. I hope the younger ones will never have to learn it. What folly to risk throwing away all that we have gained.

'We may lose the greatest social and economic benefit'

Last year when I was Chancellor I described our position as brilliant but precarious. There must always be a risk, and it is surely the lesson in life not to take too much or press an advantage too far. If we do we may lose the greatest social and economic benefit that has come to us since the war – security.

The Conservative Party is not the party of any class or section. We govern in the interests of the whole nation; and we cannot forget that some sections of our people have not shared in this general prosperity. There are those who live on fixed incomes, including those who have retired from active work. We cannot, as a national party, see their interests sacrificed. The government have a clear duty in this matter and we intend to discharge it.

'Naked into the conference chamber'

Labour Party Conference, Brighton, 3 October 1957

Aneurin Bevan
on the detrimental consequences of
unilateral nuclear disarmament

In the 1950s, with the memory of the nuclear bombs that ended the war with Japan in 1945 still fresh, the Campaign for Nuclear Disarmament became a powerful force on the fringes of British politics: and much of its support came from members of the Labour Party, and from Labour MPs. Aneurin Bevan (1897–1960) had long been associated with the radical Left of his Party. A compelling and outspoken orator from South Wales, he had resigned from Clement Attlee's government in 1950 at the imposition of prescription charges in the National Health Service, of which he had been the principal founder.

For much of the 1950s he and the man who in 1955 became his Party leader, Hugh Gaitskell (whom Bevan characterised as 'a desiccated calculating machine'), led different factions of the Party. They were also greatly dissimilar in background and temperament – Bevan had been a coal miner and acquired a reputation for plain speaking that included, at one point, describing Conservatives as 'lower than vermin'. A rapprochement between him and Gaitskell in 1957, in an attempt to create a united front for Labour in time for the general election of 1959, led to Bevan being appointed shadow foreign secretary.

It was in this capacity that he spoke at the 1957 conference against the growing tide of unilateralism, somewhat to the chagrin of many of his erstwhile adherents. However, such was the force of his rhetoric that he managed to stave off a defeat for the leadership on a Conference motion calling for a unilateralist policy – though one was passed at the 1960 conference, three months after Bevan's death, and just over a year after he had been elected unopposed as deputy leader of the Parliamentary Party.

I do not believe that this Conference ought to resolve all fundamental issues of British international relationships and British foreign policy as an incidental by-product of a resolution. Let me explain what I mean. You may decide in this country unilaterally that you will have nothing to do with experiments, nor with manufacture, nor with use. With none of those sentiments do I disagree, none of them at all. But you can't, can you, if you don't want to be guilty, appear to be benefiting by the products of somebody else's guilt? Let me put it more concretely. You will have to say at once – immediately, remember, not presently – that all the international commitments, all the international arrangements, all the international facilities afforded to your friends and allies must be immediately destroyed. (*Cries of 'Why not?'*) If you say 'Why not?', then say it in the resolution. It is not said there. It has not been said. (*A cry of 'It is implied.'*) Yes, it is implied, but nobody said it. Everybody argued about the horror that the hydrogen bomb is in reality, but what this Conference ought not to do, and I beg them not to do it now, is to decide upon the dismantling of the whole fabric of British international relationships without putting anything in its place, as a by-product of a resolution in which that was never stated at all. I say that that whole question has been hidden. I know many of my comrades believe that unilateral action of that sort will lead other nations immediately to take action of a similar sort. We can say that about the suspension of tests, but can you say it about all the rest?

I saw in the newspapers the other day that some of my actions could be explained only on the basis that I was anxious to become foreign secretary. I am bound to say that is a pretty bitter one (*sic*) to say to me. If I thought for one single moment that that consideration prevented the intelligent appreciation of this problem I would take unilateral action myself, now. Is it necessary to recall to those who said 'Hear, hear' that I myself threw up office a few years ago? And I will not take office under any circumstances to do anything that I do not believe I should do.

'You will send a British foreign secretary ... naked into the conference chamber'

But if you carry this resolution and follow out all its implications and do not run away from it you will send a British foreign secretary, whoever he may be, naked into the conference chamber. Able to preach sermons, of course; he could make good sermons. But action of that sort is not necessarily the way in which you take the menace of this bomb from the world. It might be that action of that sort will still be there available to us if our other actions fail. It is something you can always do. You can always, if the influence you have upon your allies and upon your opponents is not yielding any fruits, take unilateral action of that sort. (*A cry of 'Do it now.'*) 'Do it now', you say. This is the answer I give from the platform. Do it now as a Labour Party conference? You cannot do it now. It is not in your hands to do it. All you can do is pass a resolution. What you are saying is what was said by our friend from Hampstead, that a British foreign secretary gets up in the United Nations, without consultation – mark this; this is a responsible attitude! – without telling any members of the Commonwealth, without concerting with them, that the British Labour movement decides unilaterally that this country contracts out of all its commitments and obligations entered into with other countries and members of the Commonwealth – without consultation at all. And you call that statesmanship? I call it an emotional spasm.

Comrades, if that is what you mean, you ought to have said it, but you have not said it. It has not been said in the resolution at all. It has not been brought out in the debate. It has not been carefully considered. It has all been considered merely as a by-product of an argument about the hydrogen bomb. I am anxious to protect this country from hydrogen bombs.

If we contracted out, if we produced this diplomatic shambles it would not necessarily follow that this country would be safer from the hydrogen bomb. (*Cries of 'Nehru has no bomb.'*) No. Nehru has no bomb, but he has got all the other weapons he wants. Nehru has no bomb, but ask Nehru to disband the whole of his police forces in relation to Pakistan and see what Nehru will tell you.

The main difficulty we are in here is that in this way we shall precipitate a difficult situation with the nations that are now associated with us in a variety of treaties and alliances, most of which I do not like – I would like to substitute for them other treaties more sensible and more civilised and not chaos and a shambles. If any socialist foreign secretary is to have a chance he must be permitted to substitute good policies for bad policies. Do not disarm him diplomatically, intellectually, and in every other way before he has a chance to turn round.

'This country would be poisoned with the rest of mankind'

This country could be destroyed merely as an incident of a war between Russia and the USA. It is not necessary for any bombs to drop on us. If war broke out between the USA and the Soviet Union, this country would be poisoned with the rest of mankind. What we have, therefore, to consider is how far the policies we are considering this morning can exert an influence and a leverage over the policies of the USA and of the Soviet Union.

I do seriously believe in the rejection of the bomb. But that is not the issue. That is what I am telling you. If Resolution 24 only meant that we would have very little difficulty with it. But if Resolution 24 is read with its implications it means that as decent folk you must immediately repudiate all the protection and all the alliances and all the entanglements you have with anybody who uses or possesses or manufactures hydrogen bombs. That is our dilemma. I find it a very, very serious dilemma. This problem is without precedent in the history of the world. I consider that it is not only a question of practical statesmanship; I agree with Frank Cousins▾ and all those who have spoken this morning that it is a high moral question, too.

No nation is entitled to try to exterminate an evil by invoking a greater evil than the one it is trying to get rid of. The hydrogen bomb is, of course, a greater evil than any evil it is intended to meet. But, unfortunately, the USSR and the USA are in possession of this weapon, and we are in danger of being exterminated as a consequence of their rivalries and their antagonisms. What I would like to have is the opportunity of exerting influence upon the policies of those countries, but this is not the way to do it. You do not give us a chance. It was said to me, during the week, 'What is the use of getting up on the platform and saying you are going to stop or suspend the tests?' We have said that already. Are we thinking merely in terms of stronger and stronger resolutions accompanied by no action at all? If I may be permitted to strike a facetious note, it is like the comedian in the music hall who told his wife he was going to give her a bicycle. 'But,' she said, 'you promised me that the week before and the week before last.' He said, 'I'm a man of my word. I will promise it you next week too.' It is no use here, because we have passed a resolution, to pass a stronger one when the weaker one itself has not been started.

I am begging and praying our comrades here to consider the demands they have made because I agree that those who support Resolution No. 24 do it with complete sincerity. They do it because they believe that the resolution embodies their detestation of the bomb. But I am sure

	1939	1942	scientific director is the US physicist J. Robert Oppenheimer.
THE START OF THE ATOMIC AGE	The Einstein–Szilárd letter is sent to President Roosevelt urging research to start on an atomic bomb for fear that Germany will make one first (2 Aug.).	The Manhattan Project is set up by the USA, UK and Canada to develop the first nuclear bomb; work is co-ordinated at a secret laboratory, Los Alamos in New Mexico, and the first	**1945** The world's first atomic bomb is tested successfully near Alamogordo, New Mexico, code-named 'Trinity'

that in your secret hearts you will admit that you have not fully thought out the fact that we are in relations with other countries. I am speaking not only about Great Britain, but the Socialist Party. You are not entitled, I submit, to take action as a socialist government without giving any other members of the Commonwealth any opportunity of considering the implications of the action we ourselves decided to take.

'Technical changes in modern weapons have revolutionised international relationships'

Furthermore, I have tried to make this point and I hope it has been considered. If we decided unilaterally not to make the bomb we should only have been deciding by resolution what would naturally follow from the suspension of tests. Obviously if we decide we will not use the bomb I want you to face up to the fact that unfortunately this sort of weapon is not a weapon you can decide not to use or to use. That is the damnable nature of the bomb. Clem Attlee pointed out in the House of Commons that the great danger of the existence of these deadly weapons is the problem of anticipation. You have already had articles written in the newspapers by soldiers. You had an article the other day in the *Telegraph* in which a soldier pointed out that the decision to use the bomb will never be a decision taken by parliaments; it will not even be a decision taken by Cabinets. It may be a decision taken by an individual man who, acting upon some report of some of his spies, maybe by telephone tapping, will have been made to fear that the other chap is going to drop his bomb. (*A cry of 'Do not give it to him.'*) We do not give it to him. He has got it. And we are not speaking about their bomb.

(*A voice: 'Give an example!'*)

All right: We are endeavouring to. I am endeavouring to face you with the fact that the most important feature of this problem is not what we are going to do in this country, because that lies within our control. What we have to discuss is what is the consequence of the action upon other nations with far more deadly weapons than we have. I do beg and pray the conference to reconsider its mood in this matter, and to try and provide us with a workable policy, with a policy which in the consequence I believe will be more effective in getting rid of the bomb than Resolution 24 if it is carried.

(16 July); an enriched uranium bomb ('Little Boy') is detonated over the Japanese city of Hiroshima (6 Aug.); a plutonium bomb ('Fat Man') is dropped over Nagasaki in Japan (9 Aug.).

1946
The US Atomic Energy Commission is set up, the successor to the Manhattan Project.

1949
The first Soviet atom bomb ('Joe-1') is tested in Kazakhstan (29 Aug.), several years earlier than the USA expected, and espionage is blamed (in Britain, scientist Klaus Fuchs is jailed in March 1950 for passing on secrets); an arms race between the USA and the Soviet Union begins.

1952
Winston Churchill announces that Britain possesses the atom bomb.

In fact I would say this; I would make this statement. I have thought about this very anxiously. I knew this morning that I was going to make a speech that would offend and even hurt many of my friends. Of course. But do you think I am afraid? I shall say what I believe, and I will give the guidance that I think is the true guidance, and I do not care what happens. But I will tell you this, that in my opinion, in carrying out Resolution 24, with all the implications I have pointed out, you will do more to precipitate incidents that might easily lead to third world war – (*Cries of 'Rubbish', 'Oh', and 'Shame'*). Just listen. Just consider for a moment all the little nations running one here and one there, one running to Russia the other running to the USA, all once more clustering under the castle wall, this castle wall, or the other castle wall, because in that situation before anything else would have happened the world would have been polarised between the Soviet Union on the one side and the USA on the other. It is against that deadly dangerous negative polarisation that we would have been fighting for years. We want to have the opportunity of interposing between those two giants modifying, moderating, and mitigating influences. We have been delighted because other stations are beginning to take more and more independent stands. We are delighted because the Iron Curtain has been becoming more and more pliable. We are delighted because nations of different political complexions are arising. We are delighted because the texture of international relationships is changing. When I met Krushchev a few days ago I told him that as a Marxist he should understand that just as technical changes in society bring about revolutions in social relationships so the technical changes in modern weapons have revolutionised international relationships.

'I am deeply convinced that you are wrong'

I am convinced, profoundly convinced, that nothing would give more anxiety to many people who do not share our political beliefs than if the British nation disengaged itself from its obligations and prevented itself from influencing the course of international affairs. I know that you are deeply convinced that the action that you suggest is the most effective way of influencing international affairs. I am deeply convinced that you are wrong. It is therefore not a question of who is in favour of the hydrogen bomb and who is against the hydrogen bomb, but a question of what is the most effective way of getting the damn thing destroyed.

♥ General secretary of the Transport and General Workers' Union 1956–69, and minister of technology in Labour government 1964–6.

'This affair at Hola Camp'

House of Commons, London, 28 July 1959

Enoch Powell
on the treatment of suspected
Mau Mau in Kenya

Enoch Powell (1912–98) had already had two distinguished careers before entering politics. As Professor of Greek at the University of Sydney he had, aged 25 at his appointment, been the youngest professor in the Commonwealth. He joined the Army as a private soldier on the outbreak of war in 1939 and by 1944, aged 32, had become a brigadier on the staff in India.

On demobilisation in 1946 Powell went to work in the Conservative Research Department, under the patronage of R.A. Butler, along with such future luminaries of the Party as Iain Macleod and Reginald Maudling. Entering Parliament as part of the celebrated intake of 1950, he found his progress slow, partly because of his uncompromising manner and unclubbability, and partly because of his fastidiousness in declining office when he felt it not commensurate with either his principles or abilities.

Having resigned as a treasury minister in January 1958 over Harold Macmillan's refusal to cut public spending, he was on the back benches at the time when the Commons debated the beating to death of Mau Mau detainees at the Hola internment camp in Kenya. Powell's adamant view that the government could not operate civilised standards in Britain while countenancing uncivilised standards in the colonies deeply moved the House of Commons, which, although he spoke at 1.30am, was still well attended. The *Daily Telegraph* reported that 'as Mr Powell sat down, he put his hand across his eyes. His emotion was justified, for he had made a great and sincere speech.' Denis Healey, later defence secretary and chancellor of the exchequer, and one of the few contemporaries of Powell in the Commons who could claim to be an intellectual equal, said it was one of the finest speeches he ever heard in the Commons. Its humanity and logic moved the House and had a marked effect on colonial policy at a time when the move towards independence for colonies was gathering pace. The marked lack of racism that it displayed was conveniently forgotten by Powell's many critics after his so-called 'Rivers of Blood' speech nine years later (see page 239), when he was routinely execrated as a bigot. Powell himself thought this to be one of the two best speeches he ever made, the other being in the Commons in 1953 on the Royal Titles Bill.

' I am as certain of this as I am of anything, that my right hon. friend the secretary of state' from the beginning to the end of this affair is without any jot or title of blame for what happened in Kenya, that he could not be expected to know, that it could not be within the administrative conventions that these matters should be brought to his attention before or during the execution. When I say my right hon. friend was in this matter utterly and completely blameless, that is of a piece with his administration of his high office generally, which has been the greatest exercise of the office of colonial secretary in modern times. It is in the name of that record, it is in the name of his personal blamelessness, that I beg of him to ensure that the responsibility is recognised and carried where it properly belongs, and is seen to belong.

I have heard it suggested that there were circumstances surrounding this affair at Hola Camp which, it is argued, might justify the passing over of this responsibility – which might justify one in saying, 'Well, of course, strictly speaking, that is quite correct; but then there were special circumstances.'

'I would say that it is a fearful doctrine'

It has been said – and it is a fact – that these eleven men were the lowest of the low; subhuman was the word which one of my hon. friends used. So be it. But that cannot be relevant to the acceptance of responsibility for their death. I know that it does not enter into my right hon. friend's mind that it could be relevant, because it would be completely inconsistent with his whole policy of rehabilitation, which is based upon the assumption that whatever the present state of these men, they can be reclaimed. No one who supports the policy of rehabilitation can argue from the character and condition of these men that responsibility for their death should be different from the responsibility for anyone else's death. In general, I would say that it is a fearful doctrine, which must recoil upon the heads of those who pronounce it, to stand in judgment on a fellow human-being and to say, 'Because he was such-and-such, therefore the consequences which would otherwise flow from his death shall not flow.'

It is then said that the morale of the prison service, the morale of the whole colonial service, is above all important and that whatever we say, should have regard to that morale. 'Amen' say I. But is it for the morale of the prison service that those who executed a policy should suffer – whether inadequately or not is another question – and those who authorised it, those to whom they appealed, should be passed over? I cannot believe that that supports the morale of a service.

Going on beyond that, my hon. friend the Member for Leicester, South-East (Mr Peel), reminded the House how proud the colonial

THE MAU MAU REVOLT

1952
The colonial office in London receives the first indication of the seriousness of the insurgency by Kenyan rebels (mainly from the Kikuyu tribe) against British rule and European settlers (17 Aug.); Governor Evelyn Baring declares a state of emergency (20 Oct.), and nearly 100 presumed leaders are arrested the same day, including Jomo Kenyatta, president of the Kenya African Union, who is later imprisoned (1953–61); British troops arrive, and up to 8,000 people are arrested in the first 25 days of the Emergency.

1953
Mau Mau (possibly former servants) kill the white settlers Mr and Mrs Ruck and their son (24 Jan.), and settlers react strongly by dismissing Kikuyu servants; nearly 3,000 rebels attack the loyalist village of Lari, killing 70 (25–26 March).

1954
Nairobi, the capital, is put under military control (24 April).

1956
The last Mau Mau leader, Dedan Kimathi, is captured, effectively ending the uprising.

1959
85 prisoners are marched outside at Hola internment camp; refusing to take orders, they are beaten for 3–4 hours: 11 die and 60 are seriously injured (3 March).

1960
The Kenyan Emergency ends (Jan.).

1963
Kenya gains independence from the UK, with Kenyatta as the first president.

service is of the integrity of its administration and its record. Nothing could be more damaging to the morale of such a service than that there should be a breath or a blemish left upon it. No, sir; that argument from the morale of the prison service and the colonial service stands on its head if what we mean is that therefore the consequences of responsibility should not follow in this case as they would in any other similar case.

Finally it is argued that this is Africa, that things are different there. Of course they are. The question is whether the difference between things there and here is such that the taking of responsibility there and here should be upon different principles. We claim that it is our object – and this is something which unites both sides of the House – to leave representative institutions behind us wherever we give up our rule. I cannot imagine that it is a way to plant representative institutions to be seen to shirk the acceptance and the assignment of responsibility, which is the very essence of responsible government.

'We must be consistent with ourselves everywhere'

Nor can we ourselves pick and choose where and in what parts of the world we shall use this or that kind of standard. We cannot say, 'We will have African standards in Africa, Asian standards in Asia and perhaps British standards here at home.' We have not that choice to make. We must be consistent with ourselves everywhere. All government, all influence of man upon man, rests upon opinion. What we can do in Africa, where we still govern and where we no longer govern, depends upon the opinion which is entertained of the way in which this country acts and the way in which Englishmen act. We cannot, we dare not, in Africa of all places, fall below our own highest standards in the acceptance of responsibility.

♥ Alan Lennox-Boyd (1904–83), colonial secretary 1954–9.

'The wind of change'

Cape Town, South Africa, 3 February 1960

Harold Macmillan
on the rise of black African
nationalist feeling

Harold Macmillan left London at New Year 1960 for a six-week tour of Africa, and chose to use his visit to South Africa – then becoming an international pariah because of apartheid (this was the year of the Sharpeville massacre) – to lecture his hosts on the need to accept black nationalism. This speech was the first public recognition by a British leader of the legitimacy of black nationalist movements in Africa: it also signalled a loss of patience with South Africa over its apartheid policies – though the parliamentarians who applauded Macmillan warmly when he spoke seem not to have recognised that. However much the speech might have offended some of them when they read the text of it at their leisure, it offended perhaps more the Right of his own Party at home, who were reconciled neither to the final winding-up of the British empire (a process that had begun in 1947 with Indian independence) nor to the notion that a black person was capable of running his own affairs.

Macmillan spoke on a Monday, and the outrage his speech caused to his more traditional colleagues led to the formation of the Monday Club. The fact was, though, that neither Macmillan nor his colleagues had the will to argue for the maintenance of a colonial empire, and the country could no longer afford to run and police one. Macmillan said of this event: 'I had approached this ordeal with much trepidation and I had taken the greatest care in the preparation of my speech.' Macmillan's biographer, Sir Alistair Horne, claims the speech was written by Britain's high commissioner to South Africa, Sir John Maud; he also recounts that so nervous was Macmillan before he made it that he was physically sick.

It is, as I have said, a special privilege for me to be here in 1960 when you are celebrating what I might call the golden wedding of the Union [of South Africa]. At such a time it is natural and right that you should pause to take stock of your position, to look back at what you have achieved, to look forward to what lies ahead. In the fifty years of their nationhood the people of South Africa have built a strong economy founded upon a healthy agriculture and thriving and resilient industries. No one could fail to be impressed with the immense material progress which has been achieved. That all this has been accomplished in so short a time is a striking testimony to the skill, energy and initiative of your people. We in Britain are proud of the contribution we have made to this remarkable achievement. Much of it has been financed by British capital …

Sir, as I have travelled round the Union I have found everywhere, as I expected, a deep preoccupation with what is happening in the rest of the African continent. I understand and sympathise with your interest in these events, and your anxiety about them. Ever since the break-up of the Roman empire one of the constant facts of political life in Europe has been the emergence of independent nations. They have come into existence over the centuries in different forms, with different kinds of government, but all have been inspired by a deep, keen feeling of nationalism, which has grown as the nations have grown.

'We have seen the awakening of national consciousness'

In the 20th century, and especially since the end of the war, the processes which gave birth to the nation states of Europe have been repeated all over the world. We have seen the awakening of national consciousness in peoples who have for centuries lived in dependence upon some other power. Fifteen years ago this movement spread through Asia. Many countries there of different races and civilisations pressed their claim to an independent national life. Today the same thing is happening in Africa, and the most striking of all the impressions I have formed since I left London a month ago is of the strength of this African national consciousness. In different places it takes different forms, but it is happening everywhere. The wind of change is blowing through this continent, and, whether we like it or not, this growth of national consciousness is a political fact. We must all accept it as a fact, and our national policies must take account of it.

Of course, you understand this better than anyone. You are sprung from Europe, the home of nationalism, and here in Africa you have yourselves created a new nation. Indeed, in the history of our times yours will be recorded as the first of the African nationalisms, and this tide of national consciousness which is now rising in Africa is a fact for which you and we and the other nations of the western world are ultimately responsible. For its causes are to be found in the achievements of western civilisation, in the pushing forward of the frontiers of knowledge, in the applying of science in the service of human needs, in the expanding of food production, in the speeding and multiplying of the means of communication, and perhaps, above all, the spread of education.

As I have said, the growth of national consciousness in Africa is a political fact, and we must accept it as such. That means, I would judge, that we must come to terms with it. I sincerely believe that if we cannot do so we may imperil the precarious balance between the East and West on which the peace of the world depends. The world today is divided into three main groups. First there are what we call the Western Powers. You in South Africa and we in Britain belong to this group, together with our friends and allies in other parts of the Commonwealth. In the United States of America and in Europe we call it the Free World. Secondly there are the Communists – Russia and her satellites in Europe and China whose population will rise by the end of the next ten years to the staggering total of 800,000,000. Thirdly, there are those parts of the world whose people are at present uncommitted either to Communism or to our Western ideas.

'Let me be very frank with you'

In this context we think first of Asia and then of Africa. As I see it the great issue in this second half of the twentieth century is whether the uncommitted peoples of Asia and Africa will swing to the East or to the West. Will they be drawn into the Communist camp? Or will the great experiments in self-government that are now being made in Asia and Africa, especially within the Commonwealth, prove so successful, and by their example so compelling, that the balance will come down in favour of freedom and order and justice?

The struggle is joined, and it is a struggle for the minds of men. What is now on trial is much more than our military strength or our diplomatic and administrative skill. It is our way of life. The uncommitted nations want to see before they choose.

What can we show them to help them choose right? Each of the independent members of the Commonwealth must answer that question for itself. It is a basic principle of our modern Commonwealth that we respect each other's sovereignty in matters of internal policy. At the same time, we must recognise that in this shrinking world in which we live today the internal policies of one nation may have effects outside it. We may sometimes be tempted to say to each other, 'Mind your own business', but in these days I would myself expand the old saying so that it runs: 'Mind your own business, but mind how it affects my business, too.'

Let me be very frank with you, my friends. What governments and parliaments in the United Kingdom have done since the war in according independence to India, Pakistan, Ceylon, Malaya and Ghana, and what they will do for Nigeria and other countries now nearing independence, all this, though we take full and sole responsibility for it, we do in the belief that it is the only way to establish the future of the Commonwealth and of the Free World on sound foundations. All this of course is also of deep and close concern to you for nothing we do in this small world can be done in a corner or remain hidden. What we do today in West, Central and East Africa becomes known tomorrow to everyone in the Union, whatever his language, colour or traditions. Let me assure you, in all friendliness, that we are well aware of this and that we have acted and will act with full knowledge of the responsibility we have to all our friends.

> *'A society in which individual merit and individual merit alone is the criterion for a man's advancement'*

Nevertheless I am sure you will agree that in our own areas of responsibility we must each do what we think right. What we think right derives from a long experience both of failure and success in the management of our own affairs. We have tried to learn and apply the lessons of our judgment of right and wrong. Our justice is rooted in the same soil as yours – in Christianity and in the rule of law as the basis of a free society. This experience of our own explains why it has been our aim in the countries for which we have borne responsibility, not only to raise the material standards of living, but also to create a society which respects the rights of individuals, a society in which men are given the opportunity to grow to their full stature – and that must in our view include the opportunity to have an increasing share in political power and responsibility, a society in which individual merit and individual merit alone is the criterion for a man's advancement, whether political or economic.

Finally in countries inhabited by several different races it has been our aim to find means by which the community can become more of a community, and fellowship can be fostered between its various parts. This problem is by no means confined to Africa. Nor is it always a problem of a European minority. In Malaya, for instance, though there are Indian and European minorities, Malays and Chinese make up the great bulk of the population, and the Chinese are not much fewer in numbers than the Malays. Yet these two peoples must learn to live together in harmony and unity and the strength of Malaya as a nation will depend on the different contributions which the two races can make.

BRITISH DECOLONISATION IN AFRICA

1957
The Gold Coast (Ghana) is the first sub-Saharan European colony to become independent.

1960
Nigeria and British Somaliland become independent.

1961
Tanganyika (a German colony under British trusteeship since 1918) and Sierra Leone gain independence; South Africa becomes a republic under the National Party and withdraws from the Commonwealth, returning in 1995 after the end of white minority rule.

1962
Uganda becomes independent.

1963
Kenya and Zanzibar achieve independence.

1964
Zanzibar merges with Tanganyika to form Tanzania; Northern Rhodesia (Zambia) and Nyasaland (Malawi) gain independence.

1965
Gambia gains independence; the colonial government of Southern Rhodesia (Zimbabwe) declares unilateral independence to preserve white minority rule, and fights a 15-year insurgency by black nationalists until accepting the end of the white regime in 1980.

1966
Bechuanaland (Botswana) and Basutoland (Lesotho) gain independence.

1968
Swaziland becomes independent.

'I have thought you would wish me to state plainly and with full candour the policy for which we in Britain stand'

The attitude of the United Kingdom towards this problem was clearly expressed by the foreign secretary, Mr Selwyn Lloyd, speaking at the United Nations General Assembly on 17 September 1959. These were his words:

> In those territories where different races or tribes live side by side the task is to ensure that all the people may enjoy security and freedom and the chance to contribute as individuals to the progress and well being of these countries. We reject the idea of any inherent superiority of one race over another. Our policy therefore is non-racial. It offers a future in which Africans, Europeans, Asians, the peoples of the Pacific and others with whom we are concerned, will all play their full part as citizens in the countries where they live, and in which feelings of race will be submerged in loyalty to new nations.

I have thought you would wish me to state plainly and with full candour the policy for which we in Britain stand. It may well be that in trying to do our duty as we see it we shall sometimes make difficulties for you. If this proves to be so we shall regret it. But I know that even so you would not ask us to flinch from doing our duty.

You, too, will do your duty as you see it. I am well aware of the peculiar nature of the problems with which you are faced here in the Union of South Africa. I know the differences between your situation and that of most of the other states in Africa. You have here some three million people of European origin. This country is their home. It has been their home for many generations. They have no other. The same is true of Europeans in Central and East Africa. In most other African states those who have come from Europe have come to work, to contribute their skills, perhaps to teach, but not to make a home.

The problems to which you as members of the Union parliament have to address yourselves are very different from those which face the Parliaments of countries with homogenous populations. These are complicated and baffling problems. It would be surprising if your interpretation of your duty did not sometimes produce very different results from ours in terms of government policies and actions.

'In the world of today this difference of outlook lies between us'

As a fellow member of the Commonwealth it is our earnest desire to give South Africa our support and encouragement, but I hope you won't mind my saying frankly that there are some aspects of your policies which make it impossible for us to do this without being false
to our own deep convictions about the political destinies of free men to which in our own territories we are trying to give effect. I think we ought, as friends, to face together, without seeking to apportion credit or blame, the fact that in the world of today this difference of outlook lies between us.

'*Fight and fight and fight again*'

Labour Party Conference, Scarborough, 6 October 1960

Hugh Gaitskell
on the folly of unilateral nuclear disarmament

In 1960 the argument within the Labour Party about nuclear disarmament (see the earlier speech by Aneurin Bevan) was still raging and, like Bevan before him, the Party leader Hugh Gaitskell (1906–63) was increasingly aware of the damage being done to the Party by its association with unilateralism. Indeed, it would not be until 23 years later, at the time of the cataclysmic electoral defeat for Labour presided over by one of CND's most prominent activists, Michael Foot, that the Party was forced to realise the massive unpopularity with the British public of the policy.

In this brave and controversial speech, Gaitskell – a sophisticated, Winchester and Oxford-educated right-winger who had briefly been chancellor of the exchequer at the end of the Attlee government, and who had succeeded Attlee as leader in 1955 – provoked the wrath of his left wing by associating them with the worst sort of pacifism and allowing it to be inferred (as Conservative politicians would do over the next quarter-century) that a unilateralist Labour would be one depicted as fellow travellers of the Soviet Union, and as a Party unprepared to take the defence of Britain seriously during the Cold War.

Gaitskell lost the vote that day, but the force of his rhetoric and the passion of his conviction played a significant part (together with another powerful speech at the 1961 conference) in having the policy reversed a year later – only for the issue to come to the fore again after the Party's defeat in the 1979 election.

I come to the main issue. The main issue is contained, of course, in paragraph (a): 'A complete rejection of any defence policy based on the threat of the use of strategic or tactical nuclear weapons.' Frank Cousins[v] was asked whether that meant only what the policy statement says, namely, that NATO should change its strategy and should in future put the emphasis upon conventional rather than nuclear weapons of defence, or whether it means – and it is a fair question in the light of all this great argument – that NATO must give up nuclear weapons unilaterally, and whether we must get out of NATO. I leave it to Conference to decide whether we have a clear answer to those questions. We can only judge. We do not know. But we cannot ignore against [sic] the fact that 60 resolutions demanding the withdrawal from NATO supported the Transport and General Workers' resolution.

Now the point about it is this. Either the difference between the policy statement and the Transport and General Workers' resolution is a minor one or it is not. If it is almost negligible, as some of my colleagues believe … if that is the case, how can one explain the determined opposition of the general secretary of the union to the policy statement? I am sure we can expect a great union of this kind to have regard to the need for unity in the Party, and if there are minor points of difference I cannot see the justification either for the resolution or for the opposition to the policy statement.

Perhaps you will say that they are not minor, that they are major differences. All right. I have given you the arguments, and if that is the case, of course we ask for the rejection of the resolution.

There is one other possibility to which I must make reference, because I have read so much about it – that the issue here is not really defence at all but the leadership of this Party ... The place to decide the leadership of this Party is not here but in the Parliamentary Party. I would not wish for one day to remain a leader who had lost the confidence of his colleagues in Parliament. It is perfectly reasonable to try to get rid of somebody, to try to get rid of a man you do not agree with, who you think perhaps is not a good leader. But there are ways of doing this. What would be wrong, in my opinion, and would not be forgiven, is if, in order to get rid of a man, you supported a policy in which you did not wholeheartedly believe, a policy which, as far as the resolution is concerned, is not clear.

'Utterly opposed to unilateralism and neutralism'

Before you take the vote on this momentous occasion, allow me a last word. Frank Cousins has said this is not the end of the problem. I agree with him. It is not the end of the problem because Labour Members of Parliament will have to consider what they do in the House of Commons. What do you expect of them? You know how they voted in June overwhelmingly for the policy statement. It is not in dispute that the vast majority of Labour Members of Parliament are utterly opposed to unilateralism and neutralism. So what do you expect them to do? Change their minds overnight? To go back on the pledges they gave to the people who elected them from their constituencies? And supposing they did do that. Supposing all of us, like well-behaved sheep were to follow the policies of unilateralism and neutralism, what kind of an impression would that make upon the British people? You do not seem to be clear in your minds about it, but I will tell you this. I do not believe that the Labour Members of Parliament are prepared to act as time servers. I do not believe they will do this, and I will tell

THE HYDROGEN BOMB

1950
US President Truman announces plans to develop the hydrogen (or fusion) bomb (31 Jan.), following Soviet testing of the atomic bomb the previous year.

1952
The USA tests the world's first hydrogen device ('Ivy Mike') in the Marshall Islands: it is 1,000 times the size of the atomic bomb dropped on Hiroshima.

1953
The Soviet Union tests its first hydrogen bomb ('Joe 4') in Kazakhstan (12 Aug.): it is not a 'true' hydrogen bomb.

1954
The USA tests a hydrogen bomb proper (the 'Shrimp') at Bikini Atoll in the Marshall Islands: its blast is twice as large as expected and causes the worst radiological disaster in US nuclear history (28 Feb.).

1955
The first Soviet test of a 'true' hydrogen bomb takes place in Kazakhstan: it is the first hydrogen bomb to be dropped from a plane (22 Nov.).

1958
The USA, Soviet Union and UK (a new nuclear power since 1952) declare a temporary testing moratorium; by 1961 it is broken by the Soviet Union.

1961
The Soviet Union tests the largest ever nuclear weapon in Novaya Zemlya in the Arctic Sea (30 Oct.).

1963
The Limited Test Ban Treaty is signed by all nuclear and many non-nuclear states, allowing only underground testing.

you why – because they are men of conscience and honour. People of the so-called Right and so-called Centre have every justification for having a conscience, as well as people of the so-called Left. I do not think they will do this because they are honest men, loyal men, steadfast men, experienced men, with a lifetime of service to the Labour movement.

> *'Do you think that we can become overnight the pacifists, unilateralists and fellow travellers that other people are?*

There are other people too, not in Parliament, in the Party who share our convictions. What sort of people do you think they are? What sort of people do you think we are? Do you think we can simply accept a decision of this kind? Do you think that we can become overnight the pacifists, unilateralists and fellow travellers that other people are? How wrong can you be? As wrong as you are about the attitude of the British people.

In a few minutes the Conference will make its decision. Most of the votes, I know, are predetermined and we have been told what is likely to happen. We know how it comes about. I sometimes think, frankly, that the system we have, by which great unions decide their policy before even their conferences can consider the Executive recommendation is not really a very wise one or a good one. Perhaps in a calmer moment this situation could be looked at.

I say this to you: we may lose the vote today and the result may deal this Party a grave blow. It may not be possible to prevent it, but I think there are many of us who will not accept that this blow need be mortal, who will not believe that such an end is inevitable. There are some of us, Mr Chairman, who will fight and fight and fight again to bring back sanity and honesty and dignity, so that our Party with its great past may retain its glory and its greatness.

> *'The suicidal path of unilateral disarmament'*

It is in that spirit that I ask delegates who are still free to decide how they vote, to support what I believe to be a realistic policy on defence, which yet could so easily have united the great Party of ours, and to reject what I regard as the suicidal path of unilateral disarmament which will leave our country defenceless and alone.

♥ Frank Cousins (1904–86), leader of the Transport and General Workers' Union 1956–69, and minister of technology 1964–6.

'The end of a thousand years of history'

Labour Party Conference, Brighton, 3 October 1962

Hugh Gaitskell
on Britain's status within a converging Europe

In the summer of 1950 there had been a debate in the Commons on whether Britain should seek to join the nascent European Coal and Steel Community, the forerunner of what became the Common Market and what is now the European Union. The Labour majority in the Commons vetoed the idea, and when the Common Market was formed after the Treaties of Rome in 1957 Britain remained on the outside.

During 1962 the Conservative government of Harold Macmillan decided to seek to negotiate with the six founding members – France, West Germany, the Netherlands, Luxembourg, Belgium and Italy – about the possibility of joining. Edward Heath was sent to Europe as the chief negotiator. A passionate pro-European, he would be the man to whom it would fall, as prime minister, eventually to take Britain in, in 1973.

Although most of Hugh Gaitskell's natural supporters on the Centre Right of the Labour Party – notably men such as Roy Jenkins – shared Heath's view, Gaitskell himself was deeply concerned about the loss of sovereignty that would follow on from a decision to join, and the rupture of relations it would cause with the Commonwealth. Many on the Left of his Party saw the Common Market then, and for some decades afterwards, as a capitalist conspiracy that would seek to break down trading barriers and deregulate at the expense of organised Labour.

Gaitskell made this uncompromising speech to his Party at their annual conference, to the intense dismay of people like Jenkins, who recounted in his memoirs that during the ovation that followed it he stood, as a mark of respect to the man, but did not applaud, which might have been taken as a display of sympathy with the speech. Gaitskell's wife Dora famously turned to his colleague Charles Pannell during the ovation and said with concern, 'Charlie, all the wrong people are cheering.' (Labour was to be opposed to the European project until 1988, when the socialist president of the European Commission, Jacques Delors, used a speech to that year's TUC conference to argue that the intervention of Brussels could help liberate Britain, and the British Left, from the yoke of Thatcherism.)

Just over three months after he made this speech Gaitskell was dead, suddenly, from the rare disease lupus. Days later, General Charles de Gaulle, the French president, vetoed Britain's application to join the Six.

The European Economic Community has come to stay. We are not passing judgment on that; it is not our affair. It may well be that political union will follow. It would be the height of folly to deny that therefore in the centre of Western Europe there will in all probability develop a new powerful combination, which may be a single state, and it would, of course, be absurd to question the immense impact that this can have upon world affairs.

Nor would I for one moment question the force of the argument so frequently put that it would be better, since this thing has come to stay, that we should go in now and influence it in the best way.

These are powerful arguments and we would be very foolish to brush them aside. But that is not to say that I, for one, am prepared to accept them as overriding everything else. They must be brought into the balance, but the balancing has not been completed.

'Not all political unions are necessarily good in themselves'

And let me say this: not all political unions are necessarily good in themselves. They must surely be judged by their consequences. If, for instance, it were proposed today that Britain should join a bloc of neutral countries, which I should be strongly against, as you know, and which I think a number of those in favour of our entry into the Common Market would be strongly against, they would not say this was a good thing. If it were proposed that we should join the USA, I do not think it would be universally popular or accepted as necessarily a contribution to world peace.

It all depends, does it not? For if we were presented today with a tremendous choice, whether to go into a world federation under a world government – which alone would finally prevent war – there is not one of us who would say No.

'Is it inward-looking or is it internationally minded?'

So let us have less of this talk of narrow nationalism. It is not a matter of just any union, it is a matter of what are the effects of the union. Is it an aggressive one? Is it damaging to others? Is it selfish? Is it inward-looking or is it internationally minded? Is it power-hungry or is it satisfied? Does it erect barriers as well as pull them down? All these questions have to be asked, if we are honest, before we can decide.

There is another point: I have already said that I understand and deeply sympathise with the people of France and of Germany in their desire to get rid of the conflicts which have so often broken out between them and which indeed are all too fresh in our minds. But I sometimes wonder whether the great problems of the world today are to be found in the unity or disunity of Western Europe. I would have said there were two problems outstanding above all others: the problem of peace and the problems of poverty; the problem of East–West relations that plagues us and the problem of the division of the world into the 'haves' and the 'have nots'.

I know some will say with great sincerity: 'But we recognise that and we believe that by Britain going into Europe a great contribution can be made to these problems.' Maybe so, but it is for them to submit the proof. So far it is hard to be convinced. For although, of course,

Europe has had a great and glorious civilisation, although Europe can claim Goethe and Leonardo, Voltaire and Picasso, there have been evil features in European history too – Hitler and Mussolini and today the attitude of some Europeans to the Congo problem, the attitude of at least one European government to the United Nations. You cannot say what this Europe will be: it has its two faces and we do not know as yet which is the one which will dominate …

But here is another question we have to ask; what exactly is involved in the concept of political union? …

'The end of a thousand years of history'

We must be clear about this: it does mean, if this is the idea, the end of Britain as an independent European state. I make no apology for repeating it. It means the end of a thousand years of history. You may say, 'Let it end', but, my goodness, it is a decision that needs a little care and thought. And it does mean the end of the Commonwealth. How can one really seriously suppose that if the mother country, the centre of the Commonwealth, is a province of Europe (which is what federation means) it could continue to exist as the mother country of a series of independent nations? It is sheer nonsense …

Then we are told that we shall miss the political boat. This is a serious argument. But by a strange paradox I do not think it likely that so long as President de Gaulle remains in charge of affairs in France there are likely to be any very serious political developments within the Six. For he has made his position abundantly plain again and again, and I do not think he is likely to change. He will not give up any jot or tittle of French independence. He will agree to unanimity rules; he will accept arrangements where no one is committed unless all are agreed. But that is all. I do not think we need fear any immediate developments beyond that.

CO-OPERATION IN POST-WAR EUROPE

1946
Winston Churchill calls for a 'kind of United States of Europe' in a speech at Zurich University (19 Jan.).

1949
The North Atlantic Treaty Organisation (NATO) is founded, its signatories being the USA, Canada, Britain, France, Belgium, Denmark, Iceland, Italy, Luxembourg, the Netherlands, Norway and Portugal (4 April); the Council of Europe is established, its statute signed in London by Belgium, Britain, Denmark, France, Ireland, Italy, Luxembourg, the Netherlands, Norway and Sweden (12 May).

1950
The Council of Europe's Convention for the Protection of Human Rights and Fundamental Freedoms is

So all these arguments, I suggest, can be dismissed. Why then is the British government in such a hurry? I think I know the answer. They had a timetable. They wanted to get this thing agreed, to sign the Treaty of Rome, to force the legislation through Parliament, to get the whole thing finished and complete before the British people could have an opportunity to comment upon it.

I repeat again my demand: if when the final terms are known, this Party – the major opposition party, the alternative government of the country – comes to the conclusion that these terms are not good enough, if it is our conviction that we should not enter the Common Market on these terms, so that there is a clear clash of opinion between the two major political groupings in the country, then the only right and proper and democratic thing is to let the people decide the issue.

There is a pretty good precedent, you know: Stanley Baldwin in 1923, after a year in office, decided to introduce tariff reforms. The changes were not on the scale contemplated today, but they were a significant change. He insisted, despite his parliamentary majority, despite the fact that he had only been a year in office, in putting the issue to the country and he was defeated; and that is how the first Labour government came into existence. Well, I wish we had still today in Conservative leaders the kind of honourable approach which used to exist.

'What an odious piece of hypocritical, supercilious, arrogant rubbish'

Of course, Mr Macmillan has given a pledge in his broadcast. He said: 'When we know the final position, then it will be for us here in Britain to decide what to do.' For us here in Britain? Who does he mean? Does he mean the government? Or the Tory Party? Or the British people?

---

signed in Rome – the first international legal instrument safeguarding human rights (4 Nov.).

1951
The Treaty of Paris is signed by the Six (Belgium, France, Italy, Luxembourg, the Netherlands and West Germany), establishing the European Coal and Steel Community (ECSC) (18 April), coming into force in 1952.

1952
The Six sign the European Defence Community (EDC) Treaty in Paris (27 May).

1957
The Six sign the Treaties of Rome, establishing the European Economic Community (EEC) and the European Atomic Energy Community (Euratom) (25 March), which come into force 1 Jan. 1958.

1959
The European Court of Human Rights is established by the Council of Europe in Strasbourg (18 Sept.).

1960
The European Free Trade Association (EFTA) comes into force, its members being Austria, Britain, Denmark, Norway, Portugal, Sweden and Switzerland (3 May).

We are now being told that the British people are not capable of judging this issue – the government knows best; the top people are the only people who can understand it; it is too difficult for the rest. This is the classic argument of every tyranny in history. It begins as a refined, intellectual argument, and it moves into a one-man dictatorship; 'We know best' becomes 'I know best.' We did not win the political battles of the 19th and 20th centuries to have this reactionary nonsense thrust upon us again.

Of course, they extend the argument now, 'We must go in,' they say, 'not because the power of logic, of fact and conclusion suggest that it is to our advantage; we must go in because the people who really understand it, the top people, all want it.' They contradict themselves. If their minds are so arid that they can think of no other arguments, they are a long way down in the intellectual class. But what an odious piece of hypocritical, supercilious, arrogant rubbish is this! And how typical of the kind of Tory propaganda we may expect upon the subject – the appeal to snobbery, 'the big people know best; you had better follow them.' It is all on a par with the argument of inevitability. 'You cannot escape; you must be with it. You must belong, no matter to what you belong.' What a pitiful level of argument we have reached!

'I would rather work for War on Want'

It is said, of course, that the young are in favour of this. The young are idealists; they want change; we know that. We welcome it, and I have no desire to belittle this. But if I were a little younger today, and if I were looking around for a cause, I do not think I should be quite so certain that I would find it within the movement for greater unity in Europe. I think I would find it outside in the world at large. I would rather work for the Freedom from Hunger Campaign; I would rather work for War on Want. I would rather do something to solve world problems. And if we look for examples here, we can find them, as a matter of fact, in the United Kingdom.

Sometimes ugly things happen in that country. But surely we can all of us pay tribute to the fact that today no less than 10,000 young men and women from America are working and living at the same standard of living and speaking the same language after six months of rigorous training, teaching and practising agriculture in the under-developed countries of the world. That is the Peace Corps and it is a fine concept.

You may say: 'You can have this in Europe too.' Yes, but only on our conditions, only if Europe is a greater Europe, only if it is an outward-looking Europe, only if it is dedicated to the cause of relieving world poverty, only if it casts aside the ancient colonialisms, only if it gives up, and shows that it gives up, the narrow nationalism that could otherwise develop.

'We must reject the terms so far negotiated, for they are quite inadequate'

There is that possibility. But there is another side in Europe and in the European Movement – anti-American, anti-Russian, pro-colonial; the story of the Congo and Algeria, the intransigence over Berlin. We do not know which it will be; but our terms present what I believe to be the acid test.

We do not close the door. Our conditions can still be met; they are not impossible; they are not unreasonable. I profoundly hope that they can be met. Nor has the time yet come for a final decision. We are passing judgment today only on what we know so far. That judgment on what we know so far must be unfavourable. We must reject the terms so far negotiated, for they are quite inadequate, they do not fulfil either our own conditions or the government's pledges. But no final decision can be taken until we know the final terms, and when that moment comes we shall judge it in the light of the conditions that we have laid down.

I still hope profoundly that there may be such a change of heart in Europe as will make this possible. I appeal to our socialist comrades to use what influence they have – alas, all too little – in the Brussels negotiations, to bring this about.

'We must stand firm by what we believe'

After all, if we could carry the Commonwealth with us, safeguarded, flourishing, prosperous, if we could safeguard our agriculture, and our EFTA♥ friends were all in it, if we were secure in our employment policy, and if we were able to maintain our independent foreign policy and yet have this wider, looser association with Europe, it would indeed be a great deal. But if this should not prove to be possible, if the Six will not give it to us; if the British government will not even ask for it, then we must stand firm by what we believe, for the sake of Britain, and the Commonwealth and the world; and we shall not flinch from our duty if that moment comes.

♥ European Free Trade Association, of which Britain was then a member.

'*Never glad confident morning again*'

House of Commons, London, 17 June 1963

Nigel Birch
on the implications of the Profumo affair

In March 1963 the secretary of state for war, John Profumo (1915–2006), made a statement to the House of Commons denying accusations of impropriety with a prostitute, Christine Keeler. Miss Keeler had also been intimate with the naval attaché at the Russian Embassy in London, and there had been fears – mainly trumped up by the Labour Party in the hope of causing political embarrassment – that she might have been the conduit of secret information between Profumo and the Russians: this was the height of the Cold War, and the immediate aftermath of the Cuban Missile Crisis.

Profumo's statement was untrue, and in early June he admitted having lied to the House of Commons, immediately resigning both from the government and from Parliament. The whole episode was a massive blow to the government and to the credibility of the prime minister, Harold Macmillan. The Labour Party, but also a number of Macmillan's own MPs on the Conservative benches, rounded on him after Profumo's admission, accusing him of complacency, naivety and downright incompetence.

The Commons debated the issue on 17 June, and this speech by one of Macmillan's sworn adversaries, former secretary of air and treasury minister Nigel Birch (1906–81), was widely perceived at the time to signal the beginning of the end for Macmillan. Although best remembered for Birch's quotation from Browning's *The Lost Leader*, the mordant tone throughout highlights a quite devastating wit and reveals the contempt in which Birch held his Party leader. It is also indicative of the way in which truly independent MPs can give free vent to their feelings – Birch knew he would never be a candidate for office again and, as an extremely wealthy man, was not remotely reliant on any earnings from politics, and therefore had nothing to fear from speaking the truth as he saw it. Macmillan left office four months later, pleading ill health.

In many organs of the press and, to a certain extent, during the latter part of the speech of the Leader of the Opposition, there has been a suggestion that the whole moral health of the nation is at stake and is concerned in this debate. I do not believe that that is true. As far as the moral health of the nation can be affected by any human agency, it is affected by prophets and priests and not by politicians. But this certainly has been one of the best field days that the self-righteous have had since [Charles Stewart] Parnell was cited as co-respondent in O'Shea's divorce case [1890]. In all these miseries, the fact that so many people have found some genuine happiness is something to which, in all charity, we have no right to object.

I must say that I view the activities of the editor of *The Times* with some distaste. (*Mr E. L. Mallalieu (Brigg): 'First-class stuff'.*) He is a man about whom it could have been predicted from his early youth that he was bound to end up sooner or later on the staff of one of the Astor papers.

Nor do I think that this debate is primarily concerned with the security aspect, although that, of course, is important. It was fully dealt with by my right hon. friend the prime minister and, for my part, I am perfectly prepared to accept everything that the prime minister said about security. I believe that what he said was right and true and I am not prepared to criticise my right hon. friend in any way concerning the question of security.

'Is it really credible that the association had no sexual content?'

What seems to me to be the real issue is something much simpler and much narrower. The real issue seems to be whether it was right to accept Profumo's personal statement. There are two aspects here. There is, first, the moral aspect of accepting that part of the statement which Profumo himself subsequently denied and there is a second issue of whether the prime minister in this case acted with good sense and with competence.

I will deal with these two issues in order. First, there is the question of accepting Profumo's statement. We know a deal more now about Profumo than we did at the time of the statement, but we have all known him pretty well for a number of years in this House. I must say that he never struck me as a man at all like a cloistered monk; and Miss Keeler was a professional prostitute.

We have had a legal disquisition from my right hon. and learned friend the Member for Chertsey˅ about the legal etiquette in all this matter, but as someone who does not understand the law, I simply approach it from the basis of what an ordinary person could or would believe. Here one had an active, busy man and a professional prostitute. On his own admission, Profumo had a number of meetings with her, and, if we are to judge by the published statements, she is not a woman who would be intellectually stimulating. Is it really credible that the association had no sexual content? There seems to me to be a certain basic improbability about the proposition that their relationship was purely platonic. What are whores about? Yet Profumo's word was accepted. It was accepted from a colleague. Would

THE EVENTFUL YEAR OF 1963	**1 JANUARY** Martin Luther King delivers his 'I have a dream' speech at the Lincoln Memorial, Washington, D.C.	**18 JANUARY** Hugh Gaitskell, leader of the Labour Party, dies suddenly, to be relaced by Harold Wilson.	closures of less-used lines and stations.
			3 JUNE Pope John XXIII dies and is succeeded by Pope Paul VI.
	14 JANUARY British entry to the European Economic Community is vetoed by France's Charles de Gaulle.	**23 APRIL** The reshaping of British railways (the Beeching Report, or 'Dr Beeching's Axe') leads to wholesale	**5 JUNE** The scandal-ridden John Profumo resigns after lying to Parliament.

that word have been accepted if Profumo had not been a colleague or even if he had been a political opponent? Everyone must, I think, make his own judgment about that.

'That protection must stop short of condoning a lie'

We were told that special consideration ought to have been given to Profumo because he was a colleague. It is certainly true that a prime minister owes his subordinates all the help, comfort and protection that he can give them. But surely that help, that comfort and that protection must stop short of condoning a lie in a personal statement to this House.

Then we are told, in many organs of the press and in many speeches, that special weight ought to have been given to Profumo's words because he was a privy councillor and a secretary of state. I am a privy councillor and I have been a secretary of state, but when I sustained the burden of both offices I did not feel that any sea change had taken place in my personality. I remained what I was, what I had always been and what I am today; and I do not believe it reasonable to suppose that any sea change took place in Mr. Profumo's personality.

He was not a man who was ever likely to tell the absolute truth in a tight corner, and at the time the statement was made he was in a very tight corner indeed. There are people – and it is to the credit of our poor, suffering humanity that it is so – who will tell the whole truth about themselves whatever the consequences may be. Of such are saints and martyrs, but most of us are not like that. Most people in a tight corner either prevaricate – if anyone is interested in prevarication they will find the *locus classicus* in the evidence given before the Bank Rate Tribunal by the Leader of the Opposition [Harold Wilson] – or, as in this case, they lie.

This lie was accepted. I have meditated very deeply on this, and though I have given some rather tough reasons for not accepting that Profumo's statement was credible, I have after deep consideration come to the conclusion that my right hon. friend did absolutely genuinely believe it. I will give my reasons now for taking that view, and these reasons concern the competence and the good sense with which the affair was handled.

30 JULY
Kim Philby, the third man in the Burgess–Maclean spy ring, is given asylum in the Soviet Union.

8 AUGUST
The Great Train Robbery takes place in Buckinghamshire, at that time the biggest theft in British history (£2.6 million).

13 OCTOBER
Beatlemania erupts, at the band's performance at the London Palladium.

16 OCTOBER
Konrad Adenauer resigns as chancellor of West Germany, an office he has held since 1949.

18 OCTOBER
Harold Macmillan resigns as prime minister, being succeeded by Alec Douglas-Home.

22 NOVEMBER
President John F. Kennedy is shot dead in Dallas, Texas, and is succeeded by Vice President Lyndon B. Johnson.

12 DECEMBER
Kenya achieves its independence, with Jomo Kenyatta as president.

Profumo on his own admission had been guilty of a very considerable indiscretion, for a minister at any rate. He was not a particularly successful minister. He had no great plans in this House or in the country. I cannot really see that the prime minister was under any obligation whatever to retain his services, nor do I think that getting rid of Mr Profumo would, in fact, have made the political situation any worse than it then was. On the other hand, to retain him entailed a colossal risk and a colossal gamble. The difficulties and dangers were obvious enough. The press were in full cry. They were in possession of letters. They were hardly likely to have bought letters unless they had something of interest in them. Miss Keeler was pretty certain to turn up again, and if she did, editors were sure to make use of her literary talent. The dangers were enormous, and yet this colossal gamble was taken, and in this gamble, as it seems to me, the possible gain was negligible and the possible loss devastating.

The conclusion I draw from that is that the course adopted by my right hon. friend the prime minister could have been adopted only by someone who genuinely and completely believed the statements of Profumo, and therefore, I absolutely acquit my right hon. friend of any sort of dishonour. On the other hand, on the question of competence and good sense I cannot think that the verdict can be favourable.

'Make way for a much younger colleague'

What is to happen now? I cannot myself see at all that we can go on acting as if nothing had happened. We cannot just have business as usual. I myself feel that the time will come very soon when my right hon. friend ought to make way for a much younger colleague. I feel that that ought to happen. I certainly will not quote at him the savage words of Cromwell, but perhaps some of the words of Browning might be appropriate in his poem on 'The Lost Leader', in which he wrote:

> ... let him never come back to us!
> There would be doubt, hesitation and pain.
> Forced praise on our part – the glimmer of twilight,
> Never glad confident morning again!

'Never glad confident morning again!' – so I hope that the change will not be too long delayed.

Ahead of us we have a Division. We have the statement of my right hon. and noble friend Lord Hailsham♦, in a personal assurance on television, that a whip is not a summons to vote but a summons to attend. I call the whips to witness that I at any rate have attended.

♥ Sir Lionel Heald (1897–1981), attorney-general 1951–4.
♦ Quintin Hogg, 2nd Viscount Hailsham (1907–2001), leader of the House of Lords 1960–3.

'*The white heat of the technological revolution*'

Labour Party Conference, Scarborough, 1 October 1963

Harold Wilson

on the economic potential of technological innovation

Harold Wilson (1916–95) had won the leadership of his Party the previous spring following the sudden death of Hugh Gaitskell. Until it happened, Wilson's victory had not seemed likely: Aneurin Bevan would probably have been the automatic choice to succeed Gaitskell, but he had died in 1960. Even so, Wilson began the contest in second place to George Brown (1914–84) – but Brown's reputation as a drinker and a philanderer was beginning to get the better of him. However, Wilson – a former Oxford don of considerable ability, who had been a Cabinet minister in Clement Attlee's government when barely into his thirties – came from behind to win, and immediately set himself and his Party up in contrast to the more elderly, aristocratic image of the Conservatives under Harold Macmillan.

Wilson was to be handed an immediate piece of good fortune in the shape of the Profumo scandal, and within days of Wilson making this speech to his first Party conference as leader Macmillan had resigned, and the Conservative government had its own leadership crisis. Even before that, though, Wilson was brimming with self-confidence, born not least of his conviction that his Party was far more in touch with the mood of the times than the Conservatives were. That was the theme of this speech, which has been read ever since as a statement of Wilson's modernising manifesto.

Labour duly won the election in October 1964, though only by the narrowest of margins – a second election victory by a more overwhelming margin in 1966 allowed Wilson the chance to try to implement his programme with greater security. Sadly for him, the reactionary tendencies of many of the trades unions and the lack of vision of British management in the 1960s would not, as it turned out, allow the country to live up to his blueprint for the future. Also, Cabinet infighting and economic crisis – notably the devaluation of the pound in 1967 – severely limited the ability of the government to live up to its reforming promises. Other promises – such as those on disarmament contained in the speech – came to nothing, the reality of the Cold War world impacting as hard on Wilson when he took office as on any of his recent predecessors.

Anyone who has discussed trade prospects with Soviet leaders, as many of us have, or with some of our great Commonwealth countries, knows that there is a great demand for new chemical industries based on British research. We have the best chemists in the world, but we have never mobilised to the full the possible resources of chemical engineering to enable us to ship complete factories to these areas on a scale commensurate with their needs or our capacities. For some reason in so many of our universities, while the chemist is exalted the chemical engineer is told to go and sit somewhere below the salt. For some reason we have not developed the chemical engineering industry of this country on an adequate scale.

The Russians have talked to me of orders amounting to hundreds of millions over the next few years. A Labour government would initiate a state-sponsored chemical engineering consortium to meet the needs, not only of Eastern Europe, but far more important, of developing Commonwealth countries. We would train and we would mobilise chemical engineers to design the plants that the world needs, plants which are at present being supplied far too often by Germany or by America on the basis of British know-how and research. And in the fabrication of this plant which the new chemical engineering industry would call into being we could bring new orders to our depressed marine and heavy engineering shops in shipbuilding and other areas.

'The Labour government will include a minister for disarmament'

Here again lies the answer to the economic problems that we are going to face when, as we all hope, the arms race ends in a comprehensive disarmament agreement. The economic consequences of disarmament cannot be dealt with except on a basis of socialist planning. Advanced capitalist countries are maintaining full employment today only by virtue of vast arms orders and panic would be the order of the day in Wall Street and other stock markets, the day peace breaks out. We have announced that the Labour government will include a minister for disarmament, and among his duties will be to prepare for the economic problems that will follow hard on the heels of massive disarmament, because Conservative economic policies, thermostatic monetary controls, cannot deal with the problems of physical adjustment of the moving of real resources that we shall have to face.

You know this is the answer to another great problem that besets this country, the problem of employment for our people. Last month the minister of labour told us that 38,000 boys and girls, who left school in July, had not found work. This figure, as we all know, excluded many who, unable to find work, had returned to schools unfitted and ill-equipped to take them back. It excludes, too, the many who found temporary employment in blind-alley jobs. That this country should not be able to provide employment for boys and girls leaving school and going out into the world for the first time is an intolerable reflection on our so-called civilisation. Galbraith* warned the world a few years ago that social imbalance is the inevitable consequence of the unplanned affluent society, and we are finding this imbalance in the growing number of young people and of old people who cannot find employment. That is why we need the new industries, the revitalisation of declining industries and declining areas, to provide new hopes for the nation's youth.

'War on world poverty'

Again we must relate our scientific planning to the problems of the war on world poverty. In a system of society beset by the delirium of advertising and the ceaseless drive to produce new and different variants of existing consumer goods and services, there is no thought being given to the research that is needed to find the means of increasing food production for those millions in Asia and Africa who are living on the poverty line and below the poverty line.

It is very nice that we should be putting so much research into colour television, it is very nice that we should be putting all our energies into producing bigger and better washing machines to sell in Dusseldorf. What we should be doing is to be developing the means of mass producing simple tractors and ploughs to increase food production. In an advanced world which has long by-passed the steam engine in favour of oil and electricity as a means of propulsion we ought to be giving more thought to developing the research of this country for producing little simple one- or two-horsepower steam engines, because that is what the world needs, able to use local fuels, and capable of lifting water from that ditch to those fields a few hundred yards away. Swift saw the answer and the problem in *Gulliver's Travels* 250 years ago when he said: 'Whoever could make two ears of corn or two blades of grass to grow upon a spot of ground where only one grew before, would deserve better of mankind and do more essential service to his country than the whole race of politicians put together.'

Again, Mr Chairman, I should like to see the scientific departments of the new universities that we have been talking about mobilised to direct their scientific research to the special problems of underdeveloped countries, the needs of biological research to provide new breakthroughs in plant breeding, in the use of fertilisers, and in animal husbandry; in all the things that are needed to increase crops and to increase production.

Then again, what is the sense of closing down railway workshops that could provide the transport equipment that would make all the difference between poverty and solvency in newly developing countries?

Labour means business about world development. We are going to establish a full-scale ministry of overseas development, with a minister of Cabinet rank, to join with the ministry of science in mobilising Britain's scientific wealth for the task of creating, not the means of human destruction, but the munitions of peace.

Mr Chairman, let me conclude with what I think the message of all this is for this Conference, because in this Conference, in all our plans for the future, we are re-defining and we are re-stating our socialism in terms of the scientific revolution. But that revolution cannot become a reality unless we are prepared to make far-reaching changes in economic and social attitudes which permeate our whole system of society.

'The white heat of this revolution'

The Britain that is going to be forged in the white heat of this revolution will be no place for restrictive practices or for outdated methods on either side of industry. We shall need a totally new attitude to the problems of apprenticeship, of training and re-training for skill. If there is one thing where the traditional philosophy of capitalism breaks down it is in training for apprenticeship, because quite frankly it does not pay any individual firm, unless it is very altruistic or quixotic or farsighted, to train apprentices if it knows at the end of the period of training they will be snapped up by some unscrupulous firm that makes no contribution to apprenticeship training. That is what economists mean when they talk about the difference between marginal private cost and net social cost.

So we are going to need a new attitude. In some industries we shall have to get right away from the idea of apprenticeship to a single firm. There will have to be apprenticeship with the

HAROLD WILSON'S 'REVOLUTION'

1964

Wilson sets up the ministry of overseas development (Oct.), with Barbara Castle as its the first minister; Wilson sets up the ministry of technology (Oct.): Frank Cousins is its first minister.

1966

Following Cousins's resignation, Tony Benn succeeds him, and the department of technology becomes one of the largest and most powerful in government.

1967

The first North Sea gas is piped to mainland Britain (4 March); the Iron and Steel Act (22 March) nationalises almost all British steelmaking, with the British Steel Corporation created soon afterwards; UK (and Ireland) apply for EEC membership (11 May); the first automatic teller machine (ATM) in Britain is installed at Barclays Bank in Enfield, North London (27 June); the pound is devalued from US$2.80 to US$2.40 (19 Nov.).

1969

Barbara Castle produces the White Paper *In Place of Strife*, outlining proposals for trade-union regulation: it is rejected by the Cabinet; the Anglo-French supersonic airliner, Concorde, makes her maiden flight (2 March); the Open University is founded (23 July), following the establishment of the universities of Sussex, Essex, York, East Anglia, Lancaster, Kent, Warwick and Stirling earlier in the 1960s.

1970

Barbara Castle introduces the Equal Pay Act; Harold Wilson loses the general election (18 June).

industry as a whole, and the industry will have to take responsibility for it. Indeed, if we are going to end demarcation and snobbery in our training for skill and for science why should not these apprenticeship contracts be signed with the state itself? Then again, in the Cabinet room and the board room alike those charged with the control of our affairs must be ready to think and to speak in the language of our scientific age.

'The energies which a free people can mobilise'

For the commanding heights of British industry to be controlled today by men whose only claim is their aristocratic connections or the power of inherited wealth or speculative finance is as irrelevant to the twentieth century as would be the continued purchase of commissions in the armed forces by lordly amateurs. At the very time that even the MCC⁺ has abolished the distinction between amateurs and professionals, in science and industry we are content to remain a nation of Gentlemen in a world of Players.

For those of us who have studied the formidable Soviet challenge in the education of scientists and technologists, and above all, in the ruthless application of scientific techniques in Soviet industry, know that our future lies not in military strength alone but in the efforts, the sacrifices, and above all the energies which a free people can mobilise for the future greatness of our country. Because we are democrats, we reject the methods which Communist countries are displaying in applying the results of scientific research to industrial life, but because we care deeply about the future of Britain, we must use all the resources of democratic planning, all the latent and underdeveloped energies and skills of our people, to ensure Britain's standing in the world. That is the message which I believe will go out from this Conference to the people of Britain and to the people of the world.

♥ J.K. Galbraith (1908–2006), the Canadian-American Keynesian economist, much admired by the British Left at the time.
♦ Marylebone Cricket Club, at that time the governing body of English cricket. It had abolished the distinction between amateurs and professionals the previous year.

'*The River Tiber foaming with much blood*'

Birmingham, 20 April 1968

Enoch Powell
on the consequences of race relations legislation

I n 1968 the Labour government of Harold Wilson was in the process of passing a Race Relations Bill, which the leading Conservative MP Enoch Powell, with his constitutional precision, felt created two classes of citizen in Britain, and which, he felt, helped compound the complacency about a mass immigration (since 1948) on which the British people had never been properly consulted.

Since 1965 Powell had been defence spokesman in the Shadow Cabinet of Edward Heath, though he had made a point of speaking out on other subjects when he felt an incorrect approach was being taken to them. He had annoyed Heath by his criticism of a prices and incomes policy and, within his own brief, by talking of the need for Britain to close down military bases east of Suez. The two men were clearly heading for a showdown, and this speech provided it.

The speech was greeted with widespread euphoria by the public, and almost unanimous condemnation by the press and other politicians. Heath, who claimed to find the speech racialist in tone, sacked Powell from the front bench the next day. Powell became a national hero and hate figure simultaneously. He strenuously denied accusations that he was a racist, claiming this speech – and others made subsequently on the same theme – were about immigration, not race. His predictions of a river foaming with blood did not come true, but the admission, even by ethnic-minority community leaders nearly 40 years later, that the multicultural society had failed suggested that Powell's predictions were far more accurate than his enemies – or even those notionally on his own side – would once have given him credit for.

Even in making a speech as supposedly populist as this, Powell's style of rhetoric remained, as always, strictly classical. Until his death in 1998 the speech was an unending source of controversy for Powell, and he never varied from its message one jot.

The supreme function of statesmanship is to provide against preventable evils. In seeking to do so, it encounters obstacles which are deeply rooted in human nature. One is that by the very order of things such evils are not demonstrable until they have occurred: at each stage in their onset there is room for doubt and for dispute whether they be real or imaginary. By the same token, they attract little attention in comparison with current troubles, which are both indisputable and pressing: whence the besetting temptation of all politics to concern itself with the immediate present at the expense of the future. Above all, people are disposed to mistake predicting troubles for causing troubles and even for desiring troubles: 'if only', they love to think, 'if only people wouldn't talk about it, it probably wouldn't happen'. Perhaps this habit goes back to the primitive belief that the word and the thing, the name and the object, are identical. At all events, the discussion of future grave but, with effort now, avoidable evils is the most unpopular and at the same time the most necessary occupation for the politician. Those who knowingly shirk it, deserve, and not infrequently receive, the curses of those who come after.

'I can already hear the chorus of execration'

A week or two ago I fell into conversation with a constituent, a middle-aged, quite ordinary working man employed in one of our nationalised industries. After a sentence or two about the weather, he suddenly said: 'If I had the money to go, I wouldn't stay in this country.' I made some deprecatory reply, to the effect that even this government wouldn't last for ever; but he took no notice, and continued: 'I have three children, all of them have been through grammar school and two of them married now, with family. I shan't be satisfied till I have seen them settled overseas. In this country in fifteen or twenty years' time the black man will have the whip hand over the white man.'

I can already hear the chorus of execration. How dare I say such a horrible thing? How dare I stir up trouble and inflame feelings by repeating such a conversation? The answer is that I do not have the right not to do so. Here is a decent, ordinary fellow Englishman, who in broad daylight in my own town says to me, his Member of Parliament, that this country will not be worth living in for his children. I simply do not have the right to shrug my shoulders and think about something else. What he is saying, thousands and hundreds of thousands are saying and thinking – not throughout Great Britain, perhaps, but in the areas that are already undergoing the total transformation to which there is no parallel in a thousand years of English history.

In fifteen or twenty years, on present trends, there will be in this country three million Commonwealth immigrants and their descendants. That is not my figure. That is the official figure given to Parliament by the spokesman of the Registrar General's office. There is no comparable official figure for the year 2000, but it must be in the region of 5–7 million, approximately one-tenth of the whole population, and approaching that of Greater London. Of course, it will not be evenly distributed from Margate to Aberystwyth and from Penzance to Aberdeen. Whole areas, towns and parts of towns across England will be occupied by different sections of the immigrant and immigrant-descended population.

'The evils to be prevented ... lie several parliaments ahead'

As time goes on, the proportion of this total who are immigrant descendants, those born in England, who arrived here by exactly the same route as the rest of us, will rapidly increase. Already by 1985 the native-born would constitute the majority. It is this fact above all which creates the extreme urgency of action now, of just that kind of action which is hardest for politicians to take, action where the difficulties lie in the present but the evils to be prevented or minimised lie several parliaments ahead.

The natural and rational first question with a nation confronted by such a prospect is to ask: 'How can its dimensions be reduced?' Granted it be not wholly preventable, can it be limited, bearing in mind that numbers are of the essence: the significance and consequences of an alien element introduced into a country or population are profoundly different according to whether that element is 1 per cent or 10 per cent. The answers to the simple and rational question are equally simple and rational: by stopping or virtually stopping further inflow, and by promoting the maximum outflow. Both answers are part of the official policy of the Conservative Party.

It almost passes belief that at this moment twenty or thirty additional immigrant children are arriving from overseas in Wolverhampton' alone every week – and that means fifteen or twenty additional families of a decade or two hence. Those whom the gods wish to destroy, they first make mad. We must be mad, literally mad, as a nation to be permitting the annual inflow of some 50,000 dependants, who are for the most part the material of the future growth of the immigrant-descended population. It is like watching a nation busily engaged in heaping up its own funeral pyre. So insane are we that we actually permit unmarried persons to immigrate for the purpose of founding a family with spouses and fiancées whom they have never seen. Let no one suppose that the flow of dependants will automatically tail off. On the contrary, even at the present admission rate of only 5,000 a year by voucher, there is sufficient for a further 325,000 dependants per annum ad infinitum, without taking into account the huge reservoir of existing relations in this country – and I am making no allowance at all for fraudulent entry. In these circumstances nothing will suffice but that the total inflow for settlement should be reduced at once to negligible proportions, and that the necessary legislative and administrative measures be taken without delay. I stress the words 'for settlement'. This has nothing to do with the entry of Commonwealth citizens, any more than of aliens, into this country, for the purposes of study or of improving their qualifications, like (for instance) the Commonwealth doctors who, to the advantage of their own countries, have enabled our hospital service to be expanded faster than would otherwise have been possible. These are not, and never have been, immigrants.

'Immigrants ... come to me, asking if I can find them assistance to return home'

RACE RELATIONS IN THE 1970s

1971	1972
In the new Immigration Bill (24 Feb.) Commonwealth citizens lose their automatic right to remain in the UK and will face the same restrictions as any other persons applying to live and work in Britain; the bill comes into force 1 Jan. 1972.	Idi Amin announces (7 Aug.) the expulsion of 80,000 African Asians from Uganda, and they are given 90 days to leave: many hold UK passports and the first arrive in the UK on 18 Sept., with 29,000 more arriving over the next two months; there

I turn to re-emigration. If all immigration ended tomorrow, the rate of growth of the immigrant and immigrant-descended population would be substantially reduced, but the prospective size of this element in the population would still leave the basic character of the national danger unaffected. This can only be tackled while a considerable proportion of the total still comprises persons who entered this country during the last ten years or so. Hence the urgency of implementing now the second element of the Conservative Party's policy: the encouragement of re-emigration. Nobody can make an estimate of the numbers which, with generous grants and assistance, would choose either to return to their countries of origin or to go to other countries anxious to receive the manpower and the skills they represent. Nobody knows, because no such policy has yet been attempted. I can only say that, even at present, immigrants in my own constituency from time to time come to me, asking if I can find them assistance to return home. If such a policy were adopted and pursued with the determination which the gravity of the alternative justifies, the resultant outflow could appreciably alter the prospects for the future.

'To enact legislation ... is to risk throwing a match on to the gunpowder'

It can be no part of any policy that existing families should be kept divided; but there are two directions in which families can be reunited, and if our former and present immigration laws have brought about the division of families, albeit voluntarily or semi-voluntarily, we ought to be prepared to arrange for them to be reunited in their countries of origin. In short, suspension of immigration and encouragement of re-emigration hang together, logically and humanly, as two aspects of the same approach.

The third element of the Conservative Party's policy is that all who are in this country as citizens should be equal before the law and that there shall be no discrimination or difference made between them by public authority. As Mr Heath has put it, we will have no 'first-class citizens' and 'second-class citizens'. This does not mean that the immigrant and his descendants should be elevated into a privileged or special class or that the citizen should be denied his right to discriminate in the management of his own affairs between one fellow citizen and another or that he should be subjected to inquisition as to his reasons and motives for behaving in one lawful manner rather than another.

are similar expulsions from Malawi in 1976.

1976
100 police officers and 60 carnival-goers are injured during riots at the Notting Hill Carnival (30 Aug.); an extension to Britain's 1965 and 1968 Race Relations Acts establishes the Commission for Racial Equality (CRE).

1978
A Birmingham nightclub is ordered to open its doors to black and Chinese people (23 Nov.), the first non-discrimination notice issued by the CRE.

1979
A teacher dies after fighting breaks out in Southall, London, when thousands gather to demonstrate against a campaign meeting being held by the right-wing anti-immigration National Front (23 April).

There could be no grosser misconception of the realities than is entertained by those who vociferously demand legislation as they call it 'against discrimination', whether they be leader-writers of the same kidney and sometimes on the same newspapers which year after year in the 1930s tried to blind this country to the rising peril which confronted it, or archbishops who live in palaces, faring delicately with the bedclothes pulled right over their heads. They have got it exactly and diametrically wrong. The discrimination and the deprivation, the sense of alarm and resentment, lies not with the immigrant population but with those among whom they have come and are still coming. This is why to enact legislation of the kind before Parliament at this moment is to risk throwing a match on to the gunpowder. The kindest thing that can be said about those who propose and support it is they know not what they do.

Nothing is more misleading than comparison between the Commonwealth immigrant in Britain and the American Negro. The Negro population of the United States, which was already in existence before the United States became a nation, started literally as slaves and were later given the franchise and other rights of citizenship, to the exercise of which they have only gradually and still incompletely come. The Commonwealth immigrant came to Britain as a full citizen, to a country which knows no discrimination between one citizen and another, and he entered instantly into the possession of the rights of every citizen, from the vote to free treatment under the National Health Service. Whatever drawbacks attended the immigrants – and they were drawbacks which did not, and do not, make admission into Britain by hook or by crook appear less than desirable – arose not from the law or from public policy or from administration but from those personal circumstances and accidents which cause, and always will cause, the fortunes and experience of one man to be different from another's.

But while to the immigrant entry to this country was admission to privileges and opportunities eagerly sought, the impact upon the existing population was very different. For reasons which they could not comprehend, and in pursuance of a decision by default, on which they were never consulted, they found themselves made strangers in their own country. They found their wives unable to obtain hospital beds in childbirth, their children unable to obtain school places, their homes and neighbourhoods changed beyond recognition, their plans and prospects for the future defeated; at work they found that employers hesitated to apply to the immigrant worker the standards of discipline and competence required of the native-born worker; they began to hear, as time went by, more and more voices which told them that they were now the unwanted. On top of this, they now learn that a one-way privilege is to be established by Act of Parliament: a law, which cannot, and is not intended to, operate to protect them or redress their grievances, is to be enacted to give the stranger, the disgruntled and the agent provocateur the power to pillory them for their private actions.

'The sense of being a persecuted minority'

In the hundreds upon hundreds of letters I received when I last spoke on this subject two or three months ago, there was one striking feature which was largely new and which I find ominous. All Members of Parliament are used to the typical anonymous correspondent; but what surprised and alarmed me was the high proportion of ordinary, decent, sensible people, writing a rational and often well-educated letter, who believed that they had to omit their address because it was dangerous to have committed themselves to paper to a Member of Parliament agreeing with the views I had expressed, and that they would risk either penalties or reprisals if they were known to have done so. The sense of being a persecuted minority which is growing among ordinary English people in the areas of the country which are affected is something that those without direct experience can hardly imagine. I am going to allow just one of those hundreds of people to speak for me. She did give her name and address, which I have detached from the letter which I am about to read. She was writing from Northumberland about something which is happening at this moment in my own constituency:

Eight years ago in a respectable street in Wolverhampton a house was sold to a Negro. Now only one white (a woman old-age pensioner) lives there. This is her story. She lost her husband and both her sons in the war. So she turned her seven-roomed house, her only asset, into a boarding house. She worked hard and did well, paid off her mortgage and began to put something by for her old age. Then the immigrants moved in. With growing fear, she saw one house after another taken over. The quiet streets became a place of noise and confusion. Regretfully, her white tenants moved out.

The day after the last one left, she was awakened at 7am by two Negroes who wanted to use her phone to contact their employer. When she refused, as she would have refused any stranger at such an hour, she was abused and feared she would have been attacked but for the chain on her door. Immigrant families have tried to rent rooms in her house, but she always refused. Her little store of money went, and after paying her rates, she had less than £2 per week. She went to apply for a rate reduction and was seen by a young girl, who on hearing she had a seven-roomed house, suggested she should let part of it. When she said the only people she could get were Negroes, the girl said 'racial prejudice won't get you anywhere in this country'. So she went home.

'We are on the verge here of a change'

The telephone is her lifeline. Her family pay the bill, and help her out as best they can. Immigrants have offered to buy her house – at a price which the prospective landlord would be able to recover from his tenants in weeks, or at most in a few months. She is becoming afraid to go out. Windows are broken. She finds excreta pushed through her letterbox. When she goes to the shops, she is followed by children, charming, wide-grinning piccaninnies. They cannot speak English, but one word they know. 'Racialist', they chant. When the new Race Relations Bill is passed, this woman is convinced she will go to prison. And is she so wrong? I begin to wonder.

The other dangerous delusion from which those who are wilfully or otherwise blind to realities suffer, is summed up in the word 'integration'. To be integrated into a population means to become for all practical purposes indistinguishable from its other members. Now, at all times, where there are marked physical differences, especially of colour, integration is difficult though, over a period, not impossible. There are among the Commonwealth immigrants who have come to live here in the last fifteen years or so, many thousands whose wish and purpose is to be integrated and whose every thought and endeavour is bent in that direction. But to imagine that such a thing enters the heads of a great and growing majority of immigrants and their descendants is a ludicrous misconception, and a dangerous one to boot.

We are on the verge here of a change. Hitherto it has been force of circumstance and of background which has rendered the very idea of integration inaccessible to the greater part of the immigrant population – that they never conceived or intended such a thing, and that their numbers and physical concentration meant the pressures towards integration which normally bear upon any small minority did not operate. Now we are seeing the growth of positive forces acting against integration, of vested interests in the preservation and sharpening of racial and religious differences, with a view to the exercise of actual domination, first over fellow immigrants and then over the rest of the population. The cloud no bigger than a man's hand, that can so rapidly overcast the sky, has been visible recently in Wolverhampton and has shown signs of spreading quickly. The words I am about to use, verbatim as they appeared in the local press on 17 February, are not mine, but those of a Labour Member of Parliament who is a minister in the present government.

> The Sikh communities' campaign to maintain customs inappropriate in Britain is much to be regretted. Working in Britain, particularly in the public services, they should be prepared to accept the terms and conditions of their employment. To claim special communal rights (or should one say rites?) leads to a dangerous fragmentation within society. This communalism is a canker: whether practised by one colour or another it is to be strongly condemned.

All credit to John Stonehouse for having had the insight to perceive that, and the courage to say it.

'Like the Roman, I seem to see "the River Tiber foaming with much blood"'

For these dangerous and divisive elements the legislation proposed in the Race Relations Bill is the very pabulum they need to flourish. Here is the means of showing that the immigrant communities can organise to consolidate their members, to agitate and campaign against their fellow citizens, and to overawe and dominate the rest with the legal weapons which the ignorant and the ill-informed have provided. As I look ahead, I am filled with foreboding. Like the Roman, I seem to see 'the River Tiber foaming with much blood'. That tragic and intractable phenomenon which we watch with horror on the other side of the Atlantic, but which there is interwoven with the history and existence of the States itself, is coming upon us here by our own volition and our own neglect. Indeed, it has all but come. In numerical terms, it will be of American proportions long before the end of the century. Only resolute and urgent action will avert it even now. Whether there will be the public will to demand and obtain that action, I do not know. All I know is that to see, and not to speak, would be the great betrayal.

♥ Wolverhampton South-West was Powell's constituency at the time.

'A seraglio of eunuchs'

House of Commons, London, 1 February 1969

Michael Foot
opposes reform proposals for the
House of Lords

There had been increasingly serious debate since the defeat of the second Irish Home Rule Bill in the 1890s about reforming the House of Lords, and removing the power of the unelected, hereditary element to hold up what was perceived to be the will of the people expressed through their representatives in the House of Commons. There had been Parliament Acts in 1911 and 1949 that restricted the delaying powers of the Lords. Non-heriditary Life Peerages had been created in 1958, and by the time the Labour government of Harold Wilson sought to bring in a permanent reform of the Lords in 1969 no hereditary peerages had been created since 1964.

The battle to prevent this reform saw an unusual alliance between the left-wing radical Michael Foot (b.1913), one of his Party's foremost orators, and the right-wing radical Conservative Enoch Powell. Powell wanted the Lords maintained in its traditional form, Foot wanted it swept away altogether. In this powerful speech on the second reading of the Parliament (No. 2) Bill, Foot – who was to become leader of his Party in 1980, and ultimately lead them to a crushing electoral defeat in 1983 – demonstrates his formidable articulacy and his knowledge of the sweep of history, as he argues that any reform that is cosily stitched up between the leaders of the two main political parties can only be against the public interest. In this case, he meant that the proposed process of nomination would lead to a docile and obedient second chamber, which would inevitably fail to give proper scrutiny to measures sent up there from the Commons.

This speech in particular had enormous influence among Foot's fellow backbenchers, and the growing disquiet among them led to Wilson's decision to withdraw the bill a few weeks later. An attempt by a later Labour prime minister, Tony Blair, to reform the Lords began in 1999 with the removal of all but 92 hereditary peers from the Lords, but at the time of writing has still to proceed much further.

I shall come in a moment to the speech of the right hon. Member for Devon North*, but I should like to begin by commenting on a remark of the right hon. Member for Barnet*. He said at the beginning and end of his speech that on his side of the House there would be a free vote. I should like to announce that there will be a free vote on this side of the House as well. I recognise that it is not the custom for these announcements to be made from where I am standing, but we have great experience in these matters and wish to make it clear that that is the position. We hope that everyone will take it fully into account. As my right hon. friend the prime minister says, we are a modernising House in a modernising generation. This is an innovation which I hope will be greatly extended in future.

The right hon. Member for Barnet also said – and in my opinion this is one of the central features of the whole debate – that great constitutional reforms are better made by agreement between the two front benches and the parties. I was somewhat surprised to hear the leader of the Liberal Party accept that view. I do not think that it would have been shared by Mr Gladstone, at any rate in his later years, or by Lord Grey at the height of his fame.

'In the teeth of opposition from the other side of the House'

If the right hon. gentleman looks back at the extremely illuminating history of his great Party, he will see that most of the major constitutional innovations for which the Liberal Party was responsible were introduced in the teeth of opposition from the other side of the House, and many of them lasted for a very long time. It was particularly strange that the right hon. gentleman should say that he hoped that this reform, in particular, would be temporary. If I agreed that it would be, I should not have such strong feelings against the bill, but I recall that the Parliament Act 1911 was introduced as a temporary measure. If the present bill passes through the House, as I trust that it will not, it will have the same possibility of survival as the ill-fated 1911 act.

The theory of the right hon. Member for Barnet that it is better for constitutional reforms to be introduced on the basis of compromise is not one that I would accept at all. Major constitutional measures which affect the whole balance of power in the state, the balance of power between different interests in the country, are matters that are resolved only by Party governments who know their own minds and are determined to carry through their leading reforms without conceding to the Oppositions of the day the requirements they may press. The whole history of this great country supports my view rather than that of the right hon. Member for Barnet.

(*Mr Thorpe: 'Is the hon. gentleman aware that historically he is incorrect, whether it was Mr Gladstone on Ireland or Mr Asquith or Mr Attlee on the reform of another place [i.e. House of Lords]? All three tried first to get all-party support. I am not responsible for the stupidity of the Tory Party on that occasion, or for its spirit of co-operation now.'*)

'Great constitutional reforms have not been put through this House by compromise'

I am not talking about the speeches made, but about the history that was made. Anyone who looks at the history of our country can see that great constitutional reforms have not been put through this House by compromise between the parties, but by great leaders, Mr Gladstone among them, who fought for their views against the blast of bitter opposition and eventually got them on the statute book. That is what a Labour government should have done in this instance.

I wish, first, to look at the bargain reached between the parties, on which my right hon. friend the home secretary spoke most strongly when he wound up the debate on the White Paper.

He asked what was wrong with a bargain. In a bargain, both sides must make some contribution. Nobody could deny that, but we are entitled to see exactly who made the bargain and who contributed most towards it. If I were discourteous, I might ask, 'Who fooled whom?' But I do not. Instead I ask, 'Who got the better of the bargain?'

My right hon. friends, including the prime minister again today, have listed the advantages which they think a Labour government obtains from the bargain. I do not say that those advantages can be dismissed, but they must be weighed carefully against the claims made by the right hon. and hon. gentlemen opposite and others who are party to the bargain. In his speech on the White Paper, the right hon. Member for Enfield, West* showed himself much more agile and skilful in these matters than the right hon. Member for Barnet, who fell off the tightrope altogether. There was no safety net under him until I came along and tried to help him. He fell off altogether ...

The main division between myself and the government is because, in my view, the Opposition have got the better of the bargain. Indeed, the right hon. Member for Enfield, West understands better than do my right hon. friends what will be the nature of the assembly to be established by the bill. The House need not take it from me. I know that, on constitutional matters, the House may not wish to do that. But perhaps right hon. and hon. Members will take it from any of a whole long list of Members of another place, giving expert opinions on the subject.

'Theoretically, the powers have been somewhat reduced but, practically, they are to be greatly increased'

I do not think that it is an exaggeration to say that the overwhelming majority of opinion in the House of Lords is that the powers are to be retained pretty well as they are, but that the possibility of using them will be greatly enhanced because the place will have been made much more respectable. Theoretically, the powers have been somewhat reduced but, practically, they are to be greatly increased, and such powers will be able to be used in

HOUSE OF LORDS REFORMS 1946–63

1946
Regular attenders at the Lords are allowed to claim travelling expenses.

1949
A further Parliament Act reduces the delaying power of the House of Lords to one year, from two.

1957
Peers are allowed to claim a maximum of three guineas a day for expenses when they attend the Lords.

1958
The Life Peerages Act permits the creation of peerages for life, with no limit on numbers, to persons of either sex – thus admitting women to the Lords for the first time.

circumstances in which they have been unable to be used during the last 30 years – increasingly so in the last five or ten years. This is the great constitutional prize to be grabbed. This is what they said there, in another place.

I recommend right hon. and hon. Members to read the speech by Lord Butler[*] in another place. Nothing has disturbed me more about this bill than the bubbling *bonhomie* with which it was received by him. He could hardly contain himself. I cannot quote him, but I can tell the House the gist of what he said.

Lord Butler told his fellow peers, 'Boys and girls, this is marvellous, absolutely marvellous. Look at what we are getting. This is the finest thing we have been offered for many a long year and if you do not seize it you will be even bigger fools than you look to me at the moment.' Lord Butler said all that from the cross-benches, mark you. He went on, 'Do not worry about composition, by the way, or about nomination by the prime minister. It is all to be done through the usual channels.' That is what Lord Butler said. I have it all here. He said that the usual channels would fix up the composition of the other place.

'A second chamber selected by the whips. A seraglio of eunuchs'

Think of it! A second chamber selected by the whips. A seraglio of eunuchs. That is roughly what Lord Butler said about it. Then he went on to deal in detail with the question of the cross-benchers. We must deal with that again. Not so much has been said about it on this occasion as on previous occasions. But it is a fact that the whole point of this extraordinary constitutional pyramid which we have the wrong way up in the bill fixes on the question of the cross-benchers and how they are to be selected and how they are to behave.

In another place, their Lordships had a lot to say about that. One noble Lord put the question, 'What are we to do about crypto cross-benchers?' He never got an answer. The question is still echoing round these empty corridors. No one knows exactly how the cross-benchers are to be selected. We had excuses given by the right hon. Member for Enfield, West, who gave a few names of those he thinks are cross-benchers. He said that it was hard that

1960
Anthony Wedgwood Benn becomes Lord Stansgate on the death of his father and is barred from taking his place in the House of Commons. He is instrumental in the passage of the Peerage Bill 1963.

1963
The Peerage Bill allows for hereditary peeresses to be members of the House, for all Scottish peers to sit, and for hereditary peerages to be disclaimed for life: as a result of the last clause, Benn stays in the Commons and Lords Home (Alec Douglas-Home) and Hailsham (Quintin Hogg) leave the Lords, Hailsham to contest the Conservative leadership following Harold Macmillan's resignation, and Home once he has been appointed Conservative leader.

these gentlemen should have strictures passed upon them, and so it is. I am not presuming to judge their private lives. I am concerned with their public appearances.

The right hon. gentleman mentioned Lord Bridges and Lord Caccia, for example. He did not mention Lord Cromer, but I am sure that every ex-governor of the Bank of England becomes a cross-bencher – whether crypto or not, I do not care. All the ex-governors of the Bank of England with whom my right hon. friend the home secretary quarrelled so fiercely when he was chancellor of the exchequer will be up there judging his policy as cross-benchers. This is not a fanciful situation. It is reality.

(Mr Kenneth Lewis (Rutland and Stamford): Is the hon. gentleman suggesting that ex-governors of the Bank of England are likely to give full time to the House of Lords?)

I do not know. However, they might be more innocently engaged there than at the Bank of England. Perhaps that is the finest argument for the whole contraption we have been offered. If it provided innocent employment for ex-governors of the Bank of England, it would be quite an achievement.

However, that is not my main point. It is no good arguing about the fact, since one can see it standing out in the speech of my noble and learned friend the lord chancellor and no one can deny it, that, in the end, if a crisis comes and if a vote arrives on a major matter of principle, it is on the votes of these cross-benchers in another place that all eyes will be fixed.

We could have a national crisis with fierce controversy in the House of Commons. The matter is then referred to the other place. Momentous issues may be at stake. We may have a situation, where, just as in the Suez and Munich crises, parties and, indeed, families are deeply divided. At that stage, everyone is waiting to see what is to be the verdict of the House of Lords.

'We would hear a falsetto chorus from these political castrati'

But the House of Lords may not only settle the issue temporarily. It is no good the government saying that the House of Lords could settle it only for six months. A matter of a few weeks may be involved. There have been many important legislative measures which governments of all kinds have required to get through Parliament within days, even within a single day. Could not such a measure be settled, in effect, permanently by the cross-benchers in the House of Lords? So, in the midst of a great national crisis, with the country aflame, with everyone having forgotten who these cross-benchers are, what would we hear as the final verdict on such great issues of national policy? We would hear a falsetto chorus from these political castrati. They would be the final arbiters of our destiny in our new constitution.

What an extraordinary arrangement to propose. I say nothing about other extraordinary features, such as the cash question. Listening to my right hon. friend the prime minister, it seemed to me that this was at least partially disposed of, although I am not sure that I heard him aright. I thought that he referred to the future and said that he was keeping an open mind. Perhaps it was 'open hand'. I am not sure. It may be that my right hon. friend the secretary of state for social services⁕⁕, who is really the father of this proposal, as we know, has dealt with this matter in another of his proposals and that by 1992 they will all be getting half pay anyway.

Nobody can seriously think that these proposals are a proper constitutional device for dealing with the problems which we face. We cannot talk about modernisation when what we are offered is a Heath Robinson House of Lords, a contraption which will fall to pieces in any crisis, which will be laughed out of court on such an occasion and which it would be better for us to laugh out of court now. That would be the best way to deal with it.

The government may say, as they have said to me so powerfully on some occasions, 'If that is your view, what is your alternative? Why do you not put forward an alternative? Why do you not suggest something to put in its place?' I will make a suggestion if the government think that it will help. I hope that it is not introducing too jarring a note, but why do the government not carry out what they put in their party election manifesto about it? They said that they would take away the powers of the House of Lords. Settle that first and then we could deal with the question – and I agree that there are many differences between us about it – of what to put in its place.

'I am a fervent abolitionist'

I am a fervent abolitionist. The notion that we cannot do away with the House of Lords because of the revising requirements is quite wrong. We could remodel the life of Parliament itself so as to deal with these problems. It might take a little time to do that, but it could be done, and in the meantime, particularly if the government are worried about the next two years and particularly because they do not even appear to have got the accommodation out of the bargain which they had hoped for in the first place, they could revert to the Party programme.

When in trouble, that is always a good thing to do. Why do they not do that? It would cause much more enthusiasm in the country and it would be a much more expeditious way of dealing with the matter. It would also save a great deal of parliamentary time. If we are to be presented with this bill, many of us will think that it is our constitutional duty to argue every clause, and in that respect, if in no other, this is a bill which offers wide opportunities.

The proposal which I am making to the government is perfectly serious. They may ask, 'Why did you not tell us earlier?' But we did tell them. We have been telling them for weeks, for months, for years. We have been telling them ever since this proposal came forward. Indeed, this was another of the jokes which Lord Butler enjoyed so much in the House of Lords.

'We should kill the bill'

Lord Butler said, 'This little bill, which is to do us' – that is, the Tories – 'so much good, and which will set up the Tory Party for the next thirty years or so, is a true lineal descendant of the Life Peerage Bill which I introduced in 1957 and which was then bitterly opposed by Labour Members, who voted against the whole measure. I told them then that if only we could get in that thin end of the wedge we would get the rest of the wedge in later' – he did not put it quite in these words. 'Here is the rest of the wedge. Now let us use it as fast as we can to make sure that we establish in this country' – and here, again, I am not using his exact words – 'a new kind of assembly, a new kind of second chamber. We will make it respectable, sedate to the point of stuffy; torpid; quick to prevent any removal of injustice, but longanimous in the toleration of mischief; a perpetual encumbrance across the path of everyone wishing to act boldly; a standing incitement to those who do not wish to act at all.'

I therefore say that we should kill the bill now if we can; that, if we cannot kill it now, we should kill it in Committee; but that, at any rate, we should prevent the country from being burdened in this modernising age by such an anachronistic and absurd institution as is proposed, not surprisingly, by the collusion between the two front benches.

♥ Jeremy Thorpe (b.1929), leader of the Liberal Party 1967–76, a colourful character who in 1979 was acquitted of conspiracy to murder his former male lover.
♦ Reginald Maudling (1917–79), former champion amateur golfer, chancellor of the exchequer in Macmillan's government 1962–4, defeated by Edward Heath in 1965 for the leadership of the Conservatives, and served in Heath's government as home secretary (1970–2) before a tenuous link to a corruption scandal forced him to resign. A popular man with a legendarily hedonistic lifestyle, he died from a drink-related illness aged only 61.
♣ Iain Macleod (1913–70), former champion bridge player, colonial secretary in Macmillan's government (in which post he was branded 'too clever by half' by the Marquess of Salisbury), he died a month after being appointed chancellor of the exchequer in Heath's government.
♠ R.A. Butler (1902–82), education secretary responsible for the 1944 Education Act, subsequently chancellor of the exchequer, home secretary and first secretary of state, twice passed over for the leadership of the Conservative Party.
♥♥ Richard Crossman (1907–73), Oxford don, who posthumously scandalised the political establishment by publishing explicit and (to many of his colleagues and officials) highly embarrassing diaries of his time in office.

'The lady's not for turning'

Conservative Party Conference, Brighton, 10 October 1980

Margaret Thatcher

on the achievements of her Conservative government

Margaret Thatcher (b.1925) was the daughter of a provincial grocer and local councillor who won a place to Oxford, was called to the Bar, and in 1959, having married and given birth to twins, was elected as Conservative MP for Finchley in north London. Harold Macmillan gave her a junior ministerial job in 1962. In 1970, when Edward Heath became prime minister, she was appointed secretary of state for education. After the fall of the Heath government she was attracted to the free-market ideas of her colleague Sir Keith Joseph (1918–95), who had himself been influenced by Enoch Powell. When Joseph decided he was unsuitable to challenge Heath for the leadership of the Party, Mrs Thatcher became the candidate of the radical Right.

In February 1975, to the shock of Heath and his supporters, she won the leadership, and in May 1979 became Britain's first, and so far only, woman prime minister. Her attempt to re-structure the economy by removing state subsidies from obsolete industries, and by shifting the burden of taxation from income tax to indirect taxes, caused huge controversy. Unemployment rose to almost 3 million and, by the autumn of 1980, there was a near-unanimous chorus from her own Party urging a policy U-turn in order to avoid an inevitable election defeat.

In this speech, delivered to her Party Conference, she advertised her determination not to change tack. It is a definitive exposition of Thatcherism, and typical of its era, at the height of the Cold War. By the time of the next election in 1983, which the Tories won by a landslide, Mrs Thatcher had been boosted not by economic revival but by a victory in the previous year's short war with Argentina over the Falkland Islands. Nonetheless, by the time she was forced out of office in 1990 her policies had changed the economic landscape of Britain, the trades unions had been neutered, nationalised industries had been privatised, and ownership of homes and shares had been widened. This growth in prosperity came, however, at a considerable cost of public disquiet, and it was against that emerging background that this speech was made.

The line by which the speech is best remembered – a pun on the best-known play by Christopher Fry, *The Lady's Not for Burning* – was reputedly written for her by playwright Ronald Millar.

It seems to me that throughout my life in politics our ambitions have steadily shrunk. Our response to disappointment has not been to lengthen our stride but to shorten the distance to be covered. But with confidence in ourselves and in our future what a nation we could be!

In its first seventeen months this government have laid the foundations for recovery. We have undertaken a heavy load of legislation, a load we do not intend to repeat because we do not share the socialist fantasy that achievement is measured by the number of laws you pass. But there was a formidable barricade of obstacles that we had to sweep aside ... Prosperity comes not from grand conferences of economists but by countless acts of personal self-confidence and self-reliance.

... Britain has repaid $3,600 million of international debt, debt which had been run up by our predecessors. And we paid quite a lot of it before it was due. In the past twelve months Geoffrey [Howe] has abolished exchange controls over which British governments have dithered for decades. Our great enterprises are now free to seek opportunities overseas. This will help to secure our living standards long after North Sea oil has run out. This government thinks about the future. We have made the first crucial changes in trade union law to remove the worst abuses of the closed shop, to restrict picketing to the place of work of the parties in dispute, and to encourage secret ballots. British Aerospace will soon be open to private investment. The monopoly of the Post Office and British Telecommunications is being diminished. The barriers to private generation of electricity for sale have been lifted. For the first time nationalised industries and public utilities can be investigated by the Monopolies Commission, a long overdue reform.

Free competition in road passenger transport promises travellers a better deal. Michael Heseltine˅ has given to millions, yes millions, of council tenants the right to buy their own homes.

It was Anthony Eden who chose for us the goal of 'a property-owning democracy'. But for all the time that I have been in public affairs that has been beyond the reach of so many, who were denied the right to the most basic ownership of all the homes in which they live.

> 'If this is the death of capitalism, I must say that it has quite a way to go'

They wanted to buy. Many could afford to buy. But they happened to live under the jurisdiction of a socialist council, which would not sell and did not believe in the independence that comes with ownership. Now Michael Heseltine has given them the chance to turn a dream into reality. And all this and a lot more in seventeen months.

The Left continues to refer with relish to the death of capitalism. Well, if this is the death of capitalism, I must say that it has quite a way to go.

But all this will avail us little unless we achieve our prime economic objective, the defeat of inflation. Inflation destroys nations and societies as surely as invading armies do. Inflation is the parent of unemployment. It is the unseen robber of those who have saved. No policy which puts at risk the defeat of inflation however great its short-term attraction can be right. Our policy for the defeat of inflation is, in fact, traditional. It existed long before Sterling M3 embellished the Bank of England *Quarterly Bulletin*, or 'monetarism' became a convenient term of political invective.

But some people talk as if control of the money supply was a revolutionary policy. Yet it was an essential condition for the recovery of much of continental Europe. Those countries knew what was required for economic stability. Previously, they had lived through rampant inflation; they knew that it led to suitcase money, massive unemployment and the breakdown of society itself. They determined never to go that way again.

Today, after many years of monetary self-discipline, they have stable, prosperous economies better able than ours to withstand the buffeting of world recession.

So at international conferences to discuss economic affairs many of my fellow heads of government find our policies not strange, unusual or revolutionary, but normal, sound and honest. And that is what they are.

Their only question is: 'Has Britain the courage and resolve to sustain the discipline for long enough to break through to success?'

Yes, Mr Chairman, we have, and we shall. This government are determined to stay with the policy and see it through to its conclusion. That is what marks this administration as one of the truly radical ministries of post-war Britain. Inflation is falling and should continue to fall. Meanwhile we are not heedless of the hardships and worries that accompany the conquest of inflation.

Foremost among these is unemployment. Today our country has more than 2 million unemployed. Now you can try to soften that figure in a dozen ways. You can point out and it is quite legitimate to do so that 2 million today does not mean what it meant in the 1930s; that the percentage of unemployment is much less now than it was then.

You can add that today many more married women go out to work.

You can stress that, because of the high birth rate in the early 1960s, there is an unusually large number of school leavers this year looking for work and that the same will be true for the next two years.

You can emphasise that about a quarter of a million people find new jobs each month and therefore go off the employment register.

And you can recall that there are nearly 25 million people in jobs compared with only about 18 million in the 1930s. You can point out that the Labour Party conveniently overlooks the fact that of the 2 million unemployed for which they blame us, nearly a million and a half were bequeathed by their government.

But when all that has been said the fact remains that the level of unemployment in our country today is a human tragedy. Let me make it clear beyond doubt. I am profoundly concerned about unemployment. Human dignity and self respect are undermined when men

A DIVIDED BRITAIN 1980

JANUARY
British Steel workers stage their first national strike for more than 50 years in support of their demand for a 20% pay rise.

APRIL
Black youths riot in the St Paul's area of Bristol after police raid a café.

MAY
The SAS storms the Iranian Embassy to end a six-day hostage crisis, killing five out of the six terrorists; the TUC holds a day of action against Conservative economic and industrial policies.

JULY–AUGUST
A British team attends the controversial Moscow Olympics, against government advice.

and women are condemned to idleness. The waste of a country's most precious assets – the talent and energy of its people – makes it the bounden duty of government to seek a real and lasting cure.

If I could press a button and genuinely solve the unemployment problem, do you think that I would not press that button this instant? Does anyone imagine that there is the smallest political gain in letting this unemployment continue, or that there is some obscure economic religion which demands this unemployment as part of its ritual? This government are pursuing the only policy which gives any hope of bringing our people back to real and lasting employment. It is no coincidence that those countries, of which I spoke earlier, which have had lower rates of inflation have also had lower levels of unemployment.

I know that there is another real worry affecting many of our people. Although they accept that our policies are right, they feel deeply that the burden of carrying them out is falling much more heavily on the private than on the public sector. They say that the public sector is enjoying advantages but the private sector is taking the knocks and at the same time maintaining those in the public sector with better pay and pensions than they enjoy.

I must tell you that I share this concern and understand the resentment. That is why I and my colleagues say that to add to public spending takes away the very money and resources that industry needs to stay in business let alone to expand. Higher public spending, far from curing unemployment, can be the very vehicle that loses jobs and causes bankruptcies in trade and commerce. That is why we warned local authorities that since rates are frequently the biggest tax that industry now faces, increases in them can cripple local businesses. Councils must, therefore, learn to cut costs in the same way that companies have to.

That is why I stress that if those who work in public authorities take for themselves large pay increases they leave less to be spent on equipment and new buildings. That in turn deprives the private sector of the orders it needs, especially some of those industries in the hard pressed regions. Those in the public sector have a duty to those in the private sector not to take out so much in pay that they cause others unemployment. That is why we point out that every time high wage settlements in nationalised monopolies lead to higher charges for telephones, electricity, coal and water, they can drive companies out of business and cost other people their jobs.

If spending money like water was the answer to our country's problems, we would have no problems now. If ever a nation has spent, spent, spent and spent again, ours has. Today that

AUGUST	**SEPTEMBER**	**OCTOBER**	Party after a fractious election.
The Employment Act bans secondary picketing and limits the closed shop; the Housing Act allows council-house tenants to buy their properties.	Protestors gather at Greenham Common to oppose the siting there of US Cruise missiles; the Consett Steelworks, a major employer in County Durham, shuts down.	In Northern Ireland, a group of IRA prisoners embark on a hunger strike. **NOVEMBER** British Airways is privatised; Michael Foot becomes leader of the Labour	**DECEMBER** Unemployment figures reach above the 2 million mark, about 1 in 11 of the British workforce.

dream is over. All of that money has got us nowhere but it still has to come from somewhere. Those who urge us to relax the squeeze, to spend yet more money indiscriminately in the belief that it will help the unemployed and the small businessman are not being kind or compassionate or caring. They are not the friends of the unemployed or the small business. They are asking us to do again the very thing that caused the problems in the first place. We have made this point repeatedly.

'The State drains society, not only of its wealth but of initiative'

I am accused of lecturing or preaching about this. I suppose it is a critic's way of saying 'Well, we know it is true, but we have to carp at something.' I do not care about that. But I do care about the future of free enterprise, the jobs and exports it provides and the independence it brings to our people. Independence? Yes, but let us be clear what we mean by that. Independence does not mean contracting out of all relationships with others. A nation can be free but it will not stay free for long if it has no friends and no alliances. Above all, it will not stay free if it cannot pay its own way in the world. By the same token, an individual needs to be part of a community and to feel that he is part of it. There is more to this than the chance to earn a living for himself and his family, essential though that is. Of course, our vision and our aims go far beyond the complex arguments of economics, but unless we get the economy right we shall deny our people the opportunity to share that vision and to see beyond the narrow horizons of economic necessity. Without a healthy economy we cannot have a healthy society. Without a healthy society the economy will not stay healthy for long. But it is not the State that creates a healthy society. When the State grows too powerful people feel that they count for less and less. The State drains society, not only of its wealth but of initiative, of energy, the will to improve and innovate as well as to preserve what is best. Our aim is to let people feel that they count for more and more. If we cannot trust the deepest instincts of our people we should not be in politics at all. Some aspects of our present society really do offend those instincts.

Decent people do want to do a proper job at work, not to be restrained or intimidated from giving value for money. They believe that honesty should be respected, not derided. They see crime and violence as a threat not just to society but to their own orderly way of life. They want to be allowed to bring up their children in these beliefs, without the fear that their efforts will be daily frustrated in the name of progress or free expression. Indeed, that is what family life is all about.

There is not a generation gap in a happy and united family. People yearn to be able to rely on some generally accepted standards. Without them you have not got a society at all, you have purposeless anarchy. A healthy society is not created by its institutions, either. Great schools and universities do not make a great nation any more than great armies do. Only a great nation can create and involve great institutions of learning, of healing, of scientific advance. And a great nation is the voluntary creation of its people, a people composed of men and women whose pride in themselves is founded on the knowledge of what they can give to a community of which they in turn can be proud.

If our people feel that they are part of a great nation and they are prepared to will the means to keep it great, a great nation we shall be, and shall remain. So, what can stop us from achieving this? What then stands in our way? The prospect of another winter of discontent?

I suppose it might. But I prefer to believe that certain lessons have been learnt from experience, that we are coming, slowly, painfully, to an autumn of understanding. And I hope that it will be followed by a winter of common sense. If it is not, we shall not be diverted from our course.

'You turn if you want to. The lady's not for turning'

To those waiting with bated breath for that favourite media catchphrase, the 'U' turn, I have only one thing to say. 'You turn if you want to. The lady's not for turning.' I say that not only to you but to our friends overseas and also to those who are not our friends ...

Long before we came into office, and therefore long before the invasion of Afghanistan, I was pointing to the threat from the East. I was accused of scaremongering. But events have more than justified my words. Soviet marxism is ideologically, politically and morally bankrupt. But militarily the Soviet Union is a powerful and growing threat.

Yet it was Mr Kosygin* who said: 'No peace loving country, no person of integrity, should remain indifferent when an aggressor holds human life and world opinion in insolent contempt.' We agree. The British government are not indifferent to the occupation of Afghanistan. We shall not allow it to be forgotten. Unless and until the Soviet troops are withdrawn other nations are bound to wonder which of them may be next. Of course there are those who say that by speaking out we are complicating East–West relations, that we are endangering detente. But the real danger would lie in keeping silent. Detente is indivisible and it is a two-way process.

The Soviet Union cannot conduct wars by proxy in South-East Asia and Africa, foment trouble in the Middle East and Caribbean and invade neighbouring countries and still expect to conduct business as usual. Unless detente is pursued by both sides it can be pursued by neither, and it is a delusion to suppose otherwise. That is the message we shall be delivering loud and clear at the meeting of the European Security Conference in Madrid in the weeks immediately ahead.

But we shall also be reminding the other parties in Madrid that the Helsinki Accord was supposed to promote the freer movement of people and ideas. The Soviet government's response so far has been a campaign of repression worse than any since Stalin's day. It had been hoped that Helsinki would open gates across Europe. In fact, the guards today are better armed and the walls are no lower. But behind those walls the human spirit is unvanquished. The workers of Poland in their millions have signalled their determination to participate in the shaping of their destiny. We salute them. Marxists claim that the capitalist system is in crisis. But the Polish workers have shown that it is the Communist system that is in crisis. The Polish people should be left to work out their own future without external interference.

... The irresponsibility of the Left on defence increases as the dangers which we face loom larger. We for our part ... have chosen a defence policy which potential foes will respect. We are acquiring, with the co-operation of the United States government, the Trident missile system. This will ensure the credibility of our strategic deterrent until the end of the century and beyond, and it was very important for the reputation of Britain abroad that we should keep our independent nuclear deterrent as well as for our citizens here.

We have agreed to the stationing of Cruise missiles in this country. The unilateralists object, but the recent willingness of the Soviet government to open a new round of arms control negotiations shows the wisdom of our firmness. We intend to maintain and, where possible, to improve our conventional forces so as to pull our weight in the Alliance. We have no wish to seek a free ride at the expense of our Allies. We will play our full part.

In Europe we have shown that it is possible to combine a vigorous defence of our own interests with a deep commitment to the idea and to the ideals of the Community.

The last government were well aware that Britain's budget contribution was grossly unfair. They failed to do anything about it. We negotiated a satisfactory arrangement which will give us and our partners time to tackle the underlying issues. We have resolved the difficulties of New Zealand's lamb trade with the Community in a way which protects the interests of the farmers in New Zealand while giving our own farmers and our own housewives an excellent deal, and Peter Walker deserves to be congratulated on his success. Now he is two-thirds on his way to success in making important progress towards agreement on a common fisheries policy. That is very important to our people. There are many, many people whose livelihoods depend on it. We face many other problems in the Community, but I am confident that they too will yield to the firm yet fair approach which has already proved so much more effective than the previous overnment's five years of procrastination.

'In the wider world we face darkening horizons'

With each day it becomes clearer that in the wider world we face darkening horizons, and the war between Iran and Iraq is the latest symptom of a deeper malady. Europe and North America are centres of stability in an increasingly anxious world. The Community and the Alliance are the guarantee to other countries that democracy and freedom of choice are still possible. They stand for order and the rule of law in an age when disorder and lawlessness are ever more widespread. The British government intend to stand by both these great institutions, the Community and NATO. We will not betray them. The restoration of Britain's place in the world and of the West's confidence in its own destiny are two aspects of the same process. No doubt there will be unexpected twists in the road, but with wisdom and resolution we can reach our goal. I believe we will show the wisdom and you may be certain that we will show the resolution.

...We close our Conference in the aftermath of that sinister Utopia unveiled at Blackpool♣. Let Labour's Orwellian nightmare of the Left be the spur for us to dedicate with a new urgency our every ounce of energy and moral strength to rebuild the fortunes of this free nation. If we were to fail, that freedom could be imperilled. So let us resist the blandishments of the faint hearts; let us ignore the howls and threats of the extremists; let us stand together and do our duty, and we shall not fail.

♥ At that time, secretary of state for the environment.
♦ Alexei Kosygin (1904–80), chairman of the Council of Ministers of the Soviet Union from 1964.
♣ At Labour's conference the previous week the left-winger Michael Foot had set out a programme of hard-line socialist measures.

'The grotesque chaos of a Labour council'

Labour Party Conference, Bournemouth, 1 October 1985

Neil Kinnock
On the Labour Party's electability

Labour suffered a humiliating defeat at the 1983 general election, which it fought on a hard-Left manifesto characterised by Labour moderate Gerald Kaufman as 'the longest suicide note in history'. Afterwards the Labour Party elected Neil Kinnock (b.1942) as its leader.

Kinnock had entered the Commons as a young man in 1970 and soon made a reputation as a left-wing firebrand – though he was dismissed by his critics as 'the Welsh Windbag' for his verbose style. He reached the summit of his Party without ever having held any government office, though he had for a year been the unpaid Parliamentary private secretary to Michael Foot. Once in charge he continued to move away from his left-wing constituency in the Party, not least because of the horror with which he saw the organised Left – notably the Party within a Party, the Militant Tendency – taking over sections of it, acting irresponsibly, and helping to make Labour continually unelectable. By the time of the 1985 Party conference at Bournemouth, Labour was in serious trouble. Although the Conservative government was slipping in popularity, Labour was fighting for second place in the opinion polls with the Liberal/Social Democratic Party Alliance.

Militant's control of Liverpool's city council was being used increasingly by the Party's enemies as a weapon against it, with the council budgeting for an illegal deficit. This tactic proved catastrophic, for the council ran out of money to pay its staff, and its deputy leader, Derek Hatton, notoriously hired a fleet of 30 taxis to deliver redundancy notices to the council's employees.

In this speech, Kinnock finally signalled that his patience was exhausted with the wreckers inside the Labour Party. It marked the beginning of a showdown with Militant that led to the expulsion of the sect's members from Labour. It was received with an ovation that many older witnesses said had not been seen in response to a leader's speech for decades. Although one hard-Left member of Labour's National Executive Committee, Eric Heffer, walked out in disgust at Kinnock's attack on Liverpool, other delegates were seen in tears of emotion.

Kinnock's deputy, Roy Hattersley, said at the time that the speech changed British politics for ever. It was a prescient remark: it was, in retrospect, the beginning of a process of moving the Labour Party away from its syndicalist and working-class roots to what was to culminate in Tony Blair's consecration of 'New Labour' a decade later. Kinnock led his Party to two defeats in succession – in 1987 and, unexpectedly, in 1992 – before making a career as a European commissioner.

Comrades, 463 resolutions have been submitted to this Conference on policy issues, committed honestly, earnestly and a lot of thought has gone into them. Of those 463, 300 refer to something called the next Labour government and they refer to what they want that next Labour government to do. I want to take on many of those commitments. I want to meet many of those demands. I want to respond to many of those calls, in practice – not in words, but in actions. But there is of course a pre-condition to honouring those or any other undertaking that we give. That precondition is unavoidable, total and insurmountable. It is the pre-condition that we win a general election. There is absolutely no other way to put any of those policies into effect. The only way to restore, the only way to rebuild, the only way to reinstate, the only way to help the poor, to help the unemployed, to help the victimised, is to get the support of those who are not poor, not unemployed, not victimised, who support our view. That means, comrades, reaching out to them and showing them that we are at one with their decent values and aims, that we are with their hopes for their children, with their needs, with their ideals of justice, improvement and prosperity in the future.

'A British public who want to know that our idealism is not lunacy'

There are some in our movement who, when I say that we must reach out in that fashion, accuse me of an obsession with electoral politics. There are some who, when I say we must reach out and make a broader appeal to those who only have their labour to sell, who are part of the working classes – no doubt about their credentials – say that I am too preoccupied with winning. There are some who say, when I reach out like that and in the course of seeking that objective, that I am prepared to compromise values. I say to them and I say to everybody else, and I mean it from the depths of my soul: there is no need to compromise values, there is no need in this task to surrender our socialism, there is no need to abandon or even try to hide any of our principles. But there is an implacable need to win and there is an equal need for us to understand that we address an electorate which is sceptical, an electorate which needs convincing, a British public who want to know that our idealism is not lunacy, our realism is not timidity, our eagerness is not extremism, a British public who want to know that our carefulness too is not nervousness.

'Elections are not won in weeks, they are won in years'

I speak to you, to this Conference. People say that leaders speak to the television cameras. All right, we have got some eavesdroppers. But my belief has always been this, and I act upon it and will always act upon it. I come here to this Conference primarily, above all, to speak to this movement at its Conference. I say to you at this Conference, the best place for me to say anything, that I will tell you what you already know, although some may need reminding. I remind you, every one of you, of something that every single one of you said in the desperate days before June 9, 1983. You said to each other on the streets, you said to each other in the cars rushing round, you said to each other in the committee rooms: elections are not won in weeks, they are won in years. That is what you said to each other. That is what you have got to remember: not in future weeks or future years; this year, this week, this Conference, now – this is where we start winning elections, not waiting until the returning officer is ready.

Secondly, something else you know. If socialism is to be successful in this country, it must relate to the practical needs and the mental and moral traditions of the men and women of this country. We must emphasise what we have in common with those people who are our neighbours, workmates and fellow countrymen and women – and we have everything in common with them – in a way we could not do if we were remote, if, like the Tories, we were in orbit around the realities of our society, if, like the Social Democrats and the Liberals, we stood off from those realities, retreated from them, deserted them. But we are of, from, for the people. That is our identity, that is our commitment, that is how much we have in common with the people. Let us emphasise that, let us demonstrate it, let us not hide it away as if it was something extraordinary or evidence of reaction. Let us emphasise what we have in common with the people of this country.

We must not dogmatise or browbeat. We have got to reason with people; we have got to persuade people. That is their due. We have voluntarily, every one of us, joined a political party. We wish a lot more people would come and join us, help us, give us their counsel, their energies, their advice, broaden our participation. But in making the choice to join a political party we took a decision, and it was that, by persuasion, we hoped that we could bring more people with us. So that is the basis on which we have got to act, want to act.

Thirdly, something else you know. There is anger in this country at the devastation brought about by these last six years of Tory government, but strangely that anger is mixed with despair, a feeling that the problems are just too great, too complex, to be dealt with by any government or any policy. That feeling is abroad. We disagree with it, we contend it, we try to give people the rational alternatives, but it exists. If our response to that despair, anger and confusion amounts to little more than slogans, if we give the impression to the British people that we believe that we can just make a loud noise and the Tory walls of Jericho will fall down, they are not going to treat us very seriously at all – and we won't deserve to be treated very seriously.

'Hiring taxis to scuttle round a city handing out redundancy notices'

Fourthly, I shall tell you again, what you know. Because you are from the people, because you are of the people, because you live with the same realities as everybody else lives with, implausible promises don't win victories. I'll tell you what happens with impossible promises. You start with far-fetched resolutions. They are then pickled into a rigid dogma, a code, and you go through the years sticking to that, out-dated, misplaced, irrelevant to the real needs, and you end in the grotesque chaos of a Labour council – a Labour council – hiring taxis to scuttle round a city handing out redundancy notices to its own workers. I am telling you, no matter how entertaining, how fulfilling to short-term egos – I'm telling you, and you'll listen – you can't play politics with people's jobs and with people's services or with their homes. Comrades, the voice of the people – not the people here; the voice of the real people with real

THE MILITANT TENDENCY

1953

The Revolutionary Socialist League is founded, one of the three leading Trotskyite groups of the late 1950s in Britain, which later becomes Militant Tendency.

1964

The newspaper *Militant* is founded by Ted Grant.

1970

From this year onwards the Labour Party's youth movement, the Labour Party Young Socialists (LPYS), is under the control of Militant.

1982

Militant is declared ineligible for affiliation to the Labour Party.

1983

Five members of *Militant's* Editorial Board are expelled from the Labour Party; two Militant members are elected as Labour MPs, Dave Nellist (Coventry) and Terry Fields (Liverpool Broadgreen); Derek Hatton becomes deputy leader of Liverpool City Council.

1985

Liverpool district Labour Party is suspended by its national leadership.

1986

Derek Hatton is expelled from the Labour Party.

1987

Pat Wall, a member of Militant, becomes MP for Bradford North.

1992

Militant abandons its entryism policy, and seeks to work as an independent body called Militant Labour.

1997

Members of Militant Labour participate in the formation of the Socialist Party, whose leader, Tommy Sheridan, is elected to the Scottish Parliament in 1999, fighting under the name of the Scottish Socialist Party.

1997

Militant is replaced by *The Socialist*.

needs – is louder than all the boos that can be assembled. Understand that, please, comrades. In your socialism, in your commitment to those people, understand it. The people will not, cannot, abide posturing. They cannot respect the gesture-generals or the tendency-tacticians.

Comrades, it seems to me lately that some of our number become like latter-day public schoolboys. It seems it matters not whether you won or lost, but how you played the game. We cannot take that inspiration from Rudyard Kipling. Those game players get isolated, hammered, blocked off. They might try to blame others – workers, trade unions, some other leadership, the people of the city – for not showing sufficient revolutionary consciousness, always somebody else, and then they claim a rampant victory. Whose victory? Not victory for the people, not victory for them. I see the casualties; we will all see the casualties. They are not to be found amongst the leaders and some of the enthusiasts; they are to be found amongst the people whose jobs are destroyed, whose services are crushed, whose living standards are pushed down to deeper depths of insecurity and misery. Comrades, these are vile times under this Tory government for local democracy, and we have got to secure power to restore real local democracy.

But I look around this country and I see Labour councils, I see socialists, as good as any other socialists, who fought the good fight and who, at the point when they thought they might jeopardise people's jobs and people's services, had the intelligence, yes, and the courage to adopt a different course. They truly put jobs and services first before other considerations. They had to make hellish choices. I understand it. You must agonise with them in the choices they had to make – very unpalatable, totally undesirable, but they did it. They found ways. They used all their creativity to find ways that would best protect those whom they employed and those whom they were elected to defend. Those people are leaders prepared to take decisions, to meet obligations, to give service. They know life is real, life is earnest – too real, too earnest to mistake a Conference resolution for an accomplished fact; too real, too earnest to mistake a slogan for a strategy; too real, too earnest to allow them to mistake their own individual enthusiasms for mass movement; too real, too earnest to mistake barking for biting. I hope that becomes universal too.

Comrades, I offer you this counsel. The victory of socialism, said a great socialist, does not have to be complete to be convincing. I have no time, he went on, for those who appear to threaten the whole of private property but who in practice would threaten nothing; they are purists and therefore barren. Not the words of some hypnotised moderate, not some petrified pragmatist, but Aneurin Bevan in 1950 at the height of his socialist vision and his radical power and conviction. There are some who will say that power and principle are somehow in conflict. Those people who think that power and principle are in conflict only demonstrate the superficiality, the shallowness of their own socialist convictions; for whilst they are bold enough to preach those convictions in little coteries, they do not have the depth of conviction to subject those convictions, those beliefs, that analysis, to the real test of putting them into operation in power.

'Principle without power is naive, idle sterility'

There is no collision between principle and power. For us as democratic socialists the two must go together, like a rich vein that passes through everything that we believe in, everything that we try to do, everything that we will implement. Principle and power, conviction and accomplishment, going together. We know that power without principle is ruthless and vicious, and hollow and sour. We know that principle without power is naive, idle sterility. That is useless – useless to us, useless to the British people to overcome their travails, useless for our purpose of changing society as democratic socialists. I tell you that now. It is what I have always said, it is what I shall go on saying, because it is what I said to you at the moment that I was elected leader.

I say to you in complete honesty, because that is the movement that I belong to, that I owe this Party everything I have got – not the job, not being leader of the Labour Party, but every life chance that I have had since the time I was a child: the life chance of a comfortable home, with working parents, people who had jobs; the life chance of moving out of a pest- and damp-invested set of rooms into a decent home, built by a Labour council under a Labour government; the life chance of an education that went on for as long as I wanted to take it. Me and millions of others of my generation got all their chances from this movement. That is why I say that this movement, its values, its policies, applied in power, gave me everything that I have got – me and millions like me of my generation and succeeding generations. That is why it is my duty to be honest and that is why it is our function, our mission, our duty – all of us – to see that those life chances exist and are enriched and extended to millions more, who without us will never get the chance of fulfilling themselves. That is why we have got to win, that is what I have always believed and that is what I put to you at the very moment that I was elected.

'We will get that victory with our policies, our principles, intact'

In 1983 I said to this Conference: 'We have to win. We must not permit any purpose to be superior for the Labour movement to that purpose.' I still believe it. I will go on saying it until we achieve that victory and I shall live with the consequences, which I know, if this movement is with me, will be victory – victory with our policies intact, no sell-outs, provided that we put nothing before the objective of explaining ourselves and reasoning with the people of this country. We will get that victory with our policies, our principles, intact. I know it can be done. Reason tells me it can be done. The people throughout this movement, who I know in huge majority share all these perceptions and visions and want to give all their energies, they know it can be done. Realism tells me it can be done, and the plain realities and needs of our country tell me it must be done. We have got to win, not for our sakes, but really, truly, to deliver the British people from evil. Let's do it.

'*Let Europe be a family of nations*'

College of Europe, Bruges, 20 September 1988

Margaret Thatcher
on her vision of Europe

Once the Conservative Party had established itself firmly in office during the 1980s, and once it had appeared to have won the support of the public over its management of the economy, vicious in-fighting broke out within Margaret Thatcher's Cabinet and the wider Party about the future of Britain in Europe.

This speech, delivered in Belgium at a time when Mrs Thatcher was coming under immense pressure to take Sterling into the European exchange rate mechanism (ERM) – thereby fixing its value against other European currencies as a prelude to monetary union – signalled her personal determination not to sacrifice economic sovereignty to Brussels. Its immediate trigger was a speech made a fortnight earlier to the Trades Union Congress by Jacques Delors, president of the European Commission. He had invited the British labour movement – which had, historically, been anti-European (see Hugh Gaitskell's 1962 speech) – to support the European project, in return for greater rights and protection for workers.

Margaret Thatcher was not hearing of such interference, and forcibly said so in this speech at Bruges. Its tone, welcomed ecstatically on the nationalist Right of her Party, angered the pro-Europeans, not least because of what they regarded as its backward-looking, historicist view of Britain's superior record of safeguarding liberty. The divisions in her Party over Europe, and her refusal to adopt a more conciliatory line towards Brussels, were some of the main reasons why she was forced from office two years later, a few weeks after finally leading Britain into the ERM in order to appease her Cabinet critics.

Two years after that, during the government of her successor John Major, Britain was ejected from the ERM because of the inherent weakness of Sterling, thereby suffering the greatest economic humiliation since the International Monetary Fund had had to save the country from bankruptcy in 1976.

'Mr Chairman, you have invited me to speak on the subject of Britain and Europe. Perhaps I should congratulate you on your courage. If you believe some of the things said and written about my views on Europe, it must seem rather like inviting Genghis Khan to speak on the virtues of peaceful coexistence!

We British are as much heirs to ... European culture as any other nation'

I want to start by disposing of some myths about my country, Britain, and its relationship with Europe and to do that, I must say something about the identity of Europe itself. Europe is not the creation of the Treaty of Rome. Nor is the European idea the property of any group or institution.

We British are as much heirs to the legacy of European culture as any other nation. Our links to the rest of Europe, the continent of Europe, have been the dominant factor in our history. For three hundred years, we were part of the Roman empire and our maps still trace the straight lines of the roads the Romans built. Our ancestors – Celts, Saxons, Danes – came from the Continent. Our nation was – in that favourite Community word – 'restructured' under the Norman and Angevin rule in the 11th and 12th centuries. This year, we celebrate the 300th anniversary of the Glorious Revolution in which the British crown passed to Prince William of Orange and Queen Mary. Visit the great churches and cathedrals of Britain, read our literature and listen to our language: all bear witness to the cultural riches which we have drawn from Europe and other Europeans from us.

We in Britain are rightly proud of the way in which, since Magna Carta in the year 1215, we have pioneered and developed representative institutions to stand as bastions of freedom. And proud too of the way in which for centuries Britain was a home for people from the rest of Europe who sought sanctuary from tyranny. But we know that without the European legacy of political ideas we could not have achieved as much as we did. From classical and mediaeval thought we have borrowed that concept of the rule of law which marks out a civilised society from barbarism. And on that idea of Christendom, to which the rector referred – Christendom for long synonymous with Europe – with its recognition of the unique and spiritual nature of the individual, on that idea, we still base our belief in personal liberty and other human rights.

'To prevent Europe from falling under the dominance of a single power'

Too often, the history of Europe is described as a series of interminable wars and quarrels. Yet from our perspective today surely what strikes us most is our common experience. For instance, the story of how Europeans explored and colonised – and yes, without apology – civilised much of the world is an extraordinary tale of talent, skill and courage.

But we British have in a very special way contributed to Europe. Over the centuries we have fought to prevent Europe from falling under the dominance of a single power. We have fought

BRITAIN AND THE COMMON MARKET 1961–90

1961
Britain, Denmark and Ireland apply to join the European Economic Community (EEC).

1963
Charles de Gaulle vetoes British membership (and again in 1967).

1967
The EEC, European Atomic Energy Community (Euratom) and European Coal and Steel Community (ECSC) are united under one umbrella, the European Community (EC).

1973
Britain, Denmark and Ireland join the EC.

1975
UK holds a referendum after renegotiating its entry terms; the result is 2:1 in favour.

and we have died for her freedom. Only miles from here, in Belgium, lie the bodies of 120,000 British soldiers who died in the First World War. Had it not been for that willingness to fight and to die, Europe would have been united long before now – but not in liberty, not in justice. It was British support to resistance movements throughout the last war that helped to keep alive the flame of liberty in so many countries until the day of liberation. Tomorrow, King Baudouin will attend a service in Brussels to commemorate the many brave Belgians who gave their lives in service with the Royal Air Force – a sacrifice which we shall never forget. And it was from our island fortress that the liberation of Europe itself was mounted. And still, today, we stand together. Nearly 70,000 British servicemen are stationed on the mainland of Europe.

All these things alone are proof of our commitment to Europe's future. The European Community is one manifestation of that European identity, but it is not the only one. We must never forget that east of the Iron Curtain, people who once enjoyed a full share of European culture, freedom and identity have been cut off from their roots. We shall always look on Warsaw, Prague and Budapest as great European cities. Nor should we forget that European values have helped to make the United States of America into the valiant defender of freedom which she has become.

'Willing and active cooperation between independent sovereign states'

This is no arid chronicle of obscure facts from the dust-filled libraries of history. It is the record of nearly two thousand years of British involvement in Europe, cooperation with Europe and contribution to Europe, a contribution which today is as valid and as strong as ever.

... This evening I want to set out some guiding principles for the future which I believe will ensure that Europe does succeed, not just in economic and defence terms but also in the quality of life and the influence of its peoples.

My first guiding principle is this: willing and active cooperation between independent sovereign states is the best way to build a successful European Community. To try to suppress

1979
The European Monetary System (EMS) is created, two features of which are the introduction of the European currency unit (Ecu) and the exchange rate mechanism (ERM): all members join except the UK.

1981
Greece becomes the EC's tenth member.

1984
Margaret Thatcher renegotiates Britain's EC payments; at Fontainebleau Summit in June, the EC agrees on an annual rebate for Britain, amounting to 66% of the difference between Britain's contributions and receipts.

1986
Spain and Portugal join the EC; the European flag is unveiled; the Single European Act (1986) is signed, the first major revision of the original Treaty of Rome; the aim of a single market by 1992 is set, and the concept of European political co-operation is deepened.

1990
Britain enters the ERM (and is ejected in 1992).

nationhood and concentrate power at the centre of a European conglomerate would be highly damaging and would jeopardise the objectives we seek to achieve. Europe will be stronger precisely because it has France as France, Spain as Spain, Britain as Britain, each with its own customs, traditions and identity. It would be folly to try to fit them into some sort of identikit European personality.

Some of the founding fathers of the Community thought that the United States of America might be its model. But the whole history of America is quite different from Europe. People went there to get away from the intolerance and constraints of life in Europe. They sought liberty and opportunity; and their strong sense of purpose has, over two centuries, helped to create a new unity and pride in being American, just as our pride lies in being British or Belgian or Dutch or German.

I am the first to say that on many great issues the countries of Europe should try to speak with a single voice. I want to see us work more closely on the things we can do better together than alone. Europe is stronger when we do so, whether it be in trade, in defence or in our relations with the rest of the world. But working more closely together does not require power to be centralised in Brussels or decisions to be taken by an appointed bureaucracy. Indeed, it is ironic that just when those countries such as the Soviet Union, which have tried to run everything from the centre, are learning that success depends on dispersing power and decisions away from the centre, there are some in the Community who seem to want to move in the opposite direction.

We have not successfully rolled back the frontiers of the state in Britain, only to see them re-imposed at a European level

We have not successfully rolled back the frontiers of the state in Britain, only to see them re-imposed at a European level with a European super-state exercising a new dominance from Brussels. Certainly we want to see Europe more united and with a greater sense of common purpose. But it must be in a way which preserves the different traditions, parliamentary powers and sense of national pride in one's own country; for these have been the source of Europe's vitality through the centuries.

My second guiding principle is this: Community policies must tackle present problems in a practical way, however difficult that may be. If we cannot reform those Community policies which are patently wrong or ineffective and which are rightly causing public disquiet, then we shall not get the public support for the Community's future development. And that is why the achievements of the European Council in Brussels last February are so important. It was not right that half the total Community budget was being spent on storing and disposing of surplus food. Now those stocks are being sharply reduced. It was absolutely right to decide that agriculture's share of the budget should be cut in order to free resources for other policies, such as helping the less well-off regions and helping training for jobs. It was right too to introduce tighter budgetary discipline to enforce these decisions and to bring the Community spending under better control.

And those who complained that the Community was spending so much time on financial detail missed the point. You cannot build on unsound foundations, financial or otherwise, and it was the fundamental reforms agreed last winter which paved the way for the remarkable progress which we have made since on the Single Market.

But we cannot rest on what we have achieved to date. For example, the task of reforming the Common Agricultural Policy is far from complete. Certainly, Europe needs a stable and efficient farming industry. But the CAP has become unwieldy, inefficient and grossly expensive. Production of unwanted surpluses safeguards neither the income nor the future of farmers themselves. We must continue to pursue policies which relate supply more closely to market requirements, and which will reduce over-production and limit costs. Of course, we must protect the villages and rural areas which are such an important part of our national life, but not by the instrument of agricultural prices. Tackling these problems requires political courage. The Community will only damage itself in the eyes of its own people and the outside world if that courage is lacking.

My third guiding principle is the need for Community policies which encourage enterprise. If Europe is to flourish and create the jobs of the future, enterprise is the key. The basic framework is there: the Treaty of Rome itself was intended as a Charter for Economic Liberty. But that it is not how it has always been read, still less applied. The lesson of the economic history of Europe in the 70s and 80s is that central planning and detailed control do not work and that personal endeavour and initiative do. That a state-controlled economy is a recipe for low growth and that free enterprise within a framework of law brings better results.

'And that means action to ... reduce government intervention'

The aim of a Europe open to enterprise is the moving force behind the creation of the Single European Market in 1992. By getting rid of barriers, by making it possible for companies to operate on a European scale, we can best compete with the United States, Japan and other new economic powers emerging in Asia and elsewhere. And that means action to free markets, action to widen choice, action to reduce government intervention. Our aim should not be more and more detailed regulation from the centre: it should be to deregulate and to remove the constraints on trade.

Britain has been in the lead in opening its markets to others. The City of London has long welcomed financial institutions from all over the world, which is why it is the biggest and most successful financial centre in Europe. We have opened our market for telecommunications equipment, introduced competition into the market services and even into the network itself – steps which others in Europe are only now beginning to face. In air transport, we have taken the lead in liberalisation and seen the benefits in cheaper fares and wider choice. Our coastal shipping trade is open to the merchant navies of Europe. We wish we could say the same of many other Community members.

... Of course, we want to make it easier for goods to pass through frontiers. Of course, we must make it easier for people to travel throughout the Community. But it is a matter of plain common sense that we cannot totally abolish frontier controls if we are also to protect our citizens from crime and stop the movement of drugs, of terrorists and of illegal immigrants.

That was underlined graphically only three weeks ago when one brave German customs officer, doing his duty on the frontier between Holland and Germany, struck a major blow against the terrorists of the IRA.

And before I leave the subject of a single market, may I say that we certainly do not need new regulations which raise the cost of employment and make Europe's labour market less flexible and less competitive with overseas suppliers. If we are to have a European Company Statute, it should contain the minimum regulations. And certainly we in Britain would fight attempts to introduce collectivism and corporatism at the European level – although what people wish to do in their own countries is a matter for them.

My fourth guiding principle is that Europe should not be protectionist. The expansion of the world economy requires us to continue the process of removing barriers to trade, and to do so in the multilateral negotiations in the GATT. It would be a betrayal if, while breaking down constraints on trade within Europe, the Community were to erect greater external protection. We must ensure that our approach to world trade is consistent with the liberalisation we preach at home. We have a responsibility to give a lead on this, a responsibility which is particularly directed towards the less developed countries. They need not only aid; more than anything, they need improved trading opportunities if they are to gain the dignity of growing economic strength and independence.

'The strength of our defence. On this, we must never falter, never fail'

My last guiding principle concerns the most fundamental issue – the European countries' role in defence. Europe must continue to maintain a sure defence through NATO. There can be no question of relaxing our efforts, even though it means taking difficult decisions and meeting heavy costs. It is to NATO that we owe the peace that has been maintained over 40 years. The fact is things are going our way: the democratic model of a free enterprise society has proved itself superior; freedom is on the offensive, a peaceful offensive the world over, for the first time in my lifetime. We must strive to maintain the United States' commitment to Europe's defence. And that means recognising the burden on their resources of the world role they undertake and their point that their allies should bear the full part of the defence of freedom, particularly as Europe grows wealthier. Increasingly, they will look to Europe to play a part in out-of-area defence, as we have recently done in the Gulf.

NATO and the Western European Union have long recognised where the problems of Europe's defence lie, and have pointed out the solutions. And the time has come when we must give substance to our declarations about a strong defence effort with better value for money. It is not an institutional problem. It is not a problem of drafting. It is something at once simpler and more profound: it is a question of political will and political courage, of convincing people in all our countries that we cannot rely for ever on others for our defence, but that each member of the Alliance must shoulder a fair share of the burden.

We must keep up public support for nuclear deterrence, remembering that obsolete weapons do not deter, hence the need for modernisation. We must meet the requirements for effective conventional defence in Europe against Soviet forces which are constantly being modernised.

We should develop the WEU [Western European Union], not as an alternative to NATO, but as a means of strengthening Europe's contribution to the common defence of the West. Above all, at a time of change and uncertainty in the Soviet Union and Eastern Europe, we must preserve Europe's unity and resolve so that whatever may happen, our defence is sure. At the same time, we must negotiate on arms control and keep the door wide open to cooperation on all the other issues covered by the Helsinki Accords. But let us never forget that our way of life, our vision and all we hope to achieve, is secured not by the rightness of our cause but by the strength of our defence. On this, we must never falter, never fail.

Mr Chairman, I believe it is not enough just to talk in general terms about a European vision or ideal. If we believe in it, we must chart the way ahead and identify the next steps. And that is what I have tried to do this evening. This approach does not require new documents: they are all there, the North Atlantic Treaty, the Revised Brussels Treaty and the Treaty of Rome, texts written by far-sighted men, a remarkable Belgian – Paul Henri Spaak – among them.

'Utopia never comes ... we should not like it if it did'

However far we may want to go, the truth is that we can only get there one step at a time. And what we need now is to take decisions on the next steps forward, rather than let ourselves be distracted by Utopian goals. Utopia never comes, because we know we should not like it if it did. Let Europe be a family of nations, understanding each other better, appreciating each other more, doing more together but relishing our national identity no less than our common European endeavour.

Let us have a Europe which plays its full part in the wider world, which looks outward not inward, and which preserves that Atlantic community – that Europe on both sides of the Atlantic – which is our noblest inheritance and our greatest strength.

'Conflict of loyalty'

House of Commons, London, 13 November 1990

Sir Geoffrey Howe

on his reasons for resigning from Margaret
Thatcher's goverment

Geoffrey Howe (b.1926) had a distinguished career as a barrister before entering politics, and soon obtained office, serving as solicitor-general in the government of Edward Heath. A committed economic liberal, he was chancellor of the exchequer in Margaret Thatcher's Cabinet from 1979 to 1983. In that post he introduced many reforms of the tax system, abolished exchange controls and established the foundations of the Thatcherite economic revival that took hold in Britain in the mid- to late 1980s.

In 1983 he became foreign secretary, and from then on he and Margaret Thatcher began to fall out over matters of high politics. They came to personify the poisonous divide in the Conservative Party over Europe, with Howe a passionate pro-European and advocate of membership of the exchange rate mechanism as a prelude to a single currency. When Mrs Thatcher, herself becoming intensely unpopular, demoted him in 1989 from the foreign office to the leadership of the House of Commons, he was the recipient of a wave of sympathy from across the Conservative Party. By the time he resigned from that post a year later, in despair at what he saw as the unacceptably nationalistic nature of Mrs Thatcher's European policy and her stubborn refusal to contemplate joining a single European currency, he had acquired the power to damage her terminally.

Using his reputation and authority to deliver this crushing attack on her, he signalled the way for dissident Conservative Michael Heseltine to launch his bid against her for the leadership of the Conservative Party and thus the prime ministership. Within a fortnight there had been a leadership contest, and though Mrs Thatcher led the poll by a margin of 204 to 152, her Parliamentary Party quickly deemed it insufficient for her survival. She resigned and, in the second round, Heseltine was beaten by John Major, who was perceived to be the Thatcherite candidate, and who became the youngest prime minister since Lord Rosebery a century earlier. Howe's speech was, and is still, regarded as the intervention that made the contest possible, and changed the course of recent British political history.

I find to my astonishment that a quarter of a century has passed since I last spoke from one of the back benches. Fortunately, however, it has been my privilege to serve for the past 12 months of that time as leader of the House of Commons, so I have been reminded quite recently of the traditional generosity and tolerance of this place. I hope that I may count on that today as I offer to the House a statement about my resignation from the government.

It has been suggested – even, indeed, by some of my right hon. and hon. friends – that I decided to resign solely because of questions of style and not on matters of substance at all. Indeed, if some of my former colleagues are to be believed, I must be the first minister in history who has resigned because he was in full agreement with government policy. The truth is that, in many aspects of politics, style and substance complement each other. Very often, they are two sides of the same coin.

'The courage and leadership of my right hon. friend'

The prime minister and I have shared something like 700 meetings of Cabinet or Shadow Cabinet during the past 18 years, and some 400 hours alongside each other at more than 30 international summit meetings. For both of us, I suspect, it is a pretty daunting record. The House might well feel that something more than simple matters of style would be necessary to rupture such a well-tried relationship. It was a privilege to serve as my right hon. friend's first chancellor of the exchequer; to share in the transformation of our industrial relations scene … to help launch our free market programme, commencing with the abolition of exchange control … and, above all, to achieve such substantial success against inflation, getting it down within four years from 22 per cent to 4 per cent upon the basis of the strict monetary discipline involved in the medium-term financial strategy. Not one of our economic achievements would have been possible without the courage and leadership of my right hon. friend – and, if I may say so, they possibly derived some little benefit from the presence of a chancellor who was not exactly a wet himself.

It was a great honour to serve for six years as foreign and commonwealth secretary and to share with my right hon. friend in some notable achievements in the European Community – from Fontainebleau to the Single European Act. But it was as we moved on to consider the crucial monetary issues in the European context that I came to feel increasing concern. Some of the reasons for that anxiety were made very clear by my right hon. friend the Member for Blaby◆ in his resignation speech just over 12 months ago. Like him, I concluded at least five years ago that the conduct of our policy against inflation could no longer rest solely on attempts to measure and control the domestic money supply. We had no doubt that we should be helped in that battle, and, indeed, in other respects, by joining the exchange rate mechanism of the European monetary system. There was, or should have been, nothing novel about joining the ERM … it has been a long-standing commitment. For a quarter of a century after the Second World War, we found that the very similar Bretton Woods◆ regime did serve as a useful discipline. Now, as my right hon. friend the prime minister acknowledged two weeks ago, our entry into the ERM can be seen as an 'extra discipline for keeping down inflation'.

However, it must be said that that practical conclusion has been achieved only at the cost of substantial damage to her administration and, more serious still, to its inflation achievements. As my right hon. friend the Member for Blaby explained … 'The real tragedy is that we did not join the exchange rate mechanism at least five years ago.' As he also made clear, 'That was not for want of trying.'

Indeed, the so-called Madrid conditions came into existence only after the then chancellor and I, as foreign secretary, made it clear that we could not continue in office unless a specific commitment to join the ERM was made.

'Today's higher rates of inflation could well have been avoided'

THE EUROPEAN UNION SINCE MARGARET THATCHER

1992

EC members sign the Treaty on European Union (or Maastricht Treaty) (7 Feb.), which revises the Treaty of Rome (1957), though John Major negotiates an opt-out on proposed monetary union and a chapter on social policy.

1992

Pressure on sterling forces the UK government to pull the pound out of the ERM.

1993

The 'Single Market' comes into force: all tariffs and restrictions on the movement of people and goods among EU member states are abolished (1 Jan.); the Maastricht Treaty – and formally the 'European Union' – comes into effect (1 Nov.).

1995

Austria, Finland and Sweden join the EU, taking its membership to 15.

1997

The Amsterdam Treaty is signed: laws on employment and discrimination are strengthened, and the social chapter of the Maastricht Treaty becomes an official part of EU law.

1999

The euro comes into existence as the official currency of 11 countries; Greece adopts it in 2001, though Sweden, Denmark and the UK stay out.

2002

National currencies are finally replaced by the euro in the 12 participating countries.

2004

Cyprus, the Czech Republic, Estonia, Hungary, Latvia, Lithuania, Malta, Poland, Slovakia and Slovenia join the EU.

2007

Romania and Bulgaria become members, so that the EU totals 27 nations.

As the House will no doubt have observed, neither member of that particular partnership now remains in office. Our successor as chancellor of the exchequer has, during the past year, had to devote a great deal of his considerable talents to demonstrating exactly how those Madrid conditions have been attained, so as to make it possible to fulfil a commitment whose achievement has long been in the national interest.

It is now, alas, impossible to resist the conclusion that today's higher rates of inflation could well have been avoided had the question of ERM membership been properly considered and resolved at a much earlier stage. There are, I fear, developing grounds for similar anxiety over the handling – not just at and after the Rome summit – of the wider, much more open question of economic and monetary union. Let me first make clear certain important points on which I have no disagreement with my right hon. friend the prime minister. I do not regard the Delors report as some kind of sacred text that has to be accepted, or even rejected, on the nod. But it is an important working document. As I have often made plain, it is seriously deficient in significant respects. I do not regard the Italian presidency's management of the Rome summit as a model of its kind – far from it. It was much the same, as my right hon. friend the prime minister will recall, in Milan some five years ago.

I do not regard it as in any sense wrong for Britain to make criticisms of that kind plainly and courteously, nor in any sense wrong for us to do so, if necessary, alone. As I have already made clear, I have, like the prime minister and other right hon. friends, fought too many European battles in a minority of one to have any illusions on that score.

But it is crucially important that we should conduct those arguments upon the basis of a clear understanding of the true relationship between this country, the Community and our Community partners. And it is here, I fear, that my right hon. friend the prime minister increasingly risks leading herself and others astray in matters of substance as well as of style.

'Not to retreat into a ghetto of sentimentality about our past'

It was the late Lord Stockton, formerly Harold Macmillan, who first put the central point clearly. As long ago as 1962, he argued that we had to place and keep ourselves within the EC. He saw it as essential then, as it is today, not to cut ourselves off from the realities of power ... not to retreat into a ghetto of sentimentality about our past and so diminish our own control over our own destiny in the future.

The pity is that the Macmillan view had not been perceived more clearly a decade before in the 1950s. It would have spared us so many of the struggles of the last 20 years had we been in the Community from the outset ... had we been ready, in the much too simple phrase, to 'surrender some sovereignty' at a much earlier stage. If we had been in from the start, as almost everybody now acknowledges, we should have had more, not less, influence over the Europe in which we live today. We should never forget the lesson of that isolation, of being on the outside looking in, for the conduct of today's affairs.

We have done best when we have seen the Community not as a static entity to be resisted and contained, but as an active process which we can shape, often decisively, provided that we allow ourselves to be fully engaged in it, with confidence, with enthusiasm and in good faith. We must at all costs avoid presenting ourselves yet again with an over-simplified choice, a false antithesis, a bogus dilemma, between one alternative, starkly labelled 'co-operation between independent sovereign states', and a second, equally crudely labelled alternative, 'centralised, federal super-state', as if there were no middle way in between.

We commit a serious error if we think always in terms of 'surrendering' sovereignty and seek to stand pat for all time on a given deal – by proclaiming, as my right hon. friend the prime minister did two weeks ago, that we have 'surrendered enough'.

'I find Winston Churchill's perception a good deal more convincing'

The European enterprise is not and should not be seen like that – as some kind of zero sum game. Sir Winston Churchill put it much more positively 40 years ago, when he said ... 'It is also possible and not less agreeable to regard' this sacrifice or merger of national sovereignty 'as the gradual assumption by all the nations concerned of that larger sovereignty which can alone protect their diverse and distinctive customs and characteristics and their national traditions.'

I have to say that I find Winston Churchill's perception a good deal more convincing, and more encouraging for the interests of our nation, than the nightmare image sometimes conjured up by my right hon. friend, who seems sometimes to look out upon a continent that is positively teeming with ill-intentioned people, scheming, in her words, to 'extinguish democracy', to 'dissolve our national identities' and to lead us 'through the back-door into a federal Europe'.

What kind of vision is that for our business people, who trade there each day, for our financiers, who seek to make London the money capital of Europe, or for all the young people of today?

These concerns are especially important as we approach the crucial topic of economic and monetary union. We must be positively and centrally involved in this debate and not fearfully and negatively detached. The costs of disengagement here could be very serious indeed.

'The real threat is that of leaving ourselves with no say in ... Europe'

There is talk, of course, of a single currency for Europe. I agree that there are many difficulties about the concept – both economic and political. Of course, as I said in my letter of resignation, none of us wants the imposition of a single currency. But that is not the real risk. The 11 others cannot impose their solution on the 12th country against its will, but they can go ahead without us. The risk is not imposition but isolation. The real threat is that of leaving ourselves with no say in the monetary arrangements that the rest of Europe chooses for itself, with Britain once again scrambling to join the club later, after the rules have been set and after the power has been distributed by others to our disadvantage. That would be the worst possible outcome.

It is to avoid just that outcome and to find a compromise both acceptable in the government and sellable in Europe that my right hon. friend the chancellor has put forward his hard ecu proposal*. This lays careful emphasis on the possibility that the hard ecu as a common currency could, given time, evolve into a single currency. I have of course supported the hard ecu plan. But after Rome, and after the comments of my right hon. friend the prime minister two weeks ago, there is a grave danger that the hard ecu proposal is becoming untenable, because two things have happened. The first is that my right hon. friend the prime minister has appeared to rule out from the start any compromise at any stage on any of the basic components that all the 11 other countries believe to be a part of EMU – a single currency or a permanently fixed exchange rate, a central bank or common monetary policy. Asked whether we would veto any arrangement that jeopardised the pound sterling, my right hon. friend replied simply, 'Yes'. That statement means not that we can block EMU but that they can go ahead without us. Is that a position that is likely to ensure, as I put it in my resignation letter, that 'we hold, and retain, a position of influence in this vital debate'?

I fear not. Rather, to do so, we must, as I said, take care not to rule in or rule out any one solution absolutely. We must be seen to be part of the same negotiation.

'Their bats have been broken before the game'

The second thing that happened was, I fear, even more disturbing. Reporting to this House, my right hon. friend almost casually remarked that she did not think that many people would want to use the hard ecu anyway – even as a common currency, let alone as a single one. It was remarkable – indeed, it was tragic – to hear my right hon. friend dismissing, with such personalised incredulity, the very idea that the hard ecu proposal might find growing favour among the peoples of Europe, just as it was extraordinary to hear her assert that the whole idea of EMU might be open for consideration only by future generations. Those future generations are with us today. How on earth are the chancellor and the governor of the Bank of England, commending the hard ecu as they strive to, to be taken as serious participants in the debate against that kind of background noise? I believe that both the chancellor and the governor are cricketing enthusiasts, so I hope that there is no monopoly of cricketing metaphors. It is rather like sending your opening batsmen to the crease only for them to find, the moment the first balls are bowled, that their bats have been broken before the game by the team captain.

The point was perhaps more sharply put by a British businessman, trading in Brussels and elsewhere, who wrote to me last week, stating … 'People throughout Europe see our prime minister's finger-wagging and hear her passionate "No, No, No" much more clearly than the content of the carefully worded formal texts.'

He went on … 'It is too easy for them to believe that we all share her attitudes … for why else has she been our prime minister for so long?' My correspondent concluded … 'This is a desperately serious situation for our country.' And sadly, I have to agree.

'If we detach ourselves completely … the effects will be incalculable'

The tragedy is – and it is for me personally, for my Party, for our whole people and for my right hon. friend herself, a very real tragedy – that the prime minister's perceived attitude towards Europe is running increasingly serious risks for the future of our nation. It risks minimising our influence and maximising our chances of being once again shut out. We have paid heavily in the past for late starts and squandered opportunities in Europe. We dare not let that happen again. If we detach ourselves completely, as a party or a nation, from the middle ground of Europe, the effects will be incalculable and very hard ever to correct.

In my letter of resignation, which I tendered with the utmost sadness and dismay, I said … 'Cabinet government is all about trying to persuade one another from within.' That was my commitment to government by persuasion – persuading colleagues and the nation. I have tried to do that as foreign secretary and since, but I realise now that the task has become futile … trying to stretch the meaning of words beyond what was credible, and trying to pretend that there was a common policy when every step forward risked being subverted by some casual comment or impulsive answer.

'The tragic conflict of loyalties with which I have myself wrestled'

The conflict of loyalty, of loyalty to my right hon. friend the prime minister – and, after all, in two decades together that instinct of loyalty is still very real – and of loyalty to what I perceive to be the true interests of the nation, has become all too great. I no longer believe it possible to resolve that conflict from within this government. That is why I have resigned. In doing so, I have done what I believe to be right for my Party and my country. The time has come for others to consider their own response to the tragic conflict of loyalties with which I have myself wrestled for perhaps too long.

♥ Nigel Lawson (b.1932), chancellor of the exchequer 1983–9.
♦ A conference held in the United States in 1944, at which the British representative was John Maynard Keynes, and where an international system of fixed exchange rates was agreed in the hope of assisting economic stability in the post-war world.
♣ A proposal by the British government that a European currency – the ecu – should circulate in competition with other European currencies.

'The extraordinary and irreplaceable Diana'

Westminster Abbey, London, 6 September 1997

The 9th Earl Spencer
on the life of Princess Diana

Lady Diana Spencer married Charles, Prince of Wales, on 29 July 1981. According to most reports the marriage soon descended into unhappiness, not least because of the prince's attachment to his married friend Camilla Parker Bowles. In 1992 the couple separated, divorcing two years later. A media battle then ensued between them, as each gave television interviews putting their sides of the story, and books and countless newspaper articles pried ever more pruriently into the dirty washing of the royal family: there had been nothing like it since the scandals between the prince regent and his estranged wife nearly 200 years earlier.

By 1997 Diana, Princess of Wales (as she was styled even after her divorce), had been associated with various other men, and she began a relationship with Dodi (al-)Fayed, 'playboy' son of Harrods owner Mohammed al-Fayed. In the early hours of Sunday 31 August 1997 a car carrying them through Paris, while being pursued by paparazzi on motorcycles, crashed at high speed into the wall of an underpass. Fayed and the driver, Henri Paul (who was found subsequently to have been drunk at the wheel), were both killed instantly; Diana died two hours later in hospital.

Britain was plunged into an unprecedented orgy of grief and of recrimination against the royal family (perceived not to be responding with sufficient sorrow), both whipped up by the same tabloid newspapers that had relied on the late princess's indiscretions for ammunition in their circulation wars. The tone was nicely encapsulated by the late princess's brother, Earl Spencer, in his address to the congregation at Diana's funeral the following Saturday. Huge crowds, watching his address relayed to giant television screens in public parks, spontaneously applauded him when he finished.

The Prince of Wales eventually married the divorced Camilla Parker Bowles, who became Duchess of Cornwall in 2005.

‘I stand before you today the representative of a family in grief, in a country in mourning before a world in shock.

We are all united not only in our desire to pay our respects to Diana but rather in our need to do so. For such was her extraordinary appeal that the tens of millions of people taking part in this service all over the world via television and radio who never actually met her, feel that they too lost someone close to them in the early hours of Sunday

‘She needed no royal title ... to generate her particular brand of magic’

morning. It is a more remarkable tribute to Diana than I can ever hope to offer her today …

Diana was the very essence of compassion, of duty, of style, of beauty. All over the world she was a symbol of selfless humanity. All over the world, a standard bearer for the rights of the truly downtrodden, a very British girl who transcended nationality. Someone with a natural nobility who was classless and who proved in the last year that she needed no royal title to continue to generate her particular brand of magic.

Today is our chance to say thank you for the way you brightened our lives, even though God granted you but half a life. We will all feel cheated always that you were taken from us so young and yet we must learn to be grateful that you came along at all. Only now that you are gone do we truly appreciate what we are now without and we want you to know that life without you is very, very difficult.

We have all despaired at our loss over the past week and only the strength of the message you gave us through your years of giving has afforded us the strength to move forward …

There is a temptation to rush to canonise your memory, there is no need to do so. You stand tall enough as a human being of unique qualities not to need to be seen as a saint. Indeed to sanctify your memory would be to miss out on the very core of your being, your wonderfully mischievous sense of humour with a laugh that bent you double.

Your joy for life transmitted whereever you took your smile and the sparkle in those unforgettable eyes. Your boundless energy which you could barely contain.

But your greatest gift was your intuition and it was a gift you used wisely. This is what underpinned all your other wonderful attributes and if we look to analyse what it was about you that had such a wide appeal we find it in your instinctive feel for what was really important in all our lives.

Without your God-given sensitivity we would be immersed in greater ignorance at the anguish of Aids and HIV sufferers, the plight of the homeless, the isolation of lepers, the random destruction of landmines.

Diana explained to me once that it was her innermost feelings of suffering that made it possible for her to connect with her constituency of the rejected.

And here we come to another truth about her. For all the status, the glamour, the applause, Diana remained throughout a very insecure person at heart, almost childlike in her desire to do good for others so she could release herself from deep feelings of unworthiness of which her eating disorders were merely a symptom.

The world sensed this part of her character and cherished her for her vulnerability whilst admiring her for her honesty.

'She remained intact, true to herself'

The last time I saw Diana was on July 1, her birthday in London, when typically she was not taking time to celebrate her special day with friends but was guest of honour at a special charity fundraising evening. She sparkled of course, but I would rather cherish the days I spent with her in March when she came to visit me and my children in our home in South

Africa. I am proud of the fact apart from when she was on display meeting President Mandela we managed to contrive to stop the ever-present paparazzi from getting a single picture of her – that meant a lot to her.

These were days I will always treasure. It was as if we had been transported back to our childhood when we spent such an enormous amount of time together – the two youngest in the family.

Fundamentally she had not changed at all from the big sister who mothered me as a baby, fought with me at school and endured those long train journeys between our parents' homes with me at weekends.

It is a tribute to her level-headedness and strength that despite the most bizarre-like life imaginable after her childhood, she remained intact, true to herself …

There is no doubt that she was looking for a new direction in her life at this time. She talked endlessly of getting away from England, mainly because of the treatment that she received at the hands of the newspapers. I don't think she ever understood why her genuinely good intentions were sneered at by the media, why there appeared to be a permanent quest on their behalf to bring her down. It is baffling.

My own and only explanation is that genuine goodness is threatening to those at the opposite end of the moral spectrum. It is a point to remember that of all the ironies about Diana, perhaps the greatest was this – a girl given the name of the ancient goddess of hunting was, in the end, the most hunted person of the modern age.

She would want us today to pledge ourselves to protecting her beloved boys William and Harry from a similar fate and I do this here Diana on your behalf. We will not allow them to suffer the anguish that used regularly to drive you to tearful despair …

And beyond that, on behalf of your mother and sisters, I pledge that we, your blood family, will do all we can to continue the imaginative way in which you were steering these two exceptional young men so that their souls are not simply immersed by duty and tradition but can sing

THE EARLY LIFE OF DIANA

1961
Born as 'the Honourable Diana Frances Spencer', the youngest of three daughters of Viscount Althorp and his first wife Frances Spencer, at Park House on the Sandringham estate in Norfolk (1 July).

1964
Her brother, Charles, is born (20 May).

1967
Her mother leaves her father for Peter Shand-Kydd.

1969
Her parents are divorced (April), and her father wins custody of the children; her mother marries Shand-Kydd, and they go to live in Scotland.

1975
Her father becomes the 8th Earl Spencer, and she moves to the ancestral home of Althorp, becoming Lady Diana Spencer.

1976
Her father marries Raine, Countess of Dartmouth, the only daughter of novelist Barbara Cartland: relations are strained between Raine and his children.

1977
Leaves West Heath school, aged 16, having failed her O-Levels; at about this time meets Prince Charles, who has been dating her sister, Lady Sarah.

1981
Marries Prince Charles at a ceremony in St Paul's Cathedral, attended by 3,500 people and watched on television by a global audience estimated at 1 billion (29 July).

openly as you planned.

We fully respect the heritage into which they have both been born and will always respect and encourage them in their royal role but we, like you, recognise the need for them to experience as many different aspects of life as possible to arm them spiritually and emotionally for the

> *'The unique, the complex, the extraordinary and irreplaceable Diana'*

years ahead. I know you would have expected nothing less from us.

William and Harry, we all care desperately for you today. We are all chewed up with the sadness at the loss of a woman who was not even our mother. How great your suffering is, we cannot even imagine.

I would like to end by thanking God for the small mercies he has shown us at this dreadful time. For taking Diana at her most beautiful and radiant and when she had joy in her private life. Above all we give thanks for the life of a woman I am so proud to be able to call my sister, the unique, the complex, the extraordinary and irreplaceable Diana whose beauty, both internal and external, will never be extinguished from our minds.

'The forces of
conservatism'

Labour Party Conference, Bournemouth, 28 September 1999

Tony Blair

on 'reactionary' forces in British society
and politics

Tony Blair (b.1953) was the inventor of 'New Labour', a Party that had disposed of all the traditional working-class, trade-union, collectivist and statist apparatus that had so discredited Labour when it was last in office in the 1970s. He replaced it with a diluted – some of his Labour critics would say scarcely diluted – version of Thatcherism, refusing to raise income tax, or to renationalise privatised industries, or to restore legal immunities to trades unions. An Oxford-educated ex-public schoolboy, he was seen as being more comfortable in the company of the rich and famous than with Labour's traditional constituency.

Perhaps for all these reasons he felt it necessary, in this his third speech as prime minister to a Party Conference, to emphasise his differences with what he termed 'the forces of conservatism'. In 1997 New Labour had won the biggest election victory since 1906, annihilating the Tories and reducing them to a rump of 165 MPs. This did not prevent Blair from kicking them while they were down – for opinion polls at the time suggested that the Conservatives had no hope of recovery in the short term, and indeed Labour won the 2001 election by a similarly crushing margin.

The speech is crafted in a way that highlights Blair's rhetorical trademarks of slogans, soundbites and a subliminal emphasis on certain key words. As well as being a definitive statement of the change he wrought on Britain after 1997, it is also a prime product of the political machine that imported the concept of the 'spin-doctor' into Britain, and which sought to destroy the distinction between Party and government. Unlike many of the speeches in this book, it is neither fine rhetoric, nor does it read well in any literary sense: it is a succession of slogans and brusque statements, issued one after the other, in the hope that they will penetrate the subconscious of the listener. The speech sums up the brutality of a style that was enormously politically successful; and the remarks at the close of the extract, about Britain being a bridge between America and Europe, would soon read very differently after the events of 11 September 2001 and the Iraq war of 2003.

‘ Today at the frontier of the new Millennium I set out for you how, as a nation, we renew British strength and confidence for the 21st century; and how, as a Party reborn, we make it a century of progressive politics after one dominated by Conservatives.

'The class war is over'

A New Britain where the extraordinary talent of the British people is liberated from the forces of conservatism that so long have held them back, to create a model 21st century nation, based not on privilege, class or background, but on the equal worth of all.

And New Labour, confident at having modernised itself, now the new progressive force in British politics which can modernise the nation, sweep away those forces of conservatism to set the people free.

.... The cause we have fought for, these 100 years, is no longer simply our cause of social justice.

It is the nation's only hope of salvation.

For how do you develop the talent of all, unless in a society that treats us all equally, where the closed doors of snobbery and prejudice, ignorance and poverty, fear and injustice no longer bar our way to fulfilment.

Not equal incomes. Not uniform lifestyles or taste or culture.

But true equality: equal worth, an equal chance of fulfilment, equal access to knowledge and opportunity.

Equal rights. Equal responsibilities.

The class war is over.

But the struggle for true equality has only just begun.

To the child who goes to school hungry for food, but thirsting for knowledge, I know the talent you were born with, and the frustration you feel that it's trapped inside. We will set your potential free.

To the women free to work, but because they are also mothers, carers, helpers barely know how to get through the day, we will give you the support to set your potential free.

To the 45 year old who came to my surgery a few months ago, scared he'll never work again, I say: you didn't become useless at 45. You deserve the chance to start afresh and we will set your potential free.

And to those who have wealth, but who say that none of it means anything if my children can't play in the park, and my mother daren't go out at night. We share your belief in a strong community. We will set your potential free.

And it is us, the new radicals, the Labour Party modernised, that must undertake this historic mission. To liberate Britain from the old class divisions, old structures, old prejudices, old ways of working and of doing things, that will not do in this world of change.

To be the progressive force that defeats the forces of conservatism.

'The forces of progress and the forces of conservatism'

For the 21st century will not be about the battle between capitalism and socialism but between the forces of progress and the forces of conservatism.

They are what hold our nation back. Not just in the Conservative Party but within us, within our nation.

The forces that do not understand that creating a new Britain of true equality is no more a betrayal of Britain's history than New Labour is of Labour's values.

The old prejudices, where foreign means bad.

Where multi culturalism is not something to celebrate, but a left-wing conspiracy to destroy their way of life.

Where women shouldn't work and those who do are responsible for the breakdown of the family.

The old elites, establishments that have run our professions and our country too long. Who have kept women and black and Asian talent out of our top jobs and senior parts of government and the Services. Who keep our bright inner city kids from our best universities. And who still think the House of Lords should be run by hereditary peers in the interests of the Tory Party.

'The old order ... held people back'

The old order, those forces of conservatism, for all their language about promoting the individual, and freedom and liberty, they held people back. They kept people down. They stunted people's potential. Year after year. Decade after decade.

Think back on some of the great achievements of this century.

To us today, it almost defies belief that people had to die to win the fight for the vote for women. But they did. That battle was a massive, heroic struggle. But why did it need such a fight? Because Tory MPs stood up in the House of Commons and said: 'voting is a man's business'. And that is why we can be so proud that it is this Labour Party that has more women MPs and more women ministers than any government before us until our record is bettered by a future Labour government.

TONY BLAIR'S FIRST TERM IN OFFICE 1997–2001

1997

The Labour Party wins landslide election, with its largest-ever majority (1 May), and Blair is the youngest prime minister since Lord Liverpool in 1812; nearly a quarter of Labour MPs are women, dubbed 'Blair's Babes', with an unprecedented five women in the Cabinet; Gordon Brown, the new chancellor of the exchequer, announces the independence of the Bank of England to set interest rates, to meet inflation target of 2.5% (6 May); Scottish voters approve the creation of a Scottish Parliament in a referendum (11 Sept.); Welsh voters narrowly approve the creation of a Welsh Assembly (18 Sept.).

Look at this Party's greatest achievement. The forces of conservatism, and the force of the Conservative Party, pulled every trick in the book – voting 51 times, yes 51 times, against the creation of the NHS. One leading Tory, Mr Henry Willink, said at the time that the NHS 'will destroy so much in this country that we value', when we knew human potential can never be realised when whether you are well or ill depends on wealth not need.

The forces of conservatism allied to racism are why one of the heroes of the 20th century, Martin Luther King, is dead.

It's why another, Nelson Mandela, spent the best years of his life in a cell the size of a bed.

And though the fact that Mandela is alive, free and became president, is a sign of the progress we have made: the fact that Stephen Lawrence is dead, for no other reason than he was born black, is a sign of how far we still have to go.

And they still keep opposing progress and justice.

What did they say about the minimum wage? The same as they said right through this century.

They tried the employment argument – it would cost jobs.

They tried the business argument – it would make them bankrupt.

They then used the economic argument – it would cause inflation.

They then resorted to the selfish argument – businesses wouldn't want to pay it.

Well, businesses are paying it. Inflation is low. Unemployment is falling. There are one million job vacancies in the country.

And two million people have had a pay rise because we believe they are worth more than poverty pay.

These forces of conservatism chain us not only to an outdated view of our people's potential but of our nation's potential. What threatens the nation-state today is not change, but the refusal to change in a world opening up, becoming ever more interdependent.

1998

100,000 supporters of the Countryside Alliance, a coalition of pressure groups, march in London (1 March) to demonstrate at perceived threats to rural ways and fox-hunting; in Belfast, the British and Irish governments and the main Northern Ireland political parties reach the Good Friday Agreement on the province's political future (12 April).

1999

The national minimum wage comes into force (1 April), set initially at £3.60 an hour; the number of hereditary peers allowed to participate in the House of Lords is reduced to 92 (11 Nov.).

2000

Devolved government is suspended in Northern Ireland (11 Feb.), then reintroduced (29 May); Ken Livingstone, standing as an independent candidate, becomes the first elected mayor of Greater London (4 May).

The old air of superiority based on past glory must give way to the ambition to succeed, based on the merit of what Britain stands for today.

For the last half century, we have been torn between Europe and the United States, searching for our identity in the post-empire world.

'Britain has the potential to be the bridge between Europe and America'

I pose this simple question: is our destiny with Europe or not?

If the answer is no, then we should leave. But we would leave an economic union in which 50 per cent of our trade is done, on which millions of British jobs depend. Our economic future would be uncertain.

But what is certain is that we would not be a power.

Britain would no longer play a determining part in the future of the Continent to which we belong. That would be the real end of one thousand years of history.

We can choose this destiny. But we should do it with our eyes open and our senses alert, not blindfold and dulled by the incessant propaganda of Europhobes.

The single currency is, of course, a decision that must be dependent on the economic conditions; and on the consent of the British people in a referendum.

If we believe our destiny is with Europe, then let us leave behind the muddling through, the hesitation, the half-heartedness which has characterised British relations with Europe for forty years and play our part with confidence and pride giving us the chance to defeat the forces of conservatism, economic and political, that hold Europe back too.

There is no choice between Europe and America.

Britain is stronger with the US today because we are strong in Europe.

Britain has the potential to be the bridge between Europe and America and for the 21st century the narrow-minded isolationism of right-wing Tories should not block our path to fulfilling it.

Index

Index of notable phrases

Take away that shining bauble there, and lock up the doors. In the name of God, go! (*Cromwell*) 27

The Angel of Death has been abroad throughout the land; you may almost hear the beating of his wings (*Bright*) 99

The Britain that is going to be forged in the white heat of this revolution will be no place for restrictive practices or outdated methods (*Wilson*) 239

The class war is over (*Blair*) 295

The cup was at her lips, and she was ready to drink it, when the hand of England rudely and ruthlessly dashed it to the ground (*Gladstone*) 122

The dark ages may return, the Stone Age may return on the gleaming wings of science (*Churchill*) 196

The Great War has been like a gigantic star shell, flashing all over the land, illuminating the country and showing up the deep, dark places (*Lloyd George*) 136

The grotesque chaos of a Labour council – a Labour council – hiring taxis to scuttle round a city handing out redundancy notices to its own workers (*Kinnock*) 268

The people will not, cannot, abide posturing. They cannot respect the gesture-generals and the tendency-tacticians (*Kinnock*) 269

The principles of the English constitution do not contemplate the absence of personal influence on the part of the sovereign (*Disraeli*) 103

The right to guide the course of world history is the noblest prize of victory (*Churchill*) 188

The time has come for others to consider their own response to the tragic conflict of loyalties with which I have myself wrestled for perhaps too long (*Howe*) 287

The touch of the soil reinvigorates and reinforces (*Lloyd George*) 138

The wind of change is blowing through this continent, and, whether we like it or not, this growth of national consciousness is a political fact (*Macmillan*) 215

The world continues to offer glittering prizes to those who have stout hearts and sharp swords (*Birkenhead*) 144

There are some of us, Mr Chairman, who will fight and fight and fight again to bring back sanity and honesty and dignity (*Gaitskell*) 222

Think of it! A second chamber selected by the whips. A seraglio of eunuchs (*Foot*) 253

This country has presented a spectacle honourable to the people of England, and worthy of the admiration of mankind (*Palmerston*) 92

This means a special relationship between the British Commonwealth and the United States (*Churchill*) 195

This was their finest hour (*Churchill*) 179

Tightening the tie is frequently the means of making it burst (*Gladstone*) 118

To be the progressive force that defeats the forces of conservatism (*Blair*) 295

Toleration is not to be regarded as a thing convenient and useful to the state, but a thing in itself essentially right and just (*Fox*) 44

Universal history, the history of what man has accomplished in this world, is at bottom the history of great men (*Carlyle*) 78

War, with all its evils, is better than a peace in which there is nothing to be seen but usurpation and injustice (*Pitt*) 62

Wars are not won by evacuations. But there was a victory inside this deliverance (*Churchill*) 168

We few, we happy few, we band of brothers (*Shakespeare's Henry V*) 17

We have given Ireland a voice: we must all listen for a moment to what she says (*Gladstone*) 122

We have not successfully rolled back the frontiers of the state in Britain, only to see them re-imposed at a European level (*Thatcher*) 276

We know that a great work of liberation has been done, in which we have had no part whatsoever (*Gladstone*) 112

We must be consistent with ourselves everywhere (*Powell*) 212

We must never cease to proclaim in fearless tones the great principles of freedom and the rights of man which are the joint inheritance of the English-speaking world (*Churchill*) 195

We shall fight on the beaches, we shall fight on the landing grounds, we shall fight in the fields and in the streets, we shall fight in the hills; we shall never surrender (*Churchill*) 171

What General Weygand called the Battle of France is over. I expect that the Battle of Britain is about to begin. (*Churchill*) 179

What is our task? To make Britain a fit country for heroes to live in (*Lloyd George*) 136

When Adam dalf, and Eve span, / Who was then a gentilman? (*Ball*) 14

When is a war not a war? When it is carried on by methods of barbarism in South Africa (*Campbell-Bannerman*) 126

Why should I place burdens on the people? I am one of the people (*Lloyd George*) 134

With reference to this war, I regard it as the greatest disaster which in modern times has befallen the British nation (*Campbell-Bannerman*) 126

You ask, what is our policy? It is to wage war ... You ask, what is our aim? I can answer in one word: it is victory (*Churchill*) 164

You turn if you want to. The lady's not for turning. (*Thatcher*) 263

You will send a British foreign secretary, whoever he may be, naked into the conference chamber (*Bevan*) 205

Your representative owes you, not his industry only, but his judgment (*Burke*) 30

Author's Acknowledgements

I am grateful to Mrs Pat Ventre, without whom this book would not have been possible; to the Museum of Labour History; to the Bodleian Library, Oxford; to Jane Robins; to Richard Thorpe; to Anthony Cheetham, Richard Milbank and Mark Hawkins-Dady at Quercus; and last and by no means least to my agent, Georgina Capel.

Picture credits

Hulton Archive/Getty Images, page 12, 21, 25, 28, 32, 43, 48, 53, 82, 88, 94, 101, 135: Hulton Archive/Illustrated London News/Getty Images, 108: Time Life Pictures/Mansell/Getty Images, 69, 77: Time Life Pictures/George Scadding/ Getty Images, 190: Time Life Pictures/ Brian Seed/Getty Images, 203, 235: Time Life Pictures/Sam Doherty/ Getty Images, 265; Rischgitz/Getty Images, 263: Central Press/Hulton Archive/ Getty Images, 128: Fox Photos/Getty Images, 145, 157, 165: Keystone/Getty Images, 152, 213: Val Doone/Getty Images, 161: Topical Press Agency/ Getty Images, 172: Monty Fresco Jnr/Getty Images, 209: Express Newspapers/Getty Images, 241: Leonard Burt/Central Press/Getty Images, 249: Anwar Hussein/Getty Images, 288: Martyn Hayhow/AFP/ Getty Images, 293; National Portrait Gallery, page 15; Fine Art Photographic Library/CORBIS, page 18: Hulton-Deutsch Collection/CORBIS, 180 and cover; Wilberforce House, Hull City Museums and Art Galleries,UK/The Bridgeman Art Library, page 38: Philip Mould Ltd, London/The Bridgeman Art Library, 58: Musée de la Ville de Paris, Musée Carnavalet, Paris, France, Archives Charmet/The Bridgeman Art Library, 64: Private Collection/The Bridgeman Art Library, 116; PA Photos, page 124, 139, 223, 230, 272, 280: AP/PA Photos, 199; Topfoto, page 257.

Design: Jane McKenna
Picture research: Elaine Willis
Editorial collaboration: Rosie
   Anderson
Proofreading: Fintan Power
Index: Zeb Korycinska

First published in Great Britain in 2007 by

Quercus
21 Bloomsbury Square
London
WC1A 2NS

A CIP catalogue reference for this book is available from the British Library

ISBN 1 84724 038 0
ISBN-13 978 1 84724 038 5

Printed and bound in Great Britain by Butler and Tanner, Frome

10 9 8 7 6 5 4 3 2 1